the

MIRACLE MORNING AFTER 50

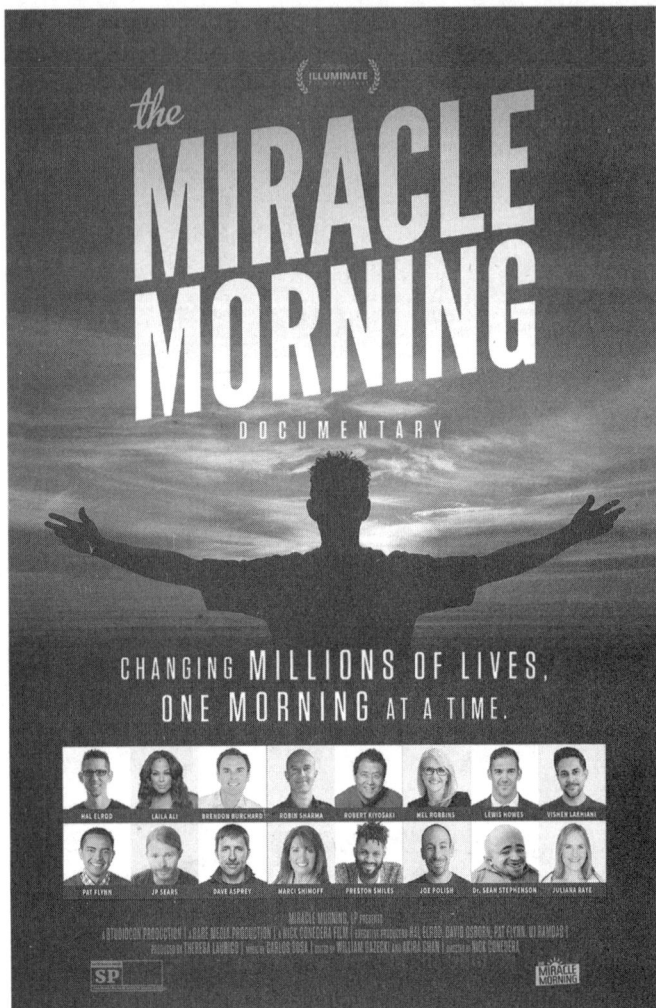

GET THE MIRACLE MORNING APP!

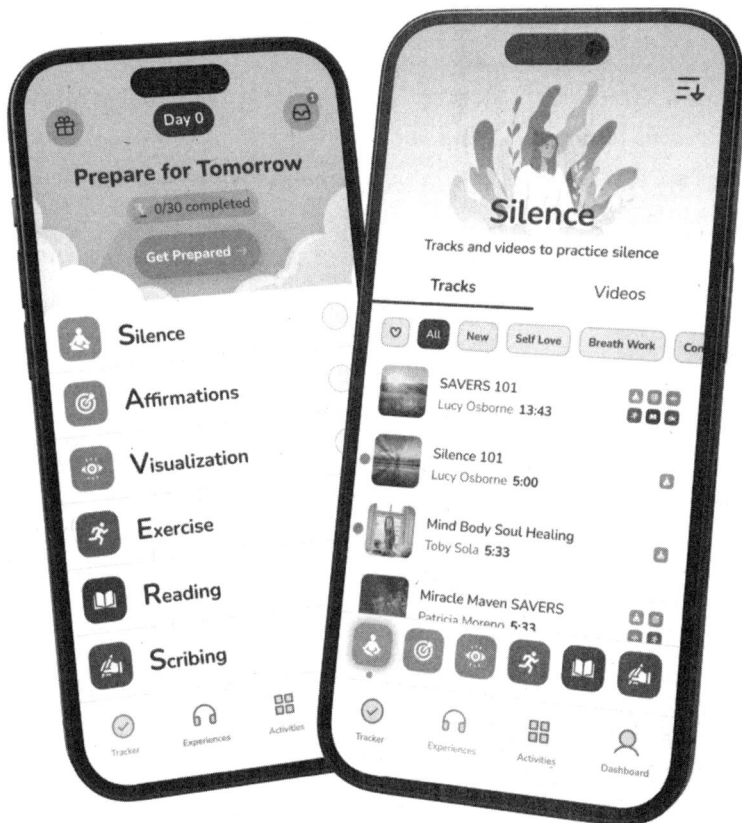

Your Morning Routine Companion

The Miracle Morning app is a resource that supports you in implementing everything you learn in the book.

Download the app at MiracleMorning.com/App

Real-Life Transformations from Miracle Morning Practitioners Over 50

"The Miracle Morning *changed my life in all aspects. I was living in so much pain from my divorce that I had lost hope, lost faith, and my business was falling. I was in such a stressful mood, had very low self-esteem, no relationship, and depression was very real . . . with suicidal thoughts.*

"My miracle started to happen the same day I got the book. My mind opened to new possibilities, and the universe started to bring me back, but not the old me, a new version—a much better one with knowledge of empathy, compassion, and love.

"The first miracle is that I now love mornings, and my life is full of purpose. I started a new career, started believing in myself again, and my relationship with my kids is 1000 percent better. I have meaningful friends, and now I really can say, I LOVE MYSELF. Miracles continue happening in my life every day. I tell everyone that this book changed my life. I guess I can say this book saved me."

—Marcia Camargo

Age 52

"I'm on Day 77 of the Miracle Morning. Given that I didn't consider myself a morning person, getting up at 6 a.m. every morning is a big transformation. I appreciate the silence and the opportunity to reflect. And while I was a little skeptical of affirmations to begin with, I admit that incorporating them into my daily S.A.V.E.R.S. routine has had a positive effect. In fact, I've been tracking my mood over the day, and I can report that it and my self-confidence have improved dramatically. I'm sticking with TMM."

—Michael Williams

Age 70

"I have been into personal development for about 30 years, give or take, but when I reached my mid-50s, I felt like I was just kind of coasting in life. Then, serendipitously, I stumbled upon The Miracle Morning, *and little did I know*

it would become my guiding light. It was so unlike any other personal development book I had read, so easy to follow and implement into my daily routine. Implementing the principles outlined in the book breathed new life into my mornings and subsequently, into every facet of my days. I embraced the power of silence, affirmations, visualization, exercise, reading, and journaling, which now form the cornerstones of my morning.

"At 64, I feel calmer, more hopeful, and more vital. I know my best years are still ahead of me! The Miracle Morning doesn't just impart knowledge. It will ignite a spark in you—a spark that will fuel a renaissance of purpose, joy, and gratitude. With each sunrise, you, too, can greet the day with renewed vigor, eager to seize the boundless opportunities it holds.

"To anyone who feels the weight of time, I offer this: The Miracle Morning After 50 isn't just a book; it's a roadmap to reclaiming your life, no matter your age. Embrace its wisdom, and watch as your mornings become miracles, and your life becomes a testament to the enduring power of possibility."

—Stephanie Blackbird
Age 64

"I am a 53-year-old father of three and grandfather of five. Recently, I transitioned to a new position in my company. My new role requires a high degree of organizational skills and holding meetings with both corporate and plant leaders. The Miracle Morning has given me focus to be able to be prepared for the day with success in my mind. It has also helped me regarding my issue with anxiety, which I struggled with for nearly two decades."

—Jym Murray
Age 53

"I'm newly retired after teaching for 38+ years. There is a vision of what retirement should be like—travel, adventure, the house perfectly cleaned and organized, projects done, the yard looking beautiful, preserving food from the garden, and time with friends and family—but it didn't pan out that way. I found myself struggling with what I envisioned and what reality was. The

Miracle Morning has helped me immensely to transition from my working self to a retirement that I'm at peace with and can enjoy, especially through the hard time of losing my mother. I'm so grateful I started TMM before she became ill because it truly helped me through that time and where I am now being there for my father as he navigates life without her. It has helped me recognize the joy in each day and realize all that I have to be grateful for."

—Linda Dunn

Age 63

"*When I first heard about* The Miracle Morning *and the results my colleagues were getting, I got the book ASAP. Being such a busy and active entrepreneur, I needed help. I convinced my wife to join me. We're 97 days in, and we look forward to our shared* Silence *each morning in our Miracle Nook in the living room. Our pets like it, too! Our relationship has significantly improved. We communicate more intimately and hold each other accountable to ensure we make time for our Miracle Morning. We are exercising, and my wife started journaling—all vast improvements. I am a believer, father of seven, husband, host of a weekly podcast, full-time IT manager, musician, and church volunteer, so maximizing our time is super important. We have more energy, are more intentional with how we spend time, and are spreading the word on my show and giving copies of the book to members of my mastermind group."*

—Paul Guyon

Age 65

"*I received* The Miracle Morning *for Christmas seven years ago, and it has changed the way I looked at my life. For the past seven years, the S.A.V.E.R.S. have become an essential part of my daily morning routine. This daily practice has seen me through a heart attack, divorce, and a stroke. Yet over those same seven years, I have written an award-winning book, achieved the rank of 6th degree black belt master instructor in Taekwondo, and successfully run my martial arts business. Today, at 75, I am as healthy as I've ever been, teaching daily in my academy as well as training and working out regularly. Life couldn't be better."*

—Lorne Davidson

Age 75

"I am a strong-headed 61-year-old female and was a chronic snooze button pusher. I have never ever been a morning person. Since starting my Miracle Morning routine, I no longer hit snooze (which I thought was impossible). I now look forward to my morning routine, including exercising. I always admired people who could exercise in the mornings but never considered myself one. Well ... here I am. The Miracle Morning DOES WORK!! I would encourage everyone to give it a try, especially people over 50 who think they can't change their life at this age. I'm here to tell you, YES, YOU CAN!! I am a living example of the wonderful changes that TMM can bring to your life!"

—JacLynne Effting

Age 61

Praise for *The Miracle Morning After 50*

"In *The Miracle Morning After 50*, Hal Elrod and Dwayne J. Clark offer a transformative guide for those of us navigating midlife and beyond. Their unique approach aligns perfectly with my philosophy of aging powerfully. This book is a must-read for anyone looking to redefine their mornings and, by extension, their lives."

—JJ Virgin, four-time *New York Times* bestselling
author and Fitness Hall of Famer

"*The Miracle Morning After 50* is the perfect companion for anyone on the midlife journey. Hal Elrod has teamed up with Dwayne J. Clark to offer a powerful daily practice that aligns beautifully with the ethos of the Modern Elder Academy—where aging is seen as a time of growth, wisdom, and reinvention. This book shows you how to wake up to make the next chapter of your life the *best* chapter of your life.

—Chip Conley, author of *Learning to Love Midlife*
and founder of the Modern Elder Academy

"I've come to learn what a privilege it is to even be able to age—a privilege denied to far too many. *The Miracle Morning After 50* is a wonderful tool for those of us in the second half of life, helping us to age with as much grace, joy, and purpose as possible."

—Ally Svenson, cofounder of MOD Pizza

"From sleep quality to morning clarity, this book nails what so many miss—it's not just about waking up early; it's about waking up well. The emphasis on intentionality, recovery, and natural rhythm alignment makes this a must-read. Readers will walk away with tools to sleep better, feel better, and age with more vitality."

—Raj Dasgupta, MD, FACP, FCCP, FAASM, associate program director of
internal medicine residency and associate professor of clinical medicine

"Having spent over three decades passionately believing in a vision of 'living longer better,' I can confirm that *The Miracle Morning After 50* provides older adults with an inspirational blueprint to personal transformation, renewed vitality, and joy at any age."

—**David Schless, president and CEO of the American Seniors Housing Association**

"Hal Elrod and Dwayne J. Clark aren't just giving you a morning routine—they're giving you a second act. *The Miracle Morning After 50* is the wake-up call we didn't know we needed, until now. Bold, practical, and unflinchingly optimistic, it proves that your most fascinating years are still ahead. (Coffee optional. Clarity guaranteed.)"

—**Sally Hogshead, *New York Times* bestselling author of *Fascinate: How to Make Your Brand Impossible to Resist***

"What a fantastic read! This book is an outstanding resource for anyone looking to lead a healthier, more fulfilling life. It offers practical and actionable tips to help improve well-being, boost productivity, and enhance overall happiness. As a geriatric physician, I wholeheartedly recommend it and hope more people embrace these valuable insights to optimize their healthspan at any age."

—**Ken Nishino, MD, FACP, geriatric and internal medicine physician**

"Dwayne J. Clark and Hal Elrod, two remarkable people with rich life experiences, share their insights, strategies, and wisdom for making our autumn years of life as meaningful—perhaps even more meaningful—than our spring and summer years. I can't think of two better guides to help us wake up—literally—to our full potential, every day, for the rest of our lives. Indeed, *The Miracle Morning After 50* shows us how it can be 'morning again' for each and every one of us! As a favorite teacher from long ago might have put it, 'Read and inwardly digest this book. Make it part of your being. You won't regret it.'"

—Dr. Kirtland C. Peterson, 66, former COO of Sunrise Living, former
Fortune 500 consultant, and current fifth-grade teacher on O'ahu

"In writing *The Miracle Morning After 50*, Dwayne and Hal have produced an approachable road map for navigating the process of aging in an engaged, curious, and energetic way. I suspect readers of this book will find that the best is yet to come."

—Dr. Ernest Madhavan, psychiatrist and founder
of Soundview Psychiatric Services

"Hal Elrod and Dwayne J. Clark have written a road map for anyone who's over 50 and wants more out of life. *The Miracle Morning After 50* is a powerful, practical guide that reminds us it's never too late to grow, heal, and wake up to our full potential."

—Anna David, *New York Times* bestselling author and
founder of Legacy Launch Pad Publishing

"In *The Miracle Morning After 50*, Hal Elrod and Dwayne J. Clark biohack aging itself. Because you can grow more vitality and performance at any time, even after 50."

—Dave Asprey, founder of Upgrade Labs, four-time *New York Times* bestselling
author, host of *The Human Upgrade* podcast, and the "father of biohacking"

"Hal Elrod's original book, *The Miracle Morning*, is a must-read . . . especially for success driven . . . high achievers. Hal and Dwayne Clark's latest book, *The Miracle Morning After 50* is priceless . . . especially for those who want to finish strong . . . in the second half of life."

—Robert Kiyosaki, internationally bestselling author of *Rich Dad Poor Dad*

"I'm in my 50s, and I'm not slowing down. I'm cranking it up. *The Miracle Morning After 50* showed me how to stay energized, focused, and free for the best half of my life. It will do the same for you."

—Mike Michalowicz, author of *Profit First* and *The Money Habit*

"My work as a geriatric neuropsychologist has shown me that, while an estate planning professional can help a person achieve a financially successful retirement, they don't teach how to answer the question at the heart of well-aging: Who do I want to be when I grow up? *The Miracle Morning After 50* is the book that I have been long searching for to give to my patients. It offers the practical tools and advice essential for embracing the transformative power of an optimistic future-driven mindset. *The Miracle Morning After 50* is not merely an invaluable book for well-aging; its wisdom is simply indispensable."

—Glenn A. Hammel, PhD, geriatric neuropsychologist, well-aging and wholistic retirement consultant, contributing author of *The Psychology of Existence*

Also by Hal Elrod

The Miracle Equation
Taking Life Head On

The Miracle Morning Series

The Miracle Morning Updated and Expanded Edition
The Miracle Morning for Salespeople
The Miracle Morning for Real Estate Agents
The Miracle Morning for Network Marketers
The Miracle Morning for Parents and Families
The Miracle Morning Art of Affirmations
The Miracle Morning for Entrepreneurs
The Miracle Morning Millionaires
The Miracle Morning for Addiction Recovery
The Miracle Morning for Couples
The Miracle Morning for Transforming Your Relationship
The Miracle Morning for Teachers
The Miracle Morning for College Students
The Miracle Morning Journal
The Miracle Morning Companion Planner
The Miracle Morning for Writers

Also by Dwayne J. Clark

30 Summers More: Adding Time Back to Your Aging Clock
My Mother, My Son: A True Story of Love, Determination, And Memories . . . Lost
A Big Life: Wisdom for My Grandchildren
Help Wanted: Recruiting, Hiring & Retaining Exceptional Staff
*Saturdays with GG: A Children's Book About Building
Memories with Loved Ones Even After Alzheimer's*

the

MIRACLE MORNING AFTER 50

A Proven Path to Joy, Vitality, and Purpose for Aging Adults

HAL ELROD and DWAYNE J. CLARK

BENBELLA

BenBella Books, Inc.
Dallas, TX

BENBELLA
BenBella Books, Inc.
8080 N. Central Expressway
Suite 1700
Dallas, TX 75206
benbellabooks.com
Send feedback to feedback@benbellabooks.com

BenBella is a federally registered trademark.

Printed in the United States of America
10 9 8 7 6 5 4 3 2 1

Library of Congress Control Number: 2025027080
ISBN 9781637746196 (trade paperback)
ISBN 9781637746202 (electronic)

Editing by Claire Schulz
Copyediting by Joe Rhatigan
Proofreading by Ashley Casteel and Denise Pangia
Text design and composition by Aaron Edmiston
Cover design by Brigid Pearson
Cover image © Adobe Stock / Iuliia (sun icon) and Shcherbyna (background)
Printed by Lake Book Manufacturing

Hal:

Mom and Dad, this one is dedicated to you! God blessed me with the best parents I could ever hope for, and I am forever grateful for the ways in which you've loved and supported me and taught me to serve others.

Dwayne:

For those who came before us—who built the bridges we cross, composed the symphonies we hum, and drafted the laws that protect our freedoms.
Your sacrifices shaped our present, and your vision carved the path to our future.
May we never take for granted the legacy you left—or the responsibility we now bear to carry it forward.

CONTENTS

Part 1: Waking Up to Your Full Potential at 50 and Beyond

Part 2: Not-So-Obvious Self-Care Strategies to Thrive After 50

A SPECIAL INVITATION

Join the Miracle Morning Community

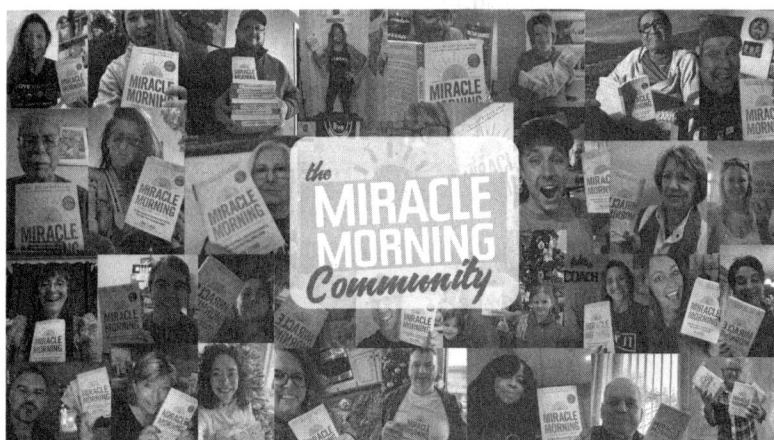

To get ongoing guidance and support, and connect with and learn from like-minded Miracle Morning practitioners of all ages as you read this book, we invite you to join the Miracle Morning Community at **MiracleMorningCommunity.com**.

What began as a Facebook group in 2012 has grown into one of the most engaged and inspiring online communities in the world, with over 300,000 members from more than one hundred countries. It's always free to join, and while you'll find many people who are just beginning their Miracle Morning journey, you'll find even more who have been practicing for years and who will happily share advice, support, best practices, and guidance to help you accelerate your success.

As the author of *The Miracle Morning*, I wanted to create a space where we can all come together to connect, ask questions, support one another, discuss the book, post videos, find an accountability partner, and even swap smoothie recipes and exercise routines. I never imagined that the Miracle Morning Community would become one of the most positive, engaged, and supportive online communities in the world, but it truly has!

You can begin connecting with other Miracle Morning practitioners today. Just visit **MiracleMorningCommunity.com** and request to join. I check in regularly, so I look forward to seeing you there!

THE MIRACLE MORNING AFTER 50
Resources and Book Bonuses

There are three additional resources that will enhance your experience you as you begin your Miracle Morning journey: *The Miracle Morning* movie, the *Miracle Morning* app, and *The Miracle Morning After 50* book bonuses—all of which are available at **TMMAfter50.com**.

The Miracle Morning Movie

The Miracle Morning movie is an inspiring feature-length documentary that takes you beyond the book and into the lives of ordinary people who have experienced extraordinary results and transformations as a result of implementing the Miracle Morning in their lives. It also provides you with exclusive insights from world-renowned authors, doctors, and experts, including Mel Robbins, Lewis Howes, Robin Sharma, Marci Shimoff, Brendon Burchard, and Dr. Michael Breus (aka the Sleep Doctor) to reveal how these highly productive individuals maximize their mornings for success.

Last but not least, you'll get a front row seat to Hal fighting for his life when, two years into filming, he was unexpectedly diagnosed with a rare form of cancer and given a dismal 30 percent chance of surviving. As a father of two young children, he focused his Miracle Mornings on beating cancer and did everything in his power to survive—combining Western medicine with the most effective holistic methods for healing.

Watch the movie today, either by yourself or with friends and family, and prepare to be inspired!

The *Miracle Morning* App

After years of requests, the *Miracle Morning* app is your all-in-one companion to help you unlock the full potential of the S.A.V.E.R.S.® practices (*Silence, Affirmations, Visualization, Exercise, Reading,* and *Scribing*) that you'll learn in this book.

Whether you have 6 minutes or 60, the app makes it effortless to stick to your Miracle Morning routine, turning each day into an opportunity to improve your physical, mental, and emotional well-being so that you can show up at your best for those you love and those you lead, beginning with yourself.

With more than 5,000 5-star ratings and even more success stories, the *Miracle Morning* app enhances your ability to implement the S.A.V.E.R.S. with ease and consistency. Available on iPhone and Android, it's the perfect companion to elevate your Miracle Morning journey. Download the app and start your free trial today!

The Miracle Morning After 50 Book Bonuses

Reading *The Miracle Morning After 50* introduces you to a series of ongoing self-care and personal development intended to optimize your physical, mental, and emotional well-being. To integrate these practices into your life long after you've read the book, we've created a set of value-added book bonuses designed to support your journey every step of the way.

To watch the movie, download the app, access all of the book bonuses and more, visit **TMMAfter50.com**.

INTRODUCTION

Notes from Dwayne and Hal

From Dwayne . . .

Imagine waking up each day with a sense of purpose, boundless energy, and the excitement of new possibilities—decade after decade! Ah, to be cruising past 50 and feeling that peculiar mix of anticipation and reflection . . . it's quite the adventure, isn't it?

Not quite a decade ago, I faced the vast expanse, teasingly wide, that separated the "me" that I was at 55 from the "me" I knew I could be at 65 and beyond. I could be more vibrant, more alive. Standing on this edge felt akin to being at the entrance of a mystical forest, with a path winding its way to a dazzling clearing where life is an endless stream of vigor, joy, and profound satisfaction. I knew living longer without all the problems aging brings was possible, but the path wasn't always clear.

I would spend countless hours—years, really—charting the steps necessary to traverse this gap, to jump from mere daydreaming to real, tangible action that made living healthier and longer possible. In addition to thinking about longevity (how long we live), I've prioritized optimizing my healthspan—how long we live *with optimal health*. Despite this, I slipped back into well-trodden habits and cozy routines (many of them bad). I slept too little and indulged too much. I prioritized unhealthy activities over self-care. I was not consistent with moving my body and settling my mind. Even though I didn't feel old in my brain, my body started sounding like an old car door creaking open. That is, until a health scare landed me squarely in the emergency room. (More on that in Chapter 7.)

Does this sound familiar? If you're reading this book, I bet it might. But know this: There is a way to break the cycle of desiring the best life without developing the habits to achieve it. The key is to start each day with a routine that sets the tone for a vibrant, fulfilling life, despite the common belief that aging inevitably sucks. A life of increasing pain and decreasing capability does not have to be your fate. This is the power of *The Miracle Morning After 50*.

> "Start each day with a routine that sets the tone for a vibrant, fulfilling life.

My world was illuminated after reading *The Miracle Morning* by Hal Elrod. His book introduced the concept of a simple morning routine that can truly change your life. It's about starting your day purposefully, incorporating activities like meditation, exercise, reading, and journaling. This routine has already helped millions of people improve their physical, mental, and emotional well-being and increase their overall quality of life. Hal's journey through adversity led to this incredible book, which proved to be an easy yet transformative read. In its pages, I discovered the key to overcoming the wellness pitfalls I had constantly encountered. And, because I knew that Hal's book could be truly transformative, particularly for those of us over age 50, I didn't want to keep this discovery to myself.

As the founder of Aegis Living, I've cared for over 80,000 aging adults, primarily focusing on nurturing longevity and healthspan. Daily, I am surrounded by Aegis Living residents, many of whom

I have taken care of for over 30 years, and I get to witness many diverse experiences of aging. With 39 communities that foster some of the best assisted living and memory care in the world, I've seen firsthand how well—and not so well—seniors can march through the decades.

Take Sam, who at 101 years old is still lively and vibrant, cracking jokes and trying to negotiate on everything at one of our communities. In contrast, I observe John, with a stooped back and trembling hands at age 67, being pushed through the halls in a wheelchair, quietly accepting his aging reality. These residents, whom I call my oracles, continuously teach me the essence of living with soulful purpose. They also helped me become a wellness warrior and sparked a profound curiosity about what it takes to be more like Sam.

Since my big health scare, I have become even more passionate about health, wellness, and everything in between. With each passing year, I've seen opportunities to improve how we age—body, mind, and spirit—personally noting micro-habits that dramatically improve a person's longevity factors. It was clear to me that I had to team up with Hal to tailor *The Miracle Morning After 50*, which is a testament to our joint vision. By starting each morning purposefully, wellness warriors at any age can enhance how well they go into each new year.

I know what you are thinking: *What I could do at 40, I can't do now at 50 (or 60, 70, 80, 90, or 100).* You may or may not be right (keep reading to discover why). Still, in either case, the routines in *The Miracle Morning* that I learned more than a decade ago are the same as those in *The Miracle Morning After 50* but modified with all the aging micro-habits you need to live vibrantly at any age.

As I look to the horizon, hopefully at 40+ more years teeming with potential, I'm filled with eagerness for what lies ahead and a fierce determination not to let a single moment slip by unused.

From Hal . . .

I love Dwayne's vision, and even more, his heart.

When Dwayne, a highly respected senior health and wellness expert, reached out and expressed with passion and conviction that people over the age of 50 could benefit greatly from a customized version of *The Miracle Morning*, I immediately agreed. I shared his vision because of the millions of people who have read the original book. I have seen countless individuals in their 50s, 60s, 70s, 80s, and beyond use the Miracle Morning practice and the S.A.V.E.R.S. routine to transform their lives (and you'll hear from many of these people throughout this book). So, customizing it for those striving to find meaning and fulfillment during the second half of this adventure we call life was a meaningful pursuit.

It was obvious that Dwayne and I were committed to the same thing: to empower ourselves and others to experience optimal levels of joy, vitality, and purpose. In other words, like you, we are striving to enjoy the life we've been blessed to live while maintaining the mental, emotional, and physical vitality to wake up and live each day with purpose. That's what this book is about. And with two decades between us, I also knew I had much to learn from Dwayne and his lifelong work with people over the age of 50.

As I write this, both of my parents are nearing 70. They are admittedly excited that I'm finally writing a book that is designed specifically to help them overcome their challenges and achieve their goals that are unique to this stage of life. Adapting the Miracle Morning to address the specific needs of those in their 50s, 60s, 70s, and beyond is deeply meaningful to me because, as you'll soon discover, I owe my health, my success, and my very life to this practice. A near-fatal car accident, financial ruin, and a deadly cancer all paved the way for the book you're reading now.

It all started in 1999, shortly after my 20th birthday, when my Ford Mustang was hit head-on by a drunk driver traveling at over

70 miles per hour, and I died as firefighters tried to free me from the wreckage. My heart stopped beating for 6 minutes. I broke 11 bones and suffered a traumatic brain injury. After being revived at the scene and airlifted to the hospital, I spent six days in a coma in critical condition and seven weeks in recovery—being told by doctors that I would never walk again—followed by years of rehabilitation.

It was in the hospital, two weeks after the crash and one week after I woke up from a coma, when I told my parents that I believed everything happens for a reason, and that it's our responsibility to choose the most empowering reasons for the challenges we face. I said, "Maybe I'm supposed to go through this in the most positive, proactive way possible so that I can help other people get through their challenges." I saw adversity as an opportunity to learn, grow, and become a better version of myself so that I could help others do the same. I assured Mom and Dad that even if I never walked another day in my life, I would be the happiest, most grateful person they had ever seen in a wheelchair. So, I had nothing to fear and they had nothing to worry about. Remarkably, defying the logic of doctors and my own temptations to be a victim, I took my first step a week later and made an almost full recovery—a true miracle.

My second life-altering challenge came at age 29, during the 2008 financial crisis. The economy crashed, and I crashed with it. I lost over half of my income, I was drowning in debt, and my house was foreclosed on. My physical and mental health, relationships, and sense of purpose crumbled. Despite trying strategies that had previously worked, nothing seemed to address the gravity of my situation.

It was then that I discovered the transformative power of a morning routine. By combining six of the most timeless, proven personal development practices—now known as the S.A.V.E.R.S. (much more on that to come)—I completely transformed my life in just two months. This routine enabled me to double my income (at the height of the Great Recession of 2008), train for an ultramarathon (even though I wasn't a runner), restore my mental health, and strengthen my relationship with my future wife, Ursula.

A key insight came from the work of entrepreneur and author Jim Rohn, who once wisely said, "Your level of success will rarely exceed your level of personal development because success is something you attract by the person you become." Those words shifted my perspective. I realized that I, like most people, wanted "level 10" success in every area of my life—health, happiness, finances, you name it—but my level of personal development was stuck at a one or two. I lacked a daily routine to cultivate the mindset, skills, and habits necessary to achieve and sustain the levels of success and fulfillment that I desired.

Determined to change, I committed to discovering and implementing the most effective personal development practices so that I could become the person I needed to be to create the life I wanted. My research led me to six of the most timeless and proven practices that successful people have relied on for centuries. Instead of choosing one or two, I decided to try all six sequentially. The next morning, I practiced *Silence*, then *Affirmations*, followed by *Visualization*, *Exercise*, *Reading*, and *Scribing*—a routine I later organized into the acronym S.A.V.E.R.S. To my surprise, I immediately experienced more clarity, energy, motivation, and improved mental health. And on days when I was pressed for time, I could effectively complete the S.A.V.E.R.S. in as little as six minutes, though I found the more time I invested into these practices, the better I felt and the more productive I was.

The results were profound. Mentally, I shifted from hopeless to confident. Physically, I became energized and started exercising regularly. The most significant transformation was with my financial situation. After struggling for six months, living on credit cards and having my house foreclosed on, I was suddenly able to more than double my income within two months by applying strategies I learned during my S.A.V.E.R.S. routine. It truly felt like a miracle! Even on bad days, the S.A.V.E.R.S. kept me focused and resilient, giving me a daily reset and ensuring that one bad day never turned into two.

I told my wife, Ursula, that the rapid transformation that resulted from my morning routine felt miraculous, prompting her to refer to it as my "miracle morning." The name stuck,

> Even on bad days, the S.A.V.E.R.S. kept me focused and resilient, giving me a daily reset and ensuring that one bad day never turned into two.

and I began writing it as such into my schedule. Inspired to share this life-changing practice, I started working on the manuscript for *The Miracle Morning: The Not-So-Obvious Secret Guaranteed to Transform Your Life (Before 8AM)*, which I published on December 12, 2012 (12/12/12). Little did I know that my little self-published book would go on to be translated into 42 languages, sell over 2 million copies worldwide, and inspire a movie, a mobile app, a podcast, a program for schools, and a series of more than a dozen additional Miracle Morning books, including the one you're reading now.

Over the past 15 years, I've personally completed more than 5,000 Miracle Mornings, implementing the S.A.V.E.R.S. each day, and the practice has helped millions of people transform their lives, simply by changing how they start their day. I am beyond excited to join forces with Dwayne to bring you this groundbreaking edition, specifically designed to empower those navigating the second half of life. This book goes far beyond generic advice—it delivers a step-by-step blueprint for achieving the vitality, clarity, happiness, and fulfillment you deserve. Whether you want to improve your health, deepen your relationships, rediscover your purpose, or launch a business, this book will equip you with the mindset and practical tools to show up at your best every single day. Imagine waking up each morning and feeling at peace—joyful, energized, inspired, ready to embrace the best years of your life. That's what this book is here to help you achieve.

Welcome to *The Miracle Morning After 50*

If you're over the age of 50, you're probably feeling a unique mix of excitement and uncertainty about what lies ahead. Maybe you're ready to finally prioritize yourself and your dreams, or perhaps you're feeling stuck—wondering if your best years are behind you. *The Miracle Morning After 50* is here to meet you exactly where you are, acknowledging the hopes, fears, and questions that come with this important chapter of life. Through powerful yet simple daily personal development practices and health optimization strategies, this book will help you reignite your purpose, reclaim your energy, and create vibrant health and happiness from the inside out. You deserve to wake up excited each morning, knowing your best years are still ahead—and this book will guide you step by step to make it happen.

We think it's safe to say that, regardless of your age, all of us have at least one thing in common: We want to improve our lives and ourselves. This is not to suggest that there is anything "wrong" with us, but as human beings, we were born with an innate desire and drive to grow and improve. We believe it's within all of us. Yet for most of us, life pretty much stays the same *because we stay the same.*

If we want to improve our lives, we have to first improve ourselves. We have to develop the mindset, habits, and capabilities that will enable us to experience and create the life we desire. Whatever your life is like now, this book will help you become the person you need to be who is capable of creating the life *you* desire. We can assure you that *The Miracle Morning After 50* contains the most practical, results-oriented, and effective methods we've ever encountered for improving any, or quite literally every, area of your life—and it will work faster than you may even believe is possible.

So, whether you're feeling perpetually stressed, overwhelmed, or unfulfilled . . .

Facing challenges in your mental or physical health, relationships, finances, or some other aspect of your life . . .

Already living a life filled with joy, purpose, meaning, and abundance . . .

Or somewhere in between—this edition is here to help you optimize your mindset, elevate your personal development, and establish habits and routines that will expand your longevity and healthspan.

Why? Because we believe that human potential is limitless; it is never too late to embody the person you're capable of becoming, and your best is yet to come.

Who Is This Book For and What Can You Expect?

The Miracle Morning After 50 is for those in the second half of life who aren't willing to leave their best years behind them and are ready to redefine what it means to age with grace, vitality, and purpose. Whether you're still working and want to set yourself up for a fulfilling retirement, a retiree yearning for new adventures, a busy grandparent wanting more energy to chase after the little ones, or a lifelong learner excited to expand your knowledge and abilities, this book is your guide. We speak to everyone over the age of 50, ensuring you can cultivate your mindset and integrate daily habits that support you in creating a vibrant, fulfilling life, no matter where you are on your journey. For anyone who believes that life after 50 is just the beginning of a new, exhilarating chapter, *The Miracle Morning After 50* is for you.

This book is organized into two parts. Part 1: Waking Up to Your Full

Potential at 50 and Beyond explores the unique benefits of implementing a Miracle Morning routine as we age, which are specific to increasing your longevity and optimizing your healthspan. It also introduces you to six timeless, proven personal development practices known as the S.A.V.E.R.S. (*Silence, Affirmations, Visualization, Exercise, Reading,* and *Scribing*), and we walk you through how to customize them for your age, lifestyle, and aspirations. We'll also address how you can implement all of this even if you've never considered yourself to be a "morning" person. Part 1 of this book will culminate with *The Miracle Morning After 50 30-Day Life Transformation Challenge* so that you can easily and effectively optimize and maintain your Miracle Morning routine.

In Part 2, we will dive deep into the Not-So-Obvious Self-Care Strategies to Thrive After 50, including *Self-Care Hours, Optimizing Your Energy, First Light and Earthing,* and *Living on Purpose with Purpose.* Most of this part of the book will go far beyond the Miracle Morning concepts and focus on scientifically proven methods for optimizing mental, emotional, spiritual, and physical well-being as you age and at every level of health.

We know these are some big promises to make, but we make them with humility and confidence because *The Miracle Morning* books and practices have already enabled millions of people to make meaningful changes in their lives. You can also feel confident knowing that more than one third of those people (roughly a million) were over the age of 50, with many well into their 60s, 70s, 80s, and beyond. Although most of them experienced some level of self-doubt and/or resistance as they began their Miracle Morning journey—similar to what you might be experiencing—now they're thriving. They're waking up each day and fulfilling more of their limitless potential. And it's not because they have any special abilities that you don't have. It's simply because they learned the Miracle Morning process and then applied what they learned in their lives, just like you're doing now.

Thank you for allowing us to join you on this meaningful journey called life. You stand at the threshold of an extraordinary chapter, ready to embrace a simple yet powerful morning routine—one specifically designed to enrich your life after 50. Day by day, morning by morning, you'll rediscover your purpose, unlock your inner vitality, and awaken to possibilities you may have never imagined. It's your time now to reclaim your mornings, realize your true potential, and start living the fulfilling, joyful life you deeply deserve.

With love and gratitude,

Hal   Dwayne

Part 1

WAKING UP TO YOUR FULL POTENTIAL AT 50 AND BEYOND

1

WHY MORNING ROUTINES ARE THE KEY TO LONGEVITY

"A human being would certainly not grow to be 70 or 80 years old if this longevity had no meaning for the species. The afternoon of human life must also have a significance of its own and cannot be merely a pitiful appendage to life's morning."
—Carl Jung, author and founder of analytic psychology

L et's talk about your relationship with mornings, a time that sets the tone for your entire day and quality of life. How do yours usually begin?

As we get older, mornings may feel more along the lines of mundane or mediocre than they do miraculous. Perhaps you're jolted from sleep by the persistent buzzing of your alarm clock, prompting you to get ready for a workday ahead—whether you were well-rested or not. Or maybe you're retired and find yourself lingering under the covers, hesitant to face the day. Rising from bed may not be as swift and energetic as it once was, with your body reminding you of the passage of time through its creaks and groans. I mean, let's be honest—who among us doesn't occasionally throw out our back just by getting out of bed the wrong way?

In all seriousness, as you transition from unconsciousness to wakefulness, your mind likely turns to the day ahead. You might feel overwhelmed grappling with a packed schedule, or you may feel a bit bored or even depressed with a lack of activities to fill your time. Mornings often bring a sense of uncertainty, possibly a lack of purpose, or feelings of stress and worry, setting the stage for the hours to come.

Too many aging adults find themselves trapped in this cycle, starting each day with a suboptimal morning and carrying that sense of unease and lack of focus throughout the day. Despite their best intentions, they often feel adrift, unable to fully enjoy or engage with their daily activities. Since passing 50, you may have noticed that time feels like it's moving faster. Maybe your body has started whispering (or shouting) reminders that you're not 25 anymore.

But here's the good news: How you start your day has a profound impact on how you age. In fact, your morning routine may be one of the most powerful, underutilized tools you have to not only extend your lifespan but to also increase the quality of your years by improving your healthspan. This chapter will show you how a few intentional habits each morning can sharpen your mind, strengthen your body, elevate your mood, and help you create the next—and possibly best—chapter of your life.

Longevity vs. Lifespan vs. Life Expectancy vs. Healthspan: Understanding the Differences

Throughout the book, we will frequently refer to four related terms: *longevity*, *lifespan*, *life expectancy*, and *healthspan*. These terms are often used synonymously, but they aren't quite the same.

- *Longevity* refers to living a long duration of life (especially beyond the average age).
- *Lifespan* refers to our lifetime (how long we live).
- *Life expectancy* assesses how long someone is expected to live based on birth year and demographics. Medical advances and living conditions have significantly increased life expectancy over the past centuries. For example, in 1900, men had a life expectancy of just 46.3 years and women 48.3 years.[1] Today, those numbers are much higher—74.8 years for men and 80.2 years for women.[2]
- *Healthspan* means living longer in optimal good health, free from chronic diseases and debilitating conditions. It generally means enjoying a life where you can remain active and fully functional. On average, there's a nine- to ten-year gap between lifespan and healthspan, meaning many of us spend nearly a decade dealing with chronic health issues. Lifestyle choices such as regular exercise, a balanced diet, and the S.A.V.E.R.S. practices you'll learn in this book are essential for improving your healthspan.

How we begin our mornings holds immense significance, particularly as we grow older. Unproductive mornings lead to unproductive days, which results in an unproductive life. But when we awaken to a powerful, predetermined morning routine, ready to craft a purposeful start to our day, we lay the groundwork for personal growth, productivity, and fulfillment. This initial spark of energy and enthusiasm not only shapes our daily experiences but also influences the trajectory of our individual development, inspiring and motivating us to make the most of every facet of our lives.

The more effective your morning routine is, the more it supports you in starting your day with clarity, purpose, and a focus on what matters most to you. It helps you cultivate an optimal mindset and emotional well-being, and it sets you on the path to increased productivity to set and achieve meaningful goals. Prioritizing personal development and self-care each morning enables you to show up as the best version of yourself throughout the day.

However, you might also be shaking your head and thinking, *Well, that's all fine and dandy, but mornings just aren't my thing. This may work for others, but I don't believe it will work for me.* Alternatively, you might find yourself saying, *Gosh, no matter what I do, I can't seem to sleep past 5:00 a.m. These early mornings are wearing me out, no matter when I go to sleep.* Or you may be thinking, *I have to listen to my body and get out of bed when it tells me to, which I don't have much control over.*

These perspectives are understandable and completely normal. Transitioning from enduring unproductive mornings to waking up with enthusiasm, intention, and structure begins with a shifting of your mindset. We are taking our time to thoroughly address and reinforce the importance of mornings while handling any and all concerns, because adopting a Miracle Morning mindset is a process, albeit a relatively straightforward and simple one. The good news is that we're just getting started. By the end of this book, you will have gradually and completely acclimated to the process of implementing the Miracle Morning and the S.A.V.E.R.S. into your life.

One key thing to understand is that benefiting from the Miracle Morning doesn't require that you sleep less, and while we will recommend rising at least 30 minutes earlier than usual to add the practice to your day, you don't *have* to wake up any earlier if you don't wish to. It's simply a matter of starting your day with personal development—specifically the S.A.V.E.R.S.—so that you can cultivate the mindset, motivation, and habits that will enable you to create and experience the life you want and deserve.

Rising early should be something we do with gratitude and enthusiasm, since we are awakening to the gift of a brand-new day. Even if we are facing challenges in our lives—and who among us isn't?—how we feel about our lives is based on what we consistently focus on. If we start our days thinking about all of our perceived problems and limitations, then we are inevitably going to feel distressed, overwhelmed, and unhappy. If, instead, we wake up and spend time focusing on (and ideally journaling about) all of our blessings and opportunities, we will generate feelings of gratitude, optimism, and happiness.

The Older We Get, the Earlier We Rise

Here is some more good news! We naturally wake up earlier as we reach 50, 60, 70, 80, and beyond. According to the National Institute on Aging, older adults need roughly the same amount of sleep as all adults—7 to 9 hours each night.[3] However, as we get older, we tend to go to sleep earlier and wake earlier than we did when we were younger. So, getting up early may not be new to your routine. However, starting your day with the S.A.V.E.R.S. (detailed in Chapter 3) likely will be.

Whatever your reasons for an earlier wake time, being intentional with what you do during your morning hours is essential. Creating a structured approach to how you rise and shine maximizes your ability to make the most of each day, which includes improving your healthspan and longevity. No one wants to get older only to feel worn out, uncomfortable, and unmotivated. With a daily personal development ritual, and specifically the Miracle Morning, we can enter each new decade wiser and more capable than the last.

Why Do Some Adults Struggle to Wake Up as They Age?

Do you wake up feeling sluggish more often than you'd like? If you're finding it more challenging to rise and shine, it might be time to investigate. Rather than resigning yourself to a cycle of daytime naps and nighttime restlessness, consider these factors that could be hindering your wake-up routine:

- **Urinary troubles:** As we age, bladder control can become less reliable, leading to more frequent trips to the bathroom at night. If this is disrupting your sleep, focus on hydrating throughout the day, and limit the amount of fluids you consume during the hours leading up to bedtime. If this issue persists, discuss it with your doctor to rule out any underlying medical conditions.
- **Sleep apnea:** A common sleep disorder affecting millions, sleep apnea can go undetected, especially for those who sleep alone. Explore this with your healthcare provider if you consistently feel tired despite a full night's sleep.
- **Nutritional deficiencies:** Our bodies process nutrients differently as we age, sometimes requiring diet or supplement adjustments. Ensure you get adequate amounts of vitamins D, E, and B, iron, calcium, and magnesium. If fatigue persists, consult your doctor for dietary guidance and bloodwork.
- **Lack of exercise:** Engaging in physical activity during the day promotes better sleep quality and duration and helps to alleviate stress. Aim for regular exercise, preferably outdoors, to support healthy sleep patterns.

- **Unsuitable mattress:** Discomfort from an unsupportive mattress can lead to restless sleep and morning stiffness. Invest in a mattress that provides proper support and comfort for a refreshing night's sleep.

Addressing these factors can help you take proactive steps to improve your sleep quality and wake up feeling refreshed each morning.

Hal says . . .

Are morning people born or made? In my case, definitely made. For most of my life, I was convinced that I was not a morning person. Most nights, I stayed up as late as possible and proudly identified as a night owl. But then I realized something true for nearly all of us: During our formative years, we were unknowingly conditioned to resist waking up. Most of us were woken up by our parents, against our will, and forced to get out of bed each morning to get ready for school. So, naturally, we resisted and even resented being woken up. Any time we were given the choice, we would continue sleeping for as long as possible. This all occurred during our youth when our brains were developing and lifelong beliefs were being instilled. Once we became adults and left home, our resistance and resentment toward waking up relatively early turned into rebellion. We stayed up late and slept in as long as possible, with no one there to tell us otherwise. "I'm not a morning person" became a false, limiting belief and part of our identity that we reinforced and perpetuated into adulthood. That was true for me, too, until I realized that if I started my day in a peak mental, emotional, physical, and spiritual state, I would be more effective and capable of creating and living the life I wanted.

Dwayne says . . .

I was the opposite. After 55, I was awake at 5:00 a.m. whether I wanted to be or not. And depending on how many times I got up during the night, I was at some level of tiredness. I'd go through seasons where I sprang out of bed and hit the ground running, while other times, it took until 11:00 a.m. to get the engine warmed up. Of course, that was before I discovered the Miracle Morning—that quiet time and space you can dedicate to showing up at your best each day for yourself and your loved ones—while the rest of the world is still asleep. More importantly, incorporating self-care factors into your Miracle Morning routine helps you maintain independence as you age.

The Power of Starting Your Day with Self-Care

If you've ever flown on a commercial airline, you've undoubtedly heard the flight attendant's friendly voice over the loudspeaker, politely reminding everyone, "If there should be a change in cabin pressure, put your oxygen mask on first before helping others." This is a near-perfect analogy for the importance of starting our mornings with self-care. To be in a position to show up at your *best* for yourself and others, you must first attend to caring for your physical, mental, emotional, and spiritual well-being.

Establishing your Miracle Morning routine ensures that you start your day with highly effective self-care. By incorporating the S.A.V.E.R.S. (*Silence, Affirmations, Visualization, Exercise, Reading,* and *Scribing*) you set a strong foundation for your overall well-being.

A 2021 study by researchers at Columbia University and Johns Hopkins University illustrates the importance of good self-care behaviors as you take each new decade by the horns![4] The study used data from the National Health and Aging Trends Study (NHATS), which included 7,609 older adults (average age 75) interviewed annually over 5 years. Researchers examined eight self-care behaviors and classified participants into favorable or unfavorable patterns. (About half of the participants had favorable self-care patterns [e.g., regular exercise and good sleep] while the other half did not.) They also tracked changes in participants' mobility and ability to perform daily activities. Their findings? Those with favorable self-care patterns were much less likely to lose their independence. They had a 92 percent lower risk of needing assistance for mobility and an 86 percent lower risk of needing assistance for daily activities. They also had a significantly lower risk of death over the five years. Favorable self-care patterns also helped participants stay healthier and have more functional years compared to those with unfavorable patterns.

The big takeaway: Routines promoting favorable self-care behaviors can dramatically enhance the quality and length of life for adults 50 and over. And yet, many aging adults don't take this simple truth to heart. They either focus on taking care of everyone else's needs and don't make time to care for themselves, or they simply fail to make self-care a priority. Over time, this can lead to exhaustion, depression, resentment, overwhelm, and burnout. If you can relate to this or would like to avoid this altogether, we will continue unpacking the not-so-obvious secrets that will turn all of this around: Improving your mornings improves your life. And once you grasp the profound benefits that make maximizing your mornings so impactful, you'll be unwilling to overlook them again.

> Routines promoting favorable self-care behaviors can dramatically enhance the quality and length of life for adults 50 and over.

Morning Routines Improve Memory, Focus, and Cognitive Abilities

A morning routine can significantly enhance our cognitive abilities through several mechanisms. First, our memory and cognitive challenges become more manageable when life is familiar and predictable. By establishing a consistent morning routine, you provide your mind with a structured approach to start the day. This consistency helps reduce decision fatigue and mental clutter, allowing you to direct your focus more effectively.

According to a 2022 study by University of Pittsburgh researchers, older adults who consistently get up early and remain active throughout the day are happier and perform better on cognitive tests than those with irregular activity patterns. "There's something about getting going early, staying active all day, and following the same routine each day that seems to protect older adults," said lead author Stephen Smagula, PhD.[5] "What's exciting about these findings is that activity patterns are under voluntary control, which means that making intentional changes to one's daily routine could improve health and wellness."

Another study, published in 2023, aimed to understand which self-care activities are most beneficial for maintaining cognitive functions like memory and attention as we get older. In this study, 105 healthy older adults (mostly women) recorded their self-care activities and underwent cognitive evaluations. Self-care activities were categorized into survival (basic daily tasks), maintenance (physical, mental, social, and spiritual activities), and personal development (reflection, new skills, and technology use). The study's key findings revealed that participants spent most of their time on survival activities, with significantly less time dedicated to maintenance and personal development. Those who engaged in personal development activities, such as learning new skills or using technology, showed better memory and attention than those who focused primarily on basic daily tasks. Additionally, a greater variety of activities, particularly those related to personal development, correlated with higher cognitive performance.[6]

Incorporating the S.A.V.E.R.S. into each morning nurtures cognitive vitality, helping you stay sharp and agile as you age. Spending time in *Silence*—using meditation, prayer, reflection, or deep breathing—calms your mind, eases stress, and enhances mental clarity. *Affirmations* reinforce positive thought patterns and create new neural pathways in your brain. *Visualization* fosters creativity and keeps the mind sharp. *Exercise* increases blood flow to the brain, elevating memory and overall cognitive function. *Reading* nourishes your intellect with fresh insights, while *Scribing* lets you capture reflections and track your progress over time. Together, these practices build a resilient and agile mind, ready to excel throughout the day.

Hal says . . .

Even though I'm still a few years away from turning 50, I already suffer from severe cognitive impairment due to a traumatic brain injury as well as brain poisoning that I experienced after enduring over 700 hours of highly toxic chemotherapy at age 37. The combined effects have left me with severely compromised mental abilities. My memory and recall are very poor, and my ability to process information isn't much better. My Miracle Mornings have proven crucial, as they enable me to start each day with structure, clarity, consistency, and focus. It's not an exaggeration to say that the S.A.V.E.R.S. have saved my life. My *Silence* practice quiets my overactive mind and improves my mental clarity. My *Affirmations* remind me of what I'm capable of and committed to. Using *Visualization* to mentally rehearse my priorities increases my productivity throughout the day. Making *Exercise* a priority in the morning boosts my energy. Being intentional about *Reading* gives me new ideas to enhance various areas of my life. And *Scribing* allows me to organize my thoughts. Making time for the S.A.V.E.R.S. each morning enables me to show up at my relative best each day, and nothing has been more effective at helping me manage my cognitive challenges. This is why I'm excited for you to experience these practices and the resulting benefits for yourself!

Morning Routines Elevate Mental and Emotional Well-Being

We all want to feel good, to be genuinely happy, and to thoroughly enjoy this one life we've been blessed to live. The primary obstacle standing in the way of feeling our best is our mindset—the mental attitude or disposition that predetermines our interpretations of and response to situations. This is evident when you consider that two people can face similar circumstances or endure similar struggles, and while one person may be miserable and constantly complain about how bad their life is, the other consciously chooses to be genuinely grateful for what they have. Though both are facing similar circumstances, two different mindsets create two very different interpretations of and responses to reality.

A person's mindset ultimately determines the quality of their mental and emotional well-being. In other words, our mindset determines what we think, how we feel, and how we behave in any given situation. No matter the circumstances, a person with a positive mindset can be genuinely grateful, happy, and at peace, even amid challenges and difficulties. No matter what happens to us, life is as good or bad as we perceive it.

Cultivating an optimal mindset begins in the morning and sets the tone for each day. By waking up and focusing on all that you have to be grateful for, choosing to be at peace with all that you don't, and actively making the most of your abilities to pursue all that you want, your mindset shapes your days and your life. No matter what your mood is upon waking, your Miracle Morning will enable you to cultivate an optimal mindset every day, allowing you to experience your life in a grateful, joyful, peaceful state no matter what your current or future circumstances might be.

Dwayne says . . .

An important point must be brought into the mindset discussion when considering aging. Depression in older adults is a complex issue often misunderstood or overlooked. Despite common misconceptions, depression is not a normal part of aging but a serious concern that requires attention. In my experience, older individuals can become reluctant to seek help or talk about their struggles. Unfortunately, this reluctance can exacerbate the problem, delaying assessment and treatment.

Several factors contribute to depression in older adults, including poor physical health, social isolation, and loss associated with aging. The loss of a companion or loved one is a major reason older adults experience depression. Chronic illnesses, medications, and reduced mobility can directly or indirectly trigger depression. Additionally, the loss of independence or one's sense of purpose can intensify feelings of sadness and hopelessness. Social isolation, exacerbated by factors such as living alone or having diminished support networks, further increases the risk of depression among older adults.

Recognizing depression in older adults can be challenging, as symptoms may differ from those in younger individuals. Rather than expressing emotional distress, older adults may exhibit physical symptoms like dizziness, aches, pains, or changes in appetite and sleep patterns. Behavioral changes, such as social withdrawal, loss of interest in once-enjoyable activities, or excessive alcohol consumption, may also signal depression. Thoughts of death or suicide should be taken seriously and addressed promptly. I resonated with Hal's original Miracle Morning book because he used the S.A.V.E.R.S. to change his mindset, which helped him overcome a six-month period of feeling depressed due to his personal financial crisis. The S.A.V.E.R.S. can grow with us and help us tap into the right mindset, energy, and productivity levels at any age and for the rest of our lives.

Morning Routines Decrease Feelings of Stress and Anxiety

As we get older, it's natural to worry about things we have little or no control over, such as our bodies aging, experiencing a loss of autonomy, or the state of the economy and the potential consequences for our retirement. Some may find themselves grappling with persistent feelings of stress and anxiety. Uncertainty about the future may become prevalent, particularly for those facing conditions like Alzheimer's disease, dementia, stroke, or other cognitive and physical impairments.

Most people, regardless of age, are uncomfortable with unpredictability and uncertainty. Establishing a well-structured morning routine can significantly reduce feelings of stress and anxiety by providing structure and a sense of control at the start of the day. When we begin our mornings with intentional activities—like meditation, exercise, journaling, or any of the other S.A.V.E.R.S.—it helps center our thoughts and calm our minds before the demands of the day take over. Engaging in these practices allows us to focus on the present moment, reducing the tendency to dwell on the past or worry about the future. A consistent morning routine also fosters a sense of accomplishment and boosts mental resilience, making it easier to handle challenges throughout the day with a clearer, more balanced mindset.

Morning Routines Increase Productivity and Fulfillment

Human beings thrive when we're proactive and making progress, especially toward predetermined goals. Whether tending to a garden or pursuing professional success, increased productivity correlates with higher levels of fulfillment. A study published in the *Journal of Applied Social Psychology* showed that early risers with established morning routines tend to be more focused, have a greater sense of what they need to accomplish throughout the day, and are more proactive.[7] Having a proactive mindset and routine leads to increased productivity and fulfillment.

Remember that how you start your day sets the tone and direction for the hours that follow. Thus, being productive in the morning fosters feelings of accomplishment and creates momentum that propels you in a positive direction through the rest of the day. Expanding on this notion, Robin Sharma, a *New York Times* bestselling author who appeared in the feature-length documentary *The Miracle Morning*, observes, "Many of the world's most productive individuals have one thing in common—they are early risers." In other words, when you win the morning, you set yourself up to win in life.

However, one of the sneaky issues we have to contend with as we age—especially after we retire—is that we often let our days go by

> When you win the morning, you set yourself up to win in life.

with a lot of "empty time." At Aegis Living, Dwayne and his team have seen that "empty time" can translate into anxiety for seniors. The lack of work, projects, and activities begins weighing heavily on their minds. This is a direct result of feeling unproductive or, perhaps, that you no longer matter as much. You retired from a job that kept your daytime hours busy. Maybe you let aches and pains keep you from hobbies or physical activities with friends. And as we age, our social circles can get smaller because people move and pass away as the years go by. So, if you're not careful, "empty time" turns into feeling empty inside and less productive. In Chapter 15, we go deep into purpose, which is essential to longevity and healthspan. But for now, we can't overemphasize the need for us all to remain as productive with our days as possible as we journey toward 100 and beyond.

As you can see, establishing your Miracle Morning routine can profoundly transform your life—enhancing your focus, memory, and mood, reducing stress and anxiety, and boosting your productivity and overall sense of fulfillment. Whether you currently consider yourself a morning person or not, in our next chapter, you're going to learn how to make waking up every day more accessible and enjoyable than ever before. We will share a little-known secret with you about early rising: *It only takes 5 minutes to become a morning person.*

What you do during the first 5 minutes after you wake determines whether or not you set yourself up to have an unproductive, mediocre morning or a highly productive Miracle Morning. We've got a lot of ground to cover in this book, so let's keep moving.

2

UNLOCKING THE MORNING PERSON WITHIN

The 5-Step Snooze-Proof Wake Up Strategy

"It is well to be up before daybreak, for such habits contribute to health, wealth, and wisdom."
—Aristotle, Greek philosopher

It's been said that nobody really likes going to the gym, but everyone loves the feeling of having gone to the gym. Similarly, we may resist the idea of waking before we *have to* and think that we prefer sleeping until the last possible minute; but the reality is that *everyone* loves the feeling of having gotten a great start to the day. We all feel better when we've had a productive morning.

When it comes to how you relate to mornings, you undoubtedly fall into one of two camps: Either you already consider yourself to be a "morning person" or you don't. There's not a whole lot of in between. Regardless of which camp you currently identify with, this chapter will enable both those who struggle with mornings as well as existing early risers to kickstart your days with newfound levels of discipline, motivation, and intention.

You're about to discover the transformative power of the Five-Step Snooze-Proof Wake Up Strategy that has helped millions of people wake up feeling rejuvenated and eager, even those who had dreaded the mornings for their entire lives. This simple approach will set you up to overcome any resistance to getting out of bed so that you can take full advantage of your Miracle Mornings—regardless of whether or not you've ever considered yourself to be a morning person.

Hal says . . .

Waking up a little earlier than you're used to for personal development is similar to beginning a running routine for physical fitness. If a person has never identified as a "runner," then they likely have a limiting belief that they could never *become* a runner or that doing so would be unpleasant. Our identity shapes our beliefs about who we are, and we tend to have a hard time seeing ourselves as capable of doing something we've never done before. As I shared earlier, this was true for me for most of my life. In high school, I dreaded running the mile. I had never been a runner and had little to no stamina. Unless someone was chasing me, you would never find me running for the sake of running.

That all changed when a friend of mine, Jon Vroman—who himself had also never been a runner—committed to completing a 52-mile ultra-marathon to raise money for charity. Although he walked as much as he jogged, he kept putting one foot in front of the other (for 15 consecutive hours) until he completed 52 consecutive miles. Afterward, he enthusiastically told me how accomplishing this seemingly impossible task completely transformed his mindset regarding what he's capable of. His experience inspired me to follow in his footsteps and do the same. (In Chapter 6, I'll share more about how *Visualization* helped me do it.)

Similarly, if you've never identified as a morning person, you may mistakenly believe that you could never become one, or that it would be too difficult. But that can change for you as it has for countless other Miracle Morning newbies who came before you. After applying the five steps you're about to learn, it's highly likely that you may soon be saying to yourself, *OMG, I can't believe it . . . I've become a morning person!*

Increasing Your Morning Motivation Level (MML)

Think about your typical morning. Whether you wake up naturally or with the assistance of an alarm clock, if you were to gauge your eagerness to get out of bed and get moving on a scale from 1 to 10 (with 10 indicating you're fully prepared to start the day and 1 meaning you're desperately longing to stay in bed), where would you place yourself?

We refer to this measurement as your morning motivation level (MML). For most of us, it's closer to the lower end of the scale, like a 1 or 2. It's completely normal to feel the urge to hit snooze and cling to sleep when you're still half asleep. This phenomenon, known as "sleep inertia," is the grogginess and disorientation that can come with waking up from a deep sleep. As you've likely experienced, it's quite difficult to muster up the drive to rise, shine, and kickstart your day when your MML is hovering around a 1 or 2 during the moments when you first awaken.

The solution lies in having a simple, predetermined strategy involving small, incremental steps that allow you to wake up gradually, one minute at a time. Each minute you're awake, your MML naturally rises as your body and brain acclimate to a wakeful state. So, although your MML may be at a 1 or 2 during the first few moments of your transition from being unconscious to conscious, after implementing the five steps you're about to learn, your MML will increase to a 5, 6, 7, or higher, giving you the energy and motivation you need to start your day powerfully.

The 5-Step Snooze-Proof Wake Up Strategy

Here are five simple steps designed to conquer morning grogginess and make waking up and getting going more accessible and enjoyable than ever before.

Step 1: Set an Empowering Intention Before Bed

Consider this: Whatever you think about before you fall asleep often reemerges as your initial thoughts as soon as you wake up. Similarly, whatever mental and emotional state you allow yourself to dwell in as you drift off to sleep (which is usually a result of what you think about) lingers while you slumber and sets the tone for how you feel in the morning. If you go to bed thinking stressful thoughts and feeling stressed and worried, you will likely wake up feeling stressed and worried. If, on the other hand, you think about what you're grateful for as you drift off to sleep, in a state of peacefulness and gratitude, you will likely wake up feeling grateful and at peace.

The problem is that most of us aren't very intentional about what we think about before bed, and we often allow our minds to wander down stress-inducing paths. If we want to optimize how we feel in the morning, we must be more disciplined and intentional about what we think about and the emotional states we experience before bed. For instance, you can set your intention to wake up feeling refreshed and energized, ready to *make* tomorrow a great day.

Similarly, our mindset and expectations about the morning often predetermine how we feel. Think back to times when you were so excited about waking up the next day that you could hardly fall asleep. Whether it was when you were a kid on Christmas Eve or the night before you were scheduled to leave for a long-awaited vacation, as soon as the morning arrived, you sprung out of bed feeling excited, energized, and ready to embrace the day! Why? Because what you focused on before you fell asleep was all positive. It becomes a self-fulfilling prophecy.

The good news is that we can recreate this experience of waking up enthusiastically and excited daily. We don't need to wait on a holiday or a vacation to set our intentions. We can also fall asleep feeling grateful and at peace simply by focusing on what we have to be thankful for. We can change what we focus on before bed, and thus how we feel in the morning, by being intentional about what we choose to think about. This is why the first step toward becoming a (happy) morning person is to consciously set an empowering intention and create a positive expectation for the following day—before you fall asleep.

For help on this and to get the precise words to say to yourself before bed, you can download a copy of The Miracle Evening Bedtime Affirmations now (that you can print and keep on your nightstand) at **TMMAfter50.com**.

Dwayne says . . .

Here's one of the ways I set an empowering intention before going to bed. I've made it a bedtime habit to post three or four sticky notes on my bathroom mirror of things that I want to see happen the next day. I write them in the past tense as if they've already happened. They may include a statement about how I want to sleep that night (*I had a great night's sleep and felt rested when I woke up*) or how I want an event to go (*The community fundraiser meeting was fruitful and productive and great ideas were shared*). This practice really helps me go to bed with the right mindset. And here's a tip from someone who's been doing this for a while: Be sure not to write "I hope" messages. "I hope" lacks certainty and takes energy out of the message and what you are looking to see happen.

Step 2: Move Your Alarm Clock Across the Room

If you use an alarm clock, this may be one of the easiest yet most effective steps to get yourself out of bed in the morning. Simply move your alarm clock as far away from where you sleep as possible. This will ensure you get out of bed as soon as the alarm sounds and immediately move your body. Movement generates energy, so getting out of bed and walking across the room helps you wake up naturally.

Think about it: If you keep your alarm clock within arm's reach of your bed, then you're still in a partial sleep state when the alarm goes off, and your MML is at its lowest point, making it much more difficult to summon up the discipline needed to get out of bed. You may turn the alarm off or hit the snooze button without realizing it. On more than a few occasions, we've all convinced ourselves that our alarm clock was merely part of the dream we were having. By getting out of bed to turn off the alarm clock, you set yourself up for early-rising success by instantly increasing your MML.

Hal was once brought in as a keynote speaker for the New York City chapter of the global Entrepreneurs' Organization (EO), and was introduced by David Schnurman, CEO of Lawline. Before David brought Hal up, he said, "There's one thing I have to mention from Hal's book that was a game changer for me, and that was his suggestion to move my alarm clock across the room. It may sound simple, but before I did that, I used to hit the snooze button repeatedly and often miss out on my Miracle Mornings. As soon as I moved my alarm clock to my bathroom counter, and I had to get out of bed to turn it off, I stopped hitting the snooze button. Now, I wake up as soon as my alarm goes off, brush my teeth, drink a glass of water, get dressed, and head into my living room to do my Miracle Morning, which has been life-changing for me. But if it wasn't for moving my alarm clock, I'd probably still be hitting the snooze button and struggling with unproductive mornings."

If you use an alarm clock, this simple strategy can be a game changer for you as well. For those who prefer not to use an alarm clock, Dwayne offers an alternative approach.

Dwayne says . . .

I want to highlight that I grew out of using an alarm clock to wake up many years ago. And here is the critical reason why: It's called first light! In Chapter 14, we cover the incredible longevity benefits of first light and exactly how to make it a part of your Miracle Morning routine. By incorporating first light as the way you wake up, you can reprogram your biology to wake up naturally while soaking in the health benefits.

One longevity benefit to waking up naturally, instead of jumping out of bed to hit the snooze button, is the opportunity to do a whole-body "stretch check-in." Bed stretching (as I call it) before getting out of bed can significantly improve balance, support healthspan, and contribute to longevity for several reasons.

Firstly, stretching helps increase blood flow to muscles and joints, reducing stiffness and improving mobility. Enhanced circulation also means that nutrients and oxygen are more efficiently delivered to tissues, promoting overall health. Stretching also improves muscle flexibility and joint range of motion, reducing the risk of injuries caused by sudden movements or falls, and helps maintain and improve the range of motion in joints, which is crucial for balance and coordination.

Moreover, stretching activates proprioceptive sensors in muscles and joints (sensory receptors that provide feedback about body and limb position), which helps the brain

> Stretching and proper hydration can improve the health and flexibility of ligaments, tendons, muscles, fascia, and joints. So stretch and stay hydrated!

understand the body's position in space, enhancing balance and coordination. It also improves neuromuscular efficiency, allowing muscles and nerves to work more efficiently, preventing falls, and improving overall stability. Additionally, stretching reduces muscle tension and stiffness, making it easier to move without discomfort. Regular stretching also combats stiffness that often occurs after prolonged inactivity, such as sleeping.

Preventing falls is crucial as we age, as falls are a leading cause of injury[1] and a leading cause of injury-related deaths among adults aged 65 and older.[2] Improving balance and flexibility through stretching can significantly reduce the risk of falls and allow us to efficiently perform daily activities and maintain our independence for longer. Staying active and mobile contributes to a higher quality of life, as individuals can engage in more activities they enjoy.

Furthermore, stretching promotes overall health by helping manage chronic conditions, such as arthritis, diabetes, and heart disease. Physical activity, including stretching, releases endorphins that can improve mood and reduce the risk of depression and anxiety. Research published in the *Journal of Aging Research* indicates that regular stretching exercises can improve flexibility, balance, and overall functional mobility in older adults, reducing the risk of falls and promoting independence.[3]

Here is a favorite bed-stretching routine of mine you can start with:

1. **Toe and ankle circles:** While lying on your back, wiggle your toes, acknowledging all 10. Then, lift one leg slightly off the bed and rotate your ankle in circles. Repeat with the other leg.

2. **Knee hugs:** Pull one knee toward your chest, hold for a few seconds, then switch to the other knee. If you can't get your knee to your chest, go as far as you can—even

just bending the knees a few times before standing helps strengthen your overall balance.

3. **Finger and arm stretches:** Extend your arms above your head and stretch as far as possible, and then wiggle each finger separately before wiggling all 10 together. Again, if you can't raise your arms above your head, go as far as you can, or simply stretch them out sideways and do the same stretch.

4. **Neck rotations:** Gently turn your head from side to side and up and down to loosen your neck muscles.

5. **Repeat:** Do this routine at least twice, if not three times, before getting out of bed to help wake up every muscle and better balance you after resting for seven to eight hours.

6. **Three cleansing breaths:** Lastly, sit up on the side of your bed and take three deep cleansing breaths. Inhale as deeply as you comfortably can through your nose, and then exhale, focusing on emptying your lungs. This will increase the oxygen in your body and help you feel more awake.

This routine makes it much more difficult to go back to sleep once you've physically woken up every inch of your body. After caring for tens of thousands of seniors in my lifetime, I've seen too many cases where seniors hurriedly get out of bed before stretching, step down without enough balance, and have a debilitating fall. This fall begins the risky landslide into countless health issues, some resulting in early death. It sounds morbid, but it is a hard truth. This is why I recommend waking up with first light and spending the first 5 minutes lying in bed doing a full-body bed stretch.

Now that you've moved your body, you've generated energy and momentum, and it's much easier to keep that momentum going, as long as you stay in motion. However, you're still just beginning to wake up and may still be feeling a bit groggy, so it's time to move on to Step 3.

Step 3: Brush Your Teeth

We know what you might be thinking: *Wait, did y'all seriously just tell me to brush my teeth? Are you suggesting that oral hygiene is the solution to this struggling to get going in the morning?*

Not exactly. Remember, the purpose of these five steps is to provide you with a handful of predetermined, nearly effortless activities to start your day so that your body and mind have time to gradually acclimate to being awake. Every minute that you remain awake and moving increases your MML. So, after turning off your alarm clock or waking naturally, head straight to the bathroom sink, grab your toothbrush, and start brushing. This will add another few minutes to the time you're awake and continue increasing your MML.

While you're at it, swish some mouthwash around in your mouth or splash some warm (or cold) water on your face for a little extra boost.

Bonus Tip: Dwayne adds something extra to this step. He brushes his teeth while standing on one foot! Besides making his wife giggle, it is an excellent longevity hack. Balancing on one foot strengthens the leg muscles, which support the joints and improve overall stability. According to the *Journal of Physical Therapy Science*, balance exercises significantly improve the strength of lower extremity muscles as we get older.[4] This is important because balance becomes critical to longevity and healthspan as we age beyond 50.

Now that your mouth is clean and minty fresh, and you're starting to feel more alert, it's time to rehydrate and reenergize.

Step 4: Drink a Glass of Water

Dehydration can cause fatigue and sluggishness. When we feel tired in the morning or at any time of the day, we often need more water, not more sleep.

Did you know that while we sleep, our bodies release water through sweat and exhalation, and the average adult can lose 8 to 10 ounces of fluid overnight? This means we wake up mildly dehydrated. That's why rehydrating as soon as possible after waking is essential. It will increase your energy and help get rid of brain fog. Dwayne recommends room temperature water because for certain individuals, including those with compromised immune systems, cold water can slow down the immune system.

So, be sure to place a full glass of water next to your bed or on the bathroom counter at night, before going to bed. Then, after you brush your teeth, drink the water as fast as is comfortable. Not only will this H_2O reduce your grogginess and raise your MML another notch, but it will also optimize your longevity and healthspan. Why? Here's the fascinating answer: Lurking throughout your body, from your liver to your brain, are zombie-like entities known as *senescent cells*. These cells release inflammatory and tissue-degrading molecules, negatively impacting health. As we age, our immune system becomes less effective at clearing these zombie cells, contributing to various age-related health problems and diseases.

> While we sleep, our bodies release water through sweat and exhalation, and the average adult can lose 8 to 10 ounces of fluid overnight.

Research reported in the *Mayo Clinic News Network* highlights the significant impact of senescent cells on aging.[5] In a recent article, they highlighted a study published in *Aging Cell* that identified proteins secreted by these cells, which serve as senescence biomarkers and predict health outcomes in older adults. Higher levels of specific senescent biomarkers, such as GDF15 and VEGFA, are linked to an increased risk of death and chronic diseases. Dr. Jennifer St. Sauver, the study's lead author, emphasizes that biological age can differ significantly from chronological age, and these biomarkers can predict future health challenges without disease.[6]

Another study published in *Nature* by Dr. Joao Passos and colleagues found that a group of mitochondria within senescent cells tries to initiate cell death, releasing their DNA into the cell's cytosol and triggering inflammation.[7] Blocking this process in older mice reduced tissue inflammation and improved overall health, including strength, balance, and bone structure.

One effective way to combat the effects of zombie cells is by drinking 8 to 12 ounces of water as soon as you get out of bed in the morning. Proper hydration plays a crucial role in fighting the detrimental effects of senescent cells via these processes:

1. **Enhanced detoxification:** Water is vital for kidney function, helping filter out toxins and waste products from the bloodstream. Drinking water first thing in the morning kickstarts this detoxification process, aiding in the removal of harmful substances released by zombie cells.

2. **Improved cellular function:** Proper hydration ensures that cells receive adequate nutrients and oxygen, which are crucial for repair and function. Well-hydrated cells are more efficient at repairing damage and maintaining their normal functions, counteracting the negative impacts of zombie cells.

3. **Reduced inflammation:** Chronic inflammation, a hallmark of senescent cells, can be mitigated by staying hydrated. Water helps balance the body's systems, reducing inflammation and supporting the immune system in removing senescent cells.

4. **Joint and muscle health:** Dehydration can worsen stiffness and pain associated with arthritis and other age-related conditions. Staying hydrated keeps joints lubricated and muscles functioning correctly, reducing discomfort from inflammation caused by zombie cells.

Studies have demonstrated the benefits of adequate hydration on overall health and longevity. For instance, an article in *Nutrition Reviews* links proper hydration to improved metabolic function, cardiovascular health, and reduced chronic disease incidence.[8] A study in *The Journal of Clinical Endocrinology & Metabolism* found that drinking water increases metabolic rate by 30 percent, enhancing the body's ability to process nutrients and eliminate toxins.[9] Dwayne also recommends waiting 30 minutes or so after drinking your water before having that morning cup of caffeine to allow the water to work its detoxing magic. You may think you can't wait that long for your coffee, but you'll find that you will actually feel better by waiting!

Level Up with Lemon and Sea Salt

If you want to get the most value from your morning water, adding lemon juice and sea salt (specifically Himalayan pink salt) is a longevity hack that has numerous benefits for overall health and wellness. Here are some of the advantages:

- **Boosts immune function:** The vitamin C content in lemon juice and the minerals in Himalayan pink salt work together to increase immune function, helping to fight off infections and diseases.
- **Reduces inflammation:** The properties of lemon juice and the minerals in Himalayan pink salt, particularly potassium and calcium, help decrease uric acid levels and alleviate inflammation in the body.
- **Improves digestion:** Lemon water with sea salt can aid digestion, reduce symptoms of indigestion and bloating, and support a healthy gut microbiome.

- **Balances body pH:** The alkaline properties of lemon juice and the minerals in Himalayan pink salt help balance the body's pH levels, promoting overall health and reducing the risk of chronic diseases.
- **Supports a healthy colon:** The fiber and minerals in lemon water with sea salt can help regulate bowel movements, reduce the risk of constipation, and support a healthy colon.
- **Increases vitality and energy:** Drinking lemon water with sea salt in the morning can help increase vitality and energy levels, making it an excellent way to start the day.

Step 5: Get Dressed in Your Exercise Clothes (or Take a Quick Shower)

The fifth step has two options. The first option is to get dressed in whatever clothing you prefer to exercise in so that you're ready to leave your bedroom and get right into your Miracle Morning practice, which will incorporate a brief period of exercise (the E in S.A.V.E.R.S.). Utilizing these additional moments to dress allows your mind and body to awaken further, elevating your MML and serving as a definitive signal to both your conscious and subconscious that you're ready to embrace the day. You can lay out your clothes before bed or even sleep in your workout clothes. (Yes, really.) And for aging adults, this "night before" prep is essential to making life easier and keeping you on track.

Option two is to jump in the shower, which is a great way to feel refreshed and push your MML to the point where the option of crawling back into bed doesn't even cross your mind.

Hal says . . .

I usually change into my exercise clothes first, since I shower before bed and prefer to shower again after working out (if I break a sweat). There is something to be said about *earning* your morning shower with a workout! But many people like to enjoy a morning shower first because it helps them wake up and gives them a fresh start to the day. The choice is entirely yours. Regardless of your choice, by the time you've executed these five simple steps, your morning motivation level will inevitably be increased so that it requires minimal discipline to stay awake and complete your S.A.V.E.R.S.

It may seem too simple for this 5-step strategy to make such a significant difference. We often mistakenly think a strategy needs to be elaborate or complicated to be effective, but the opposite is usually true. It's often the simplest, most direct path that is the *most* effective. And consistency is key. In sleep science, consistency emerges as a critical player in pursuing healthier aging. The profound impact of regular wake-up times on our cognitive and physical well-being is backed by mountains of science. By consistently waking up at the same time every morning, you can effectively synchronize your internal clock, known as your circadian rhythm, fostering better sleep quality and overall health.[10] When you maintain steady wake-up times, you'll experience improved sleep continuity and reduced sleep onset latency,[11] and you'll likely notice improvements to your memory and attention span.[12] Studies show that waking up at the same time every morning can even help adults over 50 mitigate the risk of mood disorders such as depression and anxiety.[13]

Don't Wait. Plan Your First Miracle Morning Now!

Don't wait to implement this! Your first Miracle Morning can (and should) begin tomorrow. Simply change your wake-up time to be 30 minutes earlier than usual, and prepare tonight by following the five steps covered in this chapter. Then, tomorrow morning, plan on doing just one of the S.A.V.E.R.S. (the *R* for *Reading*) and read Chapter 3: Discovering the S.A.V.E.R.S. After 50. As you learn more about each of the S.A.V.E.R.S., we suggest making it easy on yourself by gradually building your Miracle Morning, one practice at a time. Of course, you're welcome to do as many of the S.A.V.E.R.S. on day one as you'd like, but don't feel like it's an all or nothing pursuit. Your first day of the Miracle Morning can just be continuing with your *Reading* practice. Then, after you've read Chapter 4: *S Is for Silence*, you can add meditation, prayer, or deep breathing into your routine. Once you've read Chapter 5: *A Is for Affirmations*, you'll be able to create affirmations that are highly effective at optimizing your subconscious mind and directing your conscious thoughts and behavior.

There is no wrong or right way to begin your Miracle Morning routine. It's not about perfection, but about progress. What matters most is that you start as soon as possible to begin experiencing the plethora of benefits.

Miracle Morning Community Bonus Wake-Up Tips

Keep in mind that, although this simple, five-step strategy has proven to work for countless people, these five steps are not the only ways to make waking up in the morning easier. One major benefit of being part of the global Miracle Morning Community (who convene in the Facebook group at **MiracleMorningCommunity.com**) is that each person is focused on optimizing their rituals and routines, sharing what's working, and actively supporting each other. Here are a few tips we've seen shared by members of the Miracle Morning Community:

- **Use a vibrating alarm clock.** If you sleep next to a spouse or partner who is adversely affected by the sound of an alarm clock in the morning, you may need to get creative to keep in that person's good graces. Luckily, there are dozens of options for vibrating alarm clocks. There are two primary designs: wearable technology, such as a vibrating wristwatch alarm, and a vibrating pod that goes under your pillow. Just go to Google or Amazon and search "vibrating alarm clock" to see your options. (While, of course, these kinds of alarm clocks can't be placed across the room as we recommend, they can be great options if you need a silent alternative.)

- **Set a timer for your bedroom heater.** If you struggle to get out of bed in the morning because it's uncomfortably cold where you live, this tip may be useful. One member of the Miracle Morning Community said that in the winter, she keeps a portable heater next to her bed, plugged into an appliance timer that is set to turn on 15 minutes before her alarm clock sounds. That way, when she wakes up, the room is warm, and she isn't as tempted to crawl back under her covers to avoid the cold. She said it's made a huge difference!

- **Make your mornings the opposite of your evenings.** In the evening, you likely engage in activities that promote relaxation and prepare you for sleep. Conversely, in the morning, it's beneficial to incorporate stimulating practices to enhance wakefulness and alertness. For instance, if you dim the lights and avoid artificial blue light from screens and LED bulbs at night, make a point to open your blinds and curtains to let in natural sunlight upon waking. (If you're awake before sunrise, turning on several lights can simulate this effect.) Additionally, while you might listen to soothing music in the evening, playing your favorite upbeat tunes in the morning can further boost your energy, alertness, and MML. And remember this: If you're feeling groggy, move your body!

Remember, the objective of the Five-Step Snooze-Proof Wake Up Strategy is to start your day with simple, predetermined activities that require minimal effort and makes waking up and getting going as easy as possible. Next, we will cover what you'll do during your Miracle Morning. Get ready for a deep dive into six of the most potent, proven personal development practices that the world's most successful and fulfilled individuals have utilized for centuries: the S.A.V.E.R.S.

DISCOVERING THE S.A.V.E.R.S. AFTER 50

Six Timeless Practices Guaranteed to Enhance Your Life

"The way you start your day is the way you live your day. Your morning sets the tone for everything else."
—Mel Robbins, American author, podcast host, and keynote speaker

As we cross the threshold into life's second half, the landscape of our priorities begins to shift. For some, it's about savoring the fruits of decades of hard work—more time with family, hobbies long put on hold, or simply embracing a slower pace. For others, it's about redefining purpose and finding ways to contribute, grow, and live more fully than ever before. Regardless of whether you're still in the workforce or enjoying retirement, investing time in ongoing self-development is critical to being able to optimize your mental and emotional well-being so that you can feel and be at your best every day.

Life after 50 can present its own set of unique mental and emotional challenges. The older we get, the more life experiences (good and bad) we have to reflect on, and the less time we have ahead of us. Depending on what we focus on, this can create perpetual states of regret, worry, or other forms of inner turmoil based on our unchangeable past and uncertain future. Many of us have faced difficult circumstances and endured various hardships. For others, looking back may bring about feelings of resentment or regret, imagining what life might have been like had circumstances been more favorable or if they'd made different decisions along the way.

Another factor that can leave us feeling perpetually disappointed is the belief that we have yet to fulfill our potential, and that it may be too late for us to do so. Have you ever felt like there was an insurmountable gap between who you are and who you could become, or the life you're living and the one you want to be living? When you see other people who appear to be happier and more successful, do you ever feel like they seem to have it all figured out—like they must know something you don't because if you knew it as well, then you'd be enjoying the same levels of success and fulfillment?

It's a frustrating predicament, and all too often, we lack the clarity and structure needed to experience consistent motivation, and instead, we put in inconsistent effort and get inconsistent outcomes. This can be especially true for retirees; without the external clarity, structure, and motivation of a job, it can become easy to go through each day without a plan or intention, which then leads to a lack of direction. We often dwell on what we'd need to do to achieve our desired results, yet struggle to take those crucial steps forward. We understand what needs to be done, yet we don't follow through.

While we can't alter the past or turn back the hands of time, there is immense value in focusing our efforts on the present and future. Each of us has the ability to continue evolving and becoming the best version of ourselves, regardless of our age. So, rather than dwelling on what could have been, we can embrace the opportunity to make the most of each day ahead.

Enter the S.A.V.E.R.S., six of the most timeless, proven personal development practices that can become your compass, enabling you to experience new levels of fulfillment, clarity, and vitality. The S.A.V.E.R.S., which stands for *Silence, Affirmations, Visualization, Exercise, Reading,* and *Scribing,* were originally designed as a framework for creating a transformative morning routine. But their power goes far beyond mornings. These practices are universal, timeless, and adaptable to every stage of life. And they're not just habits; they're tools to help you navigate the challenges and opportunities unique to each new season.

Why do the S.A.V.E.R.S. matter so much after 50? Because this is the time to prioritize what truly matters: your physical health, mental clarity, emotional resilience, and spiritual growth. Life may have slowed down in some ways, but the world hasn't stopped moving. The S.A.V.E.R.S. empower you to stay active and intentional, ensuring that each day brings a sense of purpose and possibility, no matter what stage you're in.

Let's face it: The demands of life in your later years are different. Whether you're managing health concerns, adjusting to an empty nest, finding new meaning in your career, or navigating the complexities of retirement, it's

> The S.A.V.E.R.S. empower you to stay active and intentional, ensuring that each day brings a sense of purpose and possibility, no matter what stage you're in.

easy to feel like the best years are behind you. But the S.A.V.E.R.S. offer a powerful antidote to that mindset. They remind you that life doesn't stop improving just because you've celebrated a milestone birthday. In fact, this is the perfect time to embrace practices that help you grow into the best version of yourself.

Imagine beginning each day with a few moments of silence, clearing your mind of worry, and creating space for peace. Picture the power of affirmations to counter self-doubt and reaffirm your purpose, or the clarity that comes from visualizing the life you want and the steps you'll take to create it. Consider the vitality you'll gain from daily exercise, the inspiration of feeding your mind with reading, and the deep self-awareness that emerges from scribing (journaling). Each of these practices is simple; yet together, they create a foundation for living intentionally and meaningfully every day.

An Overview of the S.A.V.E.R.S.

In the following pages, we'll explore how each of these six practices can serve you in the context of your current life. How you approached exercise at 30 may be different from how you approach it at 60, and that's okay. The beauty of the S.A.V.E.R.S. is that they're adaptable to your unique needs and circumstances. In Chapters 4 through 9, we offer specific guidance and examples to help you implement each one. These practices are your toolkit for creating the life you deserve—one morning, one moment at a time.

- **S Is for *Silence*: Cultivate Your Calm in the Chaos.** Starting our days with peaceful, purposeful silence enables us to quiet our minds and relax our nervous systems so that we can experience inner peace and tranquility. It is a sacred time before the world stirs, offering a refuge from life's constant noise. Whether through meditation, prayer, deep breathing, or simply enjoying the stillness, it's a practice that clears the mind, soothes the soul, and brings forth a profound sense of clarity and renewal.

- **A Is for *Affirmations*: Empower Your Subconscious Mind for Success.** What we affirm repeatedly becomes our reality. The words and messages we repeat to ourselves, whether in our minds or out loud, shape our identity, cultivate our mindset, and either perpetuate our limitations or give birth to our capabilities. When we intentionally affirm perspectives and beliefs that support our mental and emotional well-being and are aligned with our aspirations, we feel better and do better. These declarations become our daily compass, moving us toward our goals and guiding us as we face life's challenges with intention and fortitude.

- *V Is for Visualization*: **Mentally Rehearse Showing Up at Your Best.** The world's greatest athletes are known for repeatedly visualizing themselves performing at their best and achieving their goals before they ever step onto the court or take the field. This method of mental rehearsal helps build their confidence and sets themselves up to perform at their best in real time. Incorporating this practice into our lives allows us to use the boundless creativity of our minds to paint pictures of our highest aspirations and then envision ourselves engaged in the behaviors that will make our dreams a reality. Visualization is a practical tool for mentally rehearsing ourselves showing up the way we want to show up, whether at work or at home with our families.

- *E Is for Exercise*: **Enhance Your Physical, Mental, and Emotional Vitality.** We've been gifted with only one physical body, and if we want it to take care of us, we are responsible for taking care of it. Exercising each morning, even for just a few minutes, not only enhances our physical and cardiovascular health, but it also increases blood flow to our brains, sharpening our minds, improving our mood, and providing us with a feeling of accomplishment. Each movement is a tribute to our bodies' resilience that invigorates our spirit and makes a declaration, each day, of our commitment to thrive.

- *R Is for Reading*: **Acquire the Knowledge to Accelerate Your Transformation.** Whether thumbing through the pages of a book like this one or perusing an article online, we have access to a limitless supply of valuable information we can use to improve any aspect of our lives. Each book, article, and story serves as a stepping stone for growth and knowledge, feeding our minds and expanding our capabilities with new perspectives and insights.

- **S Is for *Scribing*: Experience the Power of Solidifying Thoughts in Writing.** A new study suggests we have over 6,000 thoughts per day, most of which are unconscious.[1] When we become more aware of our thoughts and discern which are worthy of solidifying in writing, we can begin freeing ourselves from the burden and overwhelm perpetuated by our overactive minds. Conversely, we can strengthen positive perspectives and emotions by capturing our progress and reflecting on all we have to be grateful for. Scribing is our bridge to deeper self-awareness, chronicling our journey, celebrating our evolution, and fostering deeper states of gratitude and joy. Through writing, we capture the essence of our inner dialogue, learnings, and yearnings, turning introspection into a powerful catalyst for personal transformation.

Implementing any one of these practices consistently can enhance and even transform your life. But when you combine all six of them into a daily routine, you experience the profound benefits of each and multiply their effectiveness. When Hal was interviewed by Robert Kiyosaki, author of the #1 bestselling personal finance book of all time, *Rich Dad Poor Dad*, Robert summed it up well. As a Miracle Morning practitioner himself, he told Hal that *The Miracle Morning* was the appropriate name for his book because, while any one of the S.A.V.E.R.S. could change your life, combining all six practices changes your life so quickly and significantly that it feels like a miracle.

How S.A.V.E.R.S. Can Help Combat ANTs as We Age

Automatic negative thoughts (ANTs) are involuntary, unfavorable thoughts that can occur reflexively in response to certain situations or triggers. The *APA Dictionary of Psychology* defines them as "thoughts that are instantaneous, habitual, and nonconscious."[2] ANTs can manifest in various forms, such as:

- **Catastrophizing:** Expecting the worst possible outcome in any situation.
- **Black-and-white thinking:** Seeing things in extremes, with no middle ground.
- **Overgeneralization:** Making broad assumptions based on a single event.
- **Negative filtering:** Focusing only on the negative aspects of a situation and ignoring the positives.

ANTs are particularly important to consider after age 50 due to their impact on cognitive health, emotional well-being, and overall quality of life. For one reason, the prevalence of anxiety and depression can increase with age, and ANTs contribute significantly to these conditions in older adults.[3] Persistent negative thinking can also contribute to cognitive decline and is linked to an increased risk of dementia; ANTs can also lead to stress and inflammation, which are harmful to brain health.[4] Fortunately, addressing ANTs can create significant improvements in mood and life satisfaction.[5] And given the close link between the mind and the body, addressing ANTs can even improve physical health, too.

Here's how your S.A.V.E.R.S. practices can combat ANTs:

Silence, and specifically mindfulness meditation, enables you to quiet your mind to heighten your self-awareness. By becoming more aware of your thoughts and evaluating them without judging or condemning, you can begin to recognize and interrupt negative thought patterns. Mindfulness meditation has been shown to reduce the frequency and intensity of ANTs, thereby decreasing symptoms of anxiety, depression, and pain.[6]

Affirmations gradually improve your mindset by focusing on positive, empowering thoughts and beliefs rather than negative ones. Changing your self-talk can lead to significant improvements in mental health, and written affirmations enable you to design the self-talk that best serves your highest aspirations.[7]

Visualization can help shift focus from negative expectations to positive possibilities. It has been shown to enhance mood, increase optimism, and boost motivation, making it a valuable tool in combating negative thought patterns.[8]

Exercise increases the production of endorphins, which are natural mood lifters. It also helps reduce levels of stress hormones like cortisol, making it easier to manage negative thoughts.

Reading, particularly self-help or inspirational books, can provide new perspectives and strategies for managing ANTs. It exposes you to new ideas and positive role models that can help shift your mindset.

Scribing can help you identify negative patterns and work through them constructively. Journaling can also provide a sense of relief and clarity, making it easier to focus on positive aspects of your life. Expressive writing can reduce symptoms of anxiety, depression, and stress by helping individuals process their emotions and experiences.[9]

By incorporating the S.A.V.E.R.S. routine into your daily life, you create a comprehensive strategy to combat ANTs. The combination of *Silence*, *Affirmations*, *Visualization*, *Exercise*, *Reading*, and *Scribing* equips you with the tools you need to maintain a positive mindset and enhance your quality of life as you age.

As you navigate the coming chapters of your life, let the S.A.V.E.R.S. serve as your trustworthy companions, reshaping the narrative of aging into one of vitality, wisdom, and unbridled zest for life. Together, let's redefine what it means to grow older, not by the tally of years but by the depth of our experiences. Let us embrace each morning with purpose, each day with joy, and our lives with newfound meaning and fulfillment.

Now that you've grasped the S.A.V.E.R.S. at a high level, let's explore each practice in more detail and learn how to integrate them into your Miracle Morning.

4

S IS FOR *SILENCE*

Cultivate Your Calm in the Chaos

"In the silence, we can hear the whispers of our soul."
**—Deepak Chopra, author, integrative medicine
and personal transformation leader**

Imagine waking up to the stillness of a new day before the world rushes in with its demands and distractions. In those moments of silence, something magical happens. You create space for clarity, peace, and purpose to flow into your life. Starting your day in silence isn't just a pause from the noise, it's an invitation to connect with yourself—your highest self—on a deeper level. It's where you can listen to your inner wisdom, pray for guidance, set a peaceful tone for the day, and tap into the inherent state of love and joy that is within all of us. When you begin your morning with intentional silence, you not only calm your mind and your nervous system, but you also empower your highest self to lead the day ahead.

In a world where our daily routines are inundated with stress, starting your day with peaceful, purposeful silence can be increasingly beneficial as we grow older. Why? Because as we age, stress can affect our physical and mental well-being. Spending time in silence offers profound benefits for managing stress, acting as a sanctuary from the overwhelming pace of modern life. Silence allows your nervous system to shift out of the fight-or-flight response, lowering cortisol levels and promoting a state of relaxation.

> Silence allows your nervous system to shift out of the fight-or-flight response, lowering cortisol levels and promoting a state of relaxation.

By consistently practicing a period of silence in the morning, we can effectively reduce stress levels and cultivate a sense of calm throughout the day. This quiet space creates room for deeper reflection, helping you process your thoughts and emotions in a more grounded way, ultimately leading to a calmer, more centered approach to handling daily challenges. It allows us to escape everyday chaos, reconnect with ourselves, and savor the simple joys of existence.

Of course, harnessing the power of prayer, connecting with God, giving thanks, asking for guidance, and deepening your faith are also meaningful options during your morning *Silence*.

The Modern Challenge of Silence

Ah, the good old days. Before the invention of smartphones, countless moments of quiet contemplation were built into our daily lives. Whether waiting in line at the grocery store, sitting at the airport, or staring out the window on a bus, we had time to listen to our thoughts, engage in self-reflection, and access our inner wisdom.

Now, thanks to our digital devices, that kind of solitude, which most people nowadays call boredom, has all but disappeared. Our modern society has lost sight of the profound benefits of quiet. By distracting us with texting, playing games, checking emails, watching videos, shopping, or mindlessly scrolling through social media, our devices have ensured that we never have to be alone with our thoughts.

Unfortunately, starting your day staring at your smartphone is akin to stumbling into a stress minefield, spiking our cortisol levels before your feet even hit the floor. Stress is linked to and amplified by increased levels of cortisol, a hormone that the adrenal glands release in response to stressful feelings. While cortisol plays a vital role in the body's fight or flight response and various metabolic processes, increased cortisol levels can have several detrimental effects on health, ultimately shortening lifespan.

Seven Stress-Induced Longevity Killers

Chronic elevation of cortisol can lead to multiple health issues:

1. **Poor cardiovascular health:** Chronic high cortisol levels can lead to hypertension, a significant risk factor for heart disease and stroke. Elevated cortisol causes the blood vessels to constrict and retain sodium, raising blood pressure over time.
2. **Metabolic effects:** Cortisol influences glucose metabolism, leading to increased blood sugar levels, contributing to insulin resistance, type 2 diabetes, and damaged blood vessels and nerves, all of which increase the risk of cardiovascular diseases.
3. **Immune system suppression:** Prolonged high cortisol levels suppress the immune system, making the body more susceptible to infections and making it harder for wounds to heal and fight diseases, including cancer.

4. **Cognitive decline:** Cortisol affects brain function, particularly in the hippocampus, which is crucial for memory and learning. High levels of cortisol over extended periods can lead to brain atrophy and cognitive decline, increasing the risk of Alzheimer's disease.

5. **Bone density reduction:** High cortisol levels can decrease bone density by inhibiting bone formation and increasing bone resorption, making individuals—particularly older adults—more susceptible to osteoporosis and fractures.

6. **Weight gain and obesity:** Cortisol promotes fat storage, particularly in the abdominal area, which is associated with a higher risk of metabolic syndrome, cardiovascular disease, and mortality.

7. **Mood disorders:** Chronic stress and elevated cortisol levels are linked to mood disorders such as depression, which often leads to poor lifestyle choices, further contributing to chronic diseases and reduced lifespan.

Living in this state of constant alertness is like inviting a hormonal hurricane into your body. Therefore, incorporating a silence practice isn't just about tuning into your inner calm and giving *you* the first say in how your day unfolds . . . it's also about safeguarding your health. By spending time in silence, our cortisol is decreased, stress is lowered, self-awareness is heightened, and we regulate our nervous system, which all contribute to an extended healthspan. In other words, you'll be cultivating both optimal mental health and physical health with this one practice.

Stepping into a pocket of quiet each morning is like donning an invisible cape or activating an invisible force field. Suddenly, you're not just reacting; you're in command, navigating your day with a heightened sense of intentionality and purpose. This sense of inner peace and self-control can be incredibly empowering.

Customizing Your *Silence* Practice

So, what does silence look like as part of your Miracle Morning? As with all of the S.A.V.E.R.S., you get to customize your routine. Within the practice of silence, you can explore various techniques such as meditation, prayer, or breathwork. Here are a few options to get you started:

- Meditation
- Prayer
- Reflection
- Gratitude
- Deep Breathing and Breathwork

This list is obviously not exhaustive—there are many other practices you could choose from—but these are the five we'll explore in this chapter. The good news is that there is no right or wrong way to spend time in silence. Even just setting a timer for 5 minutes and giving yourself permission to sit and do nothing to give your mind a break from constantly thinking, worrying, and feeling overwhelmed is incredibly rewarding.

Before we talk about each of these practices, an important note: Whichever form of silence you choose (and you can select more than one on any given day or alternate from one day to the next), we recommend getting out of bed, and if possible, leaving your bedroom altogether for this and the remaining S.A.V.E.R.S. Why? The temptation to crawl back into our cozy bed and close our eyes is one that few of us can resist. So, we recommend finding your get-out-of-bed happy place—any place of comfort ideally outside of your bedroom, such as your living room couch, a comfy chair, a meditation pillow, or even outdoors if the weather permits—to complete your Miracle Morning.

Meditation

The practice of meditation dates back thousands of years. While many meditation techniques began as components of Eastern spiritual practices, these days, the term "meditation" can refer to a wide range of practices intended to calm and focus the mind and clear negative thoughts.

There is a wealth of research demonstrating meditation's profound mental, emotional, and physiological benefits. In a 2014 study published in *JAMA Internal Medicine*, researchers found that mindfulness meditation, which typically includes periods of silence, significantly reduced stress, anxiety, and depression in participants.[1] This study suggests that even short, intentional periods of silence, as part of meditation or mindfulness practice, can lead to improved mental health outcomes.

Of particular interest for us—and for you, too, since you're reading this book—is meditation's effects on cellular health. As we age, maintaining cellular health becomes crucial for optimizing our healthspan and longevity. Here are some of the key cellular benefits of meditation and how they can help you age gracefully:

- **Telomere protection:** Telomeres are the protective caps at the ends of your chromosomes. Imagine them as the plastic tips on your shoelaces, keeping everything intact. As you age, these tips wear down, leading to cellular aging and an increased risk of age-related diseases. Nobel Laureate Dr. Elizabeth Blackburn and Dr. Elissa Epel have found that meditation can boost telomerase activity, the enzyme that maintains telomere length.[2] It's like giving your shoelaces brand-new tips, helping you stay youthful at the cellular level.

- **Inflammation reduction:** Meditation has proven to be extremely effective for reducing inflammation. Chronic inflammation is a silent troublemaker, linked to many age-related diseases like heart disease, arthritis, and cancer. Research found that an eight-week mindfulness meditation program can significantly reduce inflammation markers and improve immune function.[3]
- **Mitochondrial function:** Mitochondria are known as your cells' powerhouses. These tiny engines can start to sputter as we age, leading to fatigue and decreased energy levels. Studies show that long-term meditation can enhance mitochondrial function, giving your cells the energy boost they need to keep you active and vibrant.[4]
- **Gene expression:** Think of the process of gene expression as having a remote control to your DNA, turning on the good genes that help fight stress and inflammation and turning off the ones that don't. Research has found that meditation can alter the expression of genes involved in inflammation, immune function, and overall health, leading to a more resilient you.[5]
- **Stress hormone regulation:** Mindfulness meditation significantly reduces cortisol levels, helping you manage stress more effectively and protect your brain health over the years.[6]
- **Cellular repair:** As we age, our cells' ability to repair and regenerate diminishes. Meditation promotes relaxation and reduces stress, which enhances the body's natural repair mechanisms. This means you recover more efficiently from injuries and maintain tissue health better as the years go by.[7]
- **Clearing zombie cells:** Negative thoughts and chronic stress can lead to the accumulation of zombie cells—the senescent cells we first discussed in Chapter 2 when we addressed the importance of drinking water and rehydrating first thing in the morning. Research shows that reducing stress through

meditation decreases the number of senescent cells, promoting healthier cellular function and reducing inflammation.[8]

What's more, the cumulative benefits of meditation build up over time, offering a compounding effect on your health. One unique benefit of your morning S.A.V.E.R.S. routine is that the payoff is immediate, helping you optimize your day while also serving as a daily investment in your future health. Each session of meditation not only provides immediate relaxation and clarity but also fortifies your body against the long-term effects of aging. Regular practice helps you maintain vitality, enhance resilience, promote longevity, and reduce disease risk. By making meditation a non-negotiable part of your morning routine, especially after 50, you can harness these benefits to support healthy aging and enjoy a more vibrant, fulfilling life well into your later years.

> Each session of meditation not only provides immediate relaxation and clarity but also fortifies your body against the long-term effects of aging.

While there are countless ways to practice meditation, you can separate them all into two categories: guided and self-directed. With guided meditation, you're getting instructions from someone else—whether in person or via a recording—to guide your awareness and attention. With self-directed, you meditate on your own without guidance from anyone else. Here we'd like to highlight three specific meditation techniques: mindfulness meditation, emotional optimization meditation, and Transcendental Meditation (TM).

Mindfulness Meditation

Mindfulness meditation is a practice rooted in ancient traditions but has gained significant popularity in modern life for its ability to help people manage stress, improve focus, and enhance overall well-being. At its core, mindfulness meditation is about being fully present in the moment, without judgment, and observing your thoughts, feelings, and sensations as they arise. Instead of getting caught up in distractions, overthinking, or self-judgment, the practice encourages a gentle awareness of what is happening right now, offering a powerful way to cultivate states of calm, clarity, and inner peace.

The benefits of mindfulness meditation are both psychological and physiological. Research shows that regular practice can reduce stress, improve sleep, enhance emotional regulation, and even lower blood pressure.[9] It has been linked to increased gray matter density in brain regions associated with memory, empathy, and self-awareness.[10] Additionally, it can help reduce symptoms of anxiety and depression by encouraging a healthier, more balanced perspective on difficult emotions and life circumstances. Other benefits include increased focus and concentration, greater creativity, and improved relationships, as mindfulness fosters deeper connections with others.[11]

To practice mindfulness meditation, you don't need any special equipment or experience. Here's a simple guide to get started:

1. **Find a quiet space:** Choose a comfortable place where you won't be disturbed. Sit in a chair or on the floor with your back straight.
2. **Focus on your breath:** Close your eyes and bring your attention to your breath, noticing each inhale and exhale. Feel the sensations of breathing, such as the rise and fall of your chest.
3. **Observe your thoughts:** As you meditate, thoughts will inevitably arise. Instead of trying to stop them, simply observe them without judgment and gently bring your focus back to your breath.
4. **Start small:** Begin with just 5 to 10 minutes a day and gradually increase the time as you become more comfortable with the practice.

Mindfulness meditation is about patience and consistency. Over time, the practice becomes more natural, and its benefits more profound. Whether you're seeking stress relief, emotional balance, or improved mental clarity, integrating mindfulness meditation into your routine can be a simple yet transformative way to enhance your daily life.

Emotional Optimization Meditation

Imagine possessing a superpower that enabled you to choose your optimal mental and emotional states in any set of circumstances. In other words, what would your life be like if you could consciously decide to live in perpetual states of love, joy, and inner peace regardless of any difficulties that you were facing? While most of us have been conditioned to believe that how we feel is based on what's going on outside of us, emotional optimization meditation will empower you to choose and cultivate your desired mental and emotional states, regardless of any challenges you're facing. Hal discovered this inherent ability after his car was hit head-on at 70 miles per hour. He broke 11 bones, suffered permanent brain damage, and was told he would never walk again. He realized that although his circumstances were devastating, he could choose to be the happiest and most grateful he had ever been while he endured the most difficult time in his life.

This practice works because how we feel is based primarily on what we allow ourselves to focus on. For example, when we focus on what's wrong in our lives, we experience unpleasant and often unproductive mental and emotional states such as fear, anxiety, and self-doubt. When we focus on what's right in our lives, we foster joy, gratitude, and confidence. This is the role that our attention plays in determining the quality of our life.

To clarify the subtle differences and similarities between mental and emotional states:

- *Mental state* refers to the state of your mind and the quality of your mindset, encompassing your thoughts, attitude, what you focus on, awareness, perspective, and cognitive processes.

It's about how you perceive, interpret, process, and respond to information and experiences. For example, you can choose to maintain a generally *positive* mindset in which you look for the good in life, yourself, and other people, or a *negative* mindset in which you focus on what's wrong with life, yourself, and other people.

- ***Emotional state*** refers to your feelings, emotions, and mood, encompassing your subjective emotional experience, such as happiness, sadness, anger, or fear. Your emotional state is largely influenced by your mental state. Similar to how the quality of your mindset determines the quality of your life, your emotional state *is* how you experience your life. Your emotional state is influenced by your mental state and vice versa.

When your meditation focuses on thoughts, images, and affirmations that support your optimal mental and emotional states, you generate and reinforce those states. This technique benefits you by allowing you to begin and enter into your day in an optimal mindset that supports feeling your best. Since optimal internal states lead to optimal external behaviors, this is crucial to setting yourself up for success each morning. And it benefits you even more over time because the more consistently you practice this technique, the more you hardwire your optimal mental and emotional states in your subconscious to become your default way of feeling and interpreting the world around you.

To experience emotional optimization meditation, follow these simple steps:

1. **Choose your optimal state for today:** Consider the day ahead, and ask yourself how you want to feel and which mental or emotional state would best serve you (e.g., happy, grateful, focused, confident, enthusiastic, peaceful, loving, empathetic, etc.).

2. **Focus on your breath to calm your mind:** Similar to the instructions given earlier for mindfulness meditation, simply focus on your breath, taking long, slow inhalations and exhalations. Do this for as little as 30 seconds or for as long as a few minutes—just enough to calm your nervous system and let go of any tension. Slowing down your breath slows your heart rate, which calms your nervous system. The purpose of this is to create space for you to cultivate your optimal state.

3. **Meditate in your optimal state:** Direct all of your thoughts, images, and affirmations toward your chosen state, and align your physiology (posture, breathing, facial expressions, etc.) with that state. Focus your attention on the aspects of your life that are consistent with how you want to feel. If your optimal state is gratitude, focus on things you are grateful for. If your optimal state is love, focus on the people you love and who love you. Remind yourself that you are in control of what you focus on and how you feel.

Transcendental Meditation (TM)

Imagine achieving a state of restful alertness where your body is deeply relaxed, your mind is quiet, and yet you're wide awake. TM enables you to transcend your active mind and reach a pure consciousness through the effortless repetition of a mantra. This practice brings calmness and clarity and enhances your overall well-being. Regular practice of TM has been associated with improved memory, attention, and executive function, which are crucial for maintaining independence and quality of life for folks over 50. Beyond mental health, TM positively impacts physical well-being by lowering blood pressure and reducing the risk of cardiovascular diseases. By integrating TM into your daily routines, you can experience a holistic improvement in both mental and physical health, contributing to a more fulfilling and active lifestyle.

TM is traditionally taught through personalized instruction by certified teachers, emphasizing the importance of one-on-one guidance to ensure proper technique and maximize benefits. However, some individuals choose to practice TM independently by following these general guidelines:

1. **Choose a mantra:** Select a simple, soothing word or sound to repeat silently during meditation. While official TM mantras are assigned by certified instructors, practitioners often choose sounds like "ahum" or "om" for self-guided practice.

2. **Find a quiet space:** Sit comfortably in a quiet environment where you won't be disturbed. Ensure your posture is relaxed yet upright.

3. **Set a timer:** Aim for 20-minute sessions, practicing twice daily—once in the morning and once in the evening. Setting a timer can help maintain consistency without the need to check the clock.

4. **Begin the meditation:** Close your eyes and take a few deep breaths to relax. Start repeating your chosen mantra silently, allowing it to flow naturally without force. If your mind wanders, gently return your focus to the mantra.

5. **Conclude the session:** After 20 minutes, stop repeating the mantra and sit quietly with your eyes closed for a couple of minutes before resuming your activities.

While self-guided practice can be beneficial, learning TM through a certified instructor provides personalized guidance and ensures the authenticity of the technique. Official TM courses offer comprehensive instruction and ongoing support to help achieve the full range of benefits associated with the practice.

Dwayne says . . .

Transcendental Meditation has been life-changing for me. It clears my brain of stress and distracting thoughts, lowers my blood pressure and blood sugar, and gives me much more energy, clarity, and creativity now that it's part of my daily routine. If you think you don't have time to meditate, consider this: Recent studies have shown that longtime meditators' brains are less affected by aging than those of non-meditators.[12]

If you're still feeling unsure about how to meditate—or just need a little help getting started—you're not alone. Fortunately, there are plenty of resources out there to support you. Apps like *Headspace* and *Calm* each offer their own unique approach to guided meditations. And if you're looking for something that integrates meditation into a full, life-changing morning routine, the *Miracle Morning* app offers activities and guided practices for all six S.A.V.E.R.S. Wherever you begin, the key is just to *begin*. Your mind, body, and future self will thank you for it.

Prayer

Prayer is an act of communication with a higher power, most often referred to as *God*, and usually involves expressions of gratitude or requests for guidance, comfort, or connection. It can be verbal or silent, and it varies widely across different spiritual and religious traditions.

Prayer holds deeply personal significance and is shaped by one's religious upbringing or spiritual beliefs, and for these reasons, we won't offer prescriptive advice on how to do it in this book. For some, prayer entails reciting specific sacred phrases; for others, it involves informal conversations or quiet moments of listening to a divine presence. There exists no singular method for prayer. They may be focused, addressing specific needs or desires, or open-ended, allowing for receiving guidance without a predetermined outcome. Prayer—however you choose to do it—can be an impactful and meaningful moment of silence during your S.A.V.E.R.S.

> **Hal says . . .**
>
> During my period of *Silence,* I combine prayer and meditation to experience the synergistic benefits. I start my Miracle Mornings with 5 to 10 minutes of prayer, thanking God for my life and the blessings I've experienced. Then, I ask for guidance, strength, and protection—three attributes that I've felt God has always provided for me—to fulfill my limitless potential in service of my mission to help as many people as possible. Sometimes, my request for guidance is about something specific, and other times, it is more open-ended. Then, I meditate to receive whatever comes through me, and I keep my journal nearby so that I can capture anything worthwhile. Nearly every morning, I receive valuable thoughts, perspectives, and insights during my meditation, which I refer to as downloads. The reason I call them that is because they come into my consciousness so fast that I write as quickly as I can without any conscious thought. It feels more like I'm taking dictation. Some of my most valuable wisdom and profound breakthroughs have come during these periods of peaceful, purposeful *Silence.*

Reflection

Reflecting on our past *through a positive lens* can enhance our quality of life as we age. According to the American Psychological Association, reminiscing can improve psychological well-being, and looking back on pleasant memories is especially helpful in boosting our moods.[13] This is especially true for people with memory loss conditions like dementia or Alzheimer's. Reflection includes reminiscing over memories of loved ones and meaningful life experiences, as well as recalling our past accomplishments. Our past accomplishments are often associated with positive emotions, and focusing on our achievements can promote a greater sense of satisfaction when reflecting on our lives. Thankfully, the older we get, the more we have to look back on.

Reflection is a practice you can implement internally (during your period of *Silence*) and externally, in writing (during your period of *Scribing*). Journaling or writing down a list of our accomplishments, meaningful life experiences, and aspects of life that we are grateful for becomes a resource that we can continuously revisit, reflect upon, and enjoy.

The Power of Thank You

John Kralik, a Los Angeles superior court judge, decided to transform his life by writing 365 thank-you notes over a year, beginning in 2008. This practice of daily gratitude was sparked by a difficult year in 2007 and inspired by the memory of his grandfather. Through his handwritten notes, John appreciated various people, including his son and even the barista at his local Starbucks. His journey of gratitude not only improved his outlook but also positively impacted his relationships. John's experience and insights are detailed in his book, *365 Thank Yous: The Year a Simple Act of Daily Gratitude Changed My Life*.

Dwayne also undertook a similar exercise. He was reading about the power of gratitude and an experiment that created such a wave of gratitude that he wanted to try it himself. So, he challenged himself to handwrite thank-you notes to 1,700 of his [at that time] 2,500 Aegis Living staff members. He'd write them in taxis, on airplanes, at dinner—whenever he had a few minutes. He said it was a most fulfilling experience and it was so well received.

Simple acts like these can be easily incorporated into your Miracle Morning routine for profound impact.

Gratitude

Cultivating gratitude has been associated with reduced stress, improved mood, better sleep, and enhanced mental and emotional well-being. From a practical perspective, we feel good when we focus on what we're grateful for. Our life satisfaction is improved. From a scientific viewpoint, gratitude's profound impact on healthspan is evident in various studies:

- **Improved mental health:** Research has shown that practicing gratitude through meditation can enhance overall well-being and happiness. A 2019 study published in *Frontiers in Psychology* found that gratitude meditation practices led to significant improvements in life satisfaction and reductions in depressive symptoms.[14] Participants who engaged in regular gratitude meditation experienced an uplifted mood and a greater sense of fulfillment.

- **Reduced stress and anxiety:** Gratitude meditation has been linked to lower levels of stress and anxiety. A 2019 study published in the *International Journal of Applied Positive Psychology* found that participants who practiced gratitude meditation reported reduced stress levels and increased emotional resilience.[15] The practice of focusing on gratitude helped shift attention away from worries and negative thoughts, promoting calm and relaxation.

- **Enhanced emotional regulation:** Gratitude meditation can also improve emotional regulation by fostering positive emotions and reducing negative emotional responses. A 2017 study from *Scientific Reports* demonstrated that gratitude meditation strengthens neural circuits related to positive emotions and reduces activity in brain regions associated with negative emotional responses, helping individuals manage their emotions more effectively.[16]

- **Less pain:** Yes, there is even scientific evidence connecting gratitude with reduced pain perception. A notable study published in *Personality and Individual Differences* (2012) found that individuals who regularly practiced gratitude reported experiencing less physical pain and were more willing to engage in healthier behaviors that support overall well-being. The study suggested that gratitude contributes to an enhanced psychological outlook, which can alter how people perceive and cope with pain.[17]
- Additionally, another study published in *Psychological Science* (2015) explored the neurological mechanisms behind gratitude. It found that participants who practiced gratitude showed increased activity in brain regions associated with empathy and pain modulation, suggesting that gratitude may help individuals manage pain by enhancing their emotional and psychological resilience.[18]
- These studies suggest that practicing gratitude can not only improve emotional well-being but also impact how we experience physical discomfort, reducing both the intensity and emotional distress associated with pain.[19]

Practicing gratitude during your period of *Silence* is a powerful way to enhance mental and physical health and set a positive tone for the day ahead. While there are numerous ways to practice gratitude during *Silence*, here are five that we find to be particularly effective.

1. **Gratitude meditation:** This is a meditation that focuses on cultivating feelings of appreciation, thankfulness, and of course, gratitude. Like most forms of meditation, begin by settling into a comfortable position and bringing attention to your breath, allowing your mind to calm. Next, consciously reflect on things you are grateful for, one at a time, such as relationships,

experiences, health, God, or even the moment you are currently experiencing. By visualizing these aspects through the lens of gratitude and truly allowing yourself to deeply feel the gratitude in your heart, this practice helps to shift the focus away from stress or negativity. Hal likes to place his hand on his heart during this meditation to help move from what he calls intellectual gratitude (an unemotional list of things you're thankful for) to heartfelt gratitude, which is the deeply felt love and appreciation for each aspect of your life.

2. **Gratitude walk:** Take a morning walk and reflect on the elements of nature and life that you appreciate. You can also incorporate the elements of a gratitude meditation while you walk, as well as first light and earthing, discussed more in Chapter 14. How's that for efficiency?!

3. **Grateful breathing exercise:** With each inhale, think of something you're thankful for, and with each exhale, release any negative thoughts.

4. **Appreciation in the mirror:** While getting ready, look in the mirror and acknowledge something you appreciate about yourself.

5. **Gratitude prayer:** Incorporate gratitude into your morning prayers, thanking God for your blessings.

Each of these practices encourages a habit of recognizing and appreciating the positive aspects of life, which can significantly enhance emotional well-being and may even contribute to a longer, happier, healthier life. You need not limit yourself to just one of these practices—in fact, you can incorporate any or all of them. The more gratitude, the better, as far as we're concerned!

Deep Breathing and Breathwork

Breathing is clearly essential to life, but most of us don't give it much thought, let alone take advantage of the benefits of deep breathing and breathwork.

Deep breathing generally refers to the act of intentionally taking slow, full breaths that engage the diaphragm. It's a simple practice used to calm the mind, reduce tension, or improve focus, and it can be done in a variety of contexts without specific techniques.

Breathwork, on the other hand, is a broader term that encompasses a variety of structured breathing techniques or exercises (a few of which we will explain shortly), often used for more specific purposes like emotional release, healing, or heightened states of awareness. Breathwork practices may involve different rhythms, holds, and patterns of breathing, and they are commonly found in practices like yoga, meditation, and holistic therapies.

Deep Breathing

Here are the key benefits, supported by research, of incorporating deep breathing into your life:

- **Reduced stress and anxiety:** Deep breathing activates the parasympathetic nervous system, reducing stress hormones like cortisol. A study published in *Scientific Reports* found that participants who practiced slow breathing exercises experienced significant reductions in stress and anxiety levels.[20]
- **Enhanced mental health, focus, and attention:** Studies show that deep breathing can significantly reduce symptoms of depression[21] and enhance cognitive function by increasing oxygen supply to the brain. A 2018 study published in *Consciousness and Cognition* found that breath-focused exercises improved attention and cognitive performance in participants.[22]

- **Lower blood pressure and improved heart health:** Regular deep breathing exercises help lower blood pressure and improve cardiovascular health. A 2017 review published in *Frontiers in Physiology* highlighted that breathwork can lead to significant reductions in blood pressure, particularly in individuals with hypertension.[23]
- **Improved cellular function:** Research shows deep breathing exercises can increase oxygen saturation and respiratory efficiency, enhancing overall vitality.[24]
- **Muscle relaxation and blood flow:** Deep breathing helps relax muscles, improve circulation, and release toxins. Feel the stress melt away as you breathe deeply!
- **Increased lung capacity:** Regular deep breathing helps maintain or improve lung function, supporting overall respiratory health.
- **Stimulated lymphatic system:** Deep breathing helps detoxify the body and improve the immune response. You'll feel more resilient and ready to tackle any challenges that come your way!
- **Reduced oxidative stress:** Deep breathing helps reduce oxidative stress, a significant factor in aging and chronic disease development, by lowering stress levels and enhancing oxygenation.
- **Enhanced sleep quality:** Deep breathing promotes relaxation, making it easier to fall asleep and enjoy restful, restorative sleep. Research in *Sleep Medicine* found significant improvements in sleep quality and reduced insomnia symptoms.[25]

Breathwork

If you'd like to try breathwork but aren't sure where to start, we outline three popular methods. No matter which you choose (one of these or another), in general, you'll want to make sure you are in a comfortable position, seated or lying down. Focus on your breath, taking long, slow inhalations and exhalations. And practice regularly (daily)! Aim for a few minutes each morning, and ideally, do it again in the evening, gradually increasing the duration as you become more comfortable.

Diaphragmatic Breathing (Belly Breathing)

Diaphragmatic breathing is a deep breathing exercise that fully engages the diaphragm and increases lung efficiency. This technique promotes calm relaxation, eases stress, and reduces anxiety. Unlike shallow chest breathing, which can leave you feeling anxious and drained, diaphragmatic breathing fills your lungs and energizes your body.

To practice diaphragmatic breathing:

1. **Get comfortable:** Sit or lie comfortably with one hand on your chest and the other on your abdomen.
2. **Inhale deeply:** Breathe deeply through your nose, allowing your abdomen to rise while keeping your chest still.
3. **Pause and exhale:** Pause for a moment, and then exhale slowly through your mouth.
4. **Repeat:** Continue this pattern for several breaths, focusing on the movement in your abdomen.

Box Breathing (Square Breathing)

Box breathing is a paced breathing technique that follows a four-count rhythm, bringing your body and mind into a calm state. This technique is excellent for reducing stress, clearing your mind, and restoring your natural breathing rhythm.

To practice box breathing:

1. **Get comfortable:** Sit or lie down comfortably and close your eyes.
2. **Inhale:** Slowly inhale through your nose for 4 seconds.
3. **Hold:** Hold your breath for 4 seconds.

4. **Exhale:** Slowly exhale through your mouth for 4 seconds.

5. **Hold again:** Hold your breath for another 4 seconds.

6. **Repeat:** Continue this cycle for several rounds, breathing from your belly, not your chest.

The Wim Hof Method: An Advanced Approach

The Wim Hof Method (WHM), developed by Dutch extreme athlete and motivational speaker Wim Hof, also known as "The Iceman," offers an unusual path to improving health and well-being. This method has been linked to reduced symptoms of various medical conditions, including rheumatoid arthritis, multiple sclerosis, Parkinson's disease, asthma, and sarcoidosis.

WHM works through three pillars: deep breathing, cold therapy, and commitment. To practice the Wim Hof Breathing Technique:

1. **Get comfortable:** Sit or lie down comfortably with loose clothing to allow belly expansion.

2. **30 deep breaths:** Close your eyes and clear your mind. Inhale deeply through your nose or mouth while pushing your belly outward. When your lungs are full, let your breath go through your mouth without force.

3. **Retention phase:** After the final exhalation, hold your breath until you feel the urge to breathe again.

4. **Recovery breath:** Draw a large breath, letting your belly expand fully. Hold it for 15 seconds, and then let go. This completes one round.

5. **Repeat:** Perform the cycle three to four times, adjusting the number of breaths, tempo, and cycles until you find a routine that works best for you.

Dwayne says . . .

I became a fan—and practitioner—of the Wim Hof Method after my personal trainer suggested I try it. I was already doing cold plunges and deep breathing, so it just seemed natural to try this. And the results I've experienced have just been phenomenal. It increases my lung capacity, reduces anxiety, helps me sleep more restfully, and slows my heart rate down (in a good way).

There's more to the full WHM, but the breathing technique alone is powerful. If you're feeling adventurous, try incorporating cold exposure by taking a cold shower or an ice bath for at least one minute! We dare you! You can modify the intensity of cold exposure and breathing exercises to suit your physical capabilities; pay attention to how your body responds and adjust the practice accordingly. We'll also revisit cold therapy in Chapter 7. Note: Before starting the WHM, consult a healthcare provider, especially if you have preexisting medical conditions.

Whether you prefer diaphragmatic breathing, box breathing, the WHM breathing technique, or something else, these exercises offer potent benefits to help you live a less stressful and more vibrant life and can be a valuable component of your S.A.V.E.R.S. routine.

Creating Your *Silence* Ritual

To experience the benefits of silence, here are a few simple steps to get started:

- **Choose your activity:** Choose your preferred *Silence* activity (meditation, prayer, deep breathing, etc.), and make these practices a regular part of your S.A.V.E.R.S. routine.

- **Select a quiet place:** Find a comfortable place, free of distractions, where you will complete your S.A.V.E.R.S.
- **Establish appropriate expectations:** If you're not used to regularly spending time in silence, keep in mind that anytime we incorporate a new practice into our lives, it will be accompanied by a learning curve. Ironically, the more active your mind is and the more challenging you find spending time in silence to be, the more you will benefit from sticking with it over an extended period of time (i.e., the rest of your life). Remember: Your objective is not to clear your mind and be without thought, but rather to observe your thoughts without judgment. In other words, there is no wrong way to spend time in silence. So, give yourself permission to let go of any self-imposed pressure, allow yourself to be at peace with whatever comes up, and enjoy every moment.
- **Decide on duration:** While you can experience some benefits from as little as 60 seconds of silence, we encourage you to aim for enjoying at least 5 minutes, so that you have time to calm your mind and settle into silence. Many Miracle Morning practitioners extend the duration of their S.A.V.E.R.S. on the weekends.
- **Practice regularly:** Engage in the practice consistently, preferably at the same time each day. The more consistent you are, the easier this will be, and the more your mind, body, and soul will benefit from the profound power of *Silence*.

Final Thoughts on Silence

Spending time in silence can allow you to calm your nervous system, be at peace, experience gratitude, gain clarity, and be free from your day-to-day stressors and worries. Don't be discouraged if quieting your mind is challenging at first. That's to be expected. Like anything else we want to become proficient at, doing so takes practice, consistency, patience, and time. Stick with it, and the benefits for your life will be invaluable.

The nature of physical and mental health in midlife and beyond has changed. Many diseases—even some cancers—are becoming chronic conditions that we can treat and sometimes live with into old age. All too often, though, we have been trained to quickly reach for medication when we aren't feeling quite right. In doing so, we cheat our body's natural healing abilities and become dependent on artificial means to make us feel better. Of course, there are times when medicine is needed, so please don't stop taking anything without first consulting your healthcare provider. But let's also emphasize and explore natural solutions that don't come with any detrimental side effects.

In this chapter, we examined the profound benefits of meditation, prayer, reflection, gratitude, and deep breathing as options during your period of *Silence*. Each practice offers unique advantages for enhancing mental clarity, emotional well-being, and physical health, all contributing to a longer, healthier life. Experiment with different methods to see what suits you best and enjoy the journey toward optimizing your healthspan and longevity.

A Note from a Miracle Morning Community Member

"I have always been a 'get up and go' person. I had never considered starting my day with *Silence*, *Affirmations*, or *Visualizations* for that matter. Honestly, to me it seemed like a waste of time. After reading *The Miracle Morning*, that changed. While I practice all the S.A.V.E.R.S., I have found that *Silence* is the most beneficial. It is amazing to me what 10 minutes of silence BEFORE starting my day has done for me. I am calmer, more centered, and FOCUSED."

—Maria Lopez
Age 62

5

A IS FOR *AFFIRMATIONS*

Empower Your Subconscious Mind for Success

"Every word we speak or think is an affirmation.
Every thought we think is creating our future."
—**Louise Hay, author, speaker, and publisher**

If you watched the hit television show *Saturday Night Live* in the 1990s, you may remember comedian Al Franken's popular mock self-help show, "Daily Affirmations with Stuart Smalley." Franken would begin each episode by staring at his reflection in a tall, old-fashioned mirror and enthusiastically telling himself, "I'm good enough . . . I'm smart enough . . . and doggone it, people like me!" For many people, Franken's portrayal was their first introduction to the practice of affirmations.

Despite the comedic portrayal of affirmations, they're no joke—and if you're new to the practice, you're on the brink of a profound discovery. What you tell yourself consistently may be the most powerful determining factor in the quality of your thoughts, beliefs, emotions, actions, and ultimately, the outcomes you manifest in your life. In other words, what you affirm repeatedly quite literally becomes your reality.

Understanding the Power of Affirmations

Every one of us has an internal dialogue (sometimes called an inner monologue or self-talk) that runs in our minds almost nonstop. The problem is that most of that dialogue is unconscious, meaning we aren't proactively and intentionally choosing our thoughts. Instead, we allow our past experiences, disempowering perspectives, fears about the future, and self-imposed limitations to replay in our heads. Doing this reaffirms and perpetuates our negative feelings, fears, insecurities, and limiting beliefs, causing us to limit who we are and what we experience in the present based on who we were and what we did (or didn't do) in the past. Although this is considered "normal," it can be one of the most detrimental factors in enjoying our lives and fulfilling our potential.

Thankfully, we can upgrade our self-talk (in writing) and be far more intentional about what we think, which determines how we feel and ultimately, which actions we take. In this chapter, we will address two fundamental flaws with how affirmations have been taught for many decades, which have caused people to view them as cheesy and ineffective at best, or a complete waste of time at worst. Then, we'll walk you through three very specific steps to draft powerful written affirmations that are actionable, rooted in truth, and designed to produce meaningful results.

Hal says . . .

When I first learned about affirmations, I was among the crowd who considered them cheesy and ineffective. They seemed to be nothing more than feel-good statements that had zero grounding in reality. Repeating statements such as "I am wealthy" (when you're struggling financially) or "I am happy" (when you're feeling depressed) seemed borderline delusional.

As I began studying personal development, I was reintroduced to affirmations as a legitimate tool for self-transformation and dove deeper into understanding their purpose. In doing so, I had an epiphany. I realized that the problem wasn't with affirmations themselves, but the way they were often taught that contained two major flaws. This awareness enabled me to completely change my approach. I began designing affirmations that were practical, actionable, rooted in truth, and consistently helped me overcome my self-imposed limitations and produce measurable, meaningful results.

Now, when I'm often asked if I have a "favorite" of the S.A.V.E.R.S., I don't hesitate to answer, *Affirmations*. Why? Because my affirmations are written statements that clearly articulate what I'm committed to achieving in each area of my life (health, fitness, happiness, relationships, finances, marriage, parenting, recreation, etc.) and why these commitments are an absolute must for me. They also clarify which actions I'm committed to taking to help me consistently follow through with creating my ideal life. My affirmations are like the blueprint for designing and creating the life I want, and I spend a few minutes reviewing them every morning so that I'm reminded of exactly what I want, why it's important to me, and what I need to do each day to create and live the life I want. By simply living in alignment with my affirmations, each day, I've been able to create the life I've always wanted. You can do the same.

Think Affirmations Don't Work?

The history of affirmations goes back thousands of years. The ancient Hindus and Buddhists used a form of affirmations known as mantra meditation as a way to quiet the mind and focus on higher truths. The first recorded use of affirmations dates back to 3200 BCE when the Egyptian philosopher Ptahhotep wrote *The Maxims of Ptahhotep*. This ancient text contains a number of proverbs and sayings that were designed to help people improve their lives. While Ptahhotep's affirmations were somewhat different from the ones we use today, they shared one key similarity: They were all positive statements that could be repeated to oneself in order to change the way one thinks and feels.

It wasn't until the 19th century that affirmations began to be used for personal development. The New Thought movement, which began in the United States in the 1800s, was based on the belief that positive thinking could create positive results in your life.

In the early 20th century, Napoleon Hill popularized the use of affirmations as a tool for achieving success in business and life. In his classic book *Think and Grow Rich*, Hill wrote about the power of positive thinking and included several affirmations that could be used for success in any area of life. Since then, affirmations have been used by millions of people around the world to improve their lives. There are now affirmations for everything from weight loss to attracting a soulmate to becoming wealthy.

However, despite the long history and proven track record of affirmations, many people have tried them only to be disappointed. From our vantage point, there are two fundamental flaws in the way affirmations have been (mis)taught over the years.

Flaw #1: Lying to Yourself Doesn't Work

Wording your affirmations as if you've already achieved, overcome, or become something that you haven't (yet) may be the biggest reason that affirmations are ineffective for most people. Repeating statements to yourself like, "I am wealthy," "I am happy," or "I have achieved all of my goals" when these things aren't yet true for you will likely feel inauthentic and create an internal conflict (as if we don't have enough of them). Whenever you recite an affirmation that doesn't resonate as true for you, your subconscious will resist and reject it. As an intelligent human being who isn't delusional, lying to yourself repeatedly will never be the optimal strategy. The truth will always prevail.

Flaw #2: Passive Language Doesn't Produce Meaningful Results

Similarly, affirmations like "I am a money magnet" and "Money flows to me effortlessly and in abundance" may make you feel good in the moment and even give you a false sense of relief, but they aren't likely to generate real-life results. Wealthy people didn't become financially abundant by sitting idly and telling themselves that money will magically appear in their lives. People who are fit didn't get in shape by affirming that they were fit and healthy. They got clear on what they wanted, why they wanted it, committed to the necessary actions, and actively created what they desired. That is exactly how we are going to structure your Miracle Morning Results-Oriented Affirmations.

We think you'll agree that if you're going to take time to draft, write, and recite affirmations, you'd like to see them produce meaningful results, not merely delude you into momentarily feeling better. For example, if you're reciting an affirmation about improving your financial situation, you want to see your income or bank account balance begin to increase. If you're repeating an affirmation about losing weight, you want the results of that affirmation to show up every time you step on the scale. If you're using affirmations to improve your marriage, you want your spouse to experience (and ideally reciprocate) the improvements you've made. Your affirmations must lead to improvements in both your thinking and your behaviors to achieve meaningful results.

Science Supports Affirmations

Affirmations are supported by research in psychology, neuroscience, and cardiology, showing their positive impact on mental, emotional, and physical health. These benefits contribute to increased longevity and healthspan.

- **Mind-body connection:** Research shows positive self-talk and affirmations can reduce stress and improve emotional well-being. A study reported in *Psychological Science* found that self-affirmations lower cortisol levels.[1]
- **Improved coping mechanisms:** Affirmations improve coping mechanisms by fostering resilience. Published in *PLOS ONE*, research from Carnegie Mellon University provides evidence that self-affirmation can protect against the damaging effects of stress on problem-solving performance.[2]
- **Encouraging healthy behaviors:** Affirmations promote healthier behaviors. A study reported in the *Journal of Sport & Exercise Psychology* found that self-affirmation increases physical activity levels, which is crucial for maintaining health and preventing age-related diseases.[3]
- **Sustaining motivation:** Affirmations sustain motivation for long-term health goals, enhancing adherence to health-related behaviors, such as diet and exercise.
- **Neuroplasticity:** Affirmations influence the brain's ability to form new neural connections. Research published in *Social Cognitive and Affective Neuroscience* found that self-affirmation activates the brain's reward centers.[4]
- **Cognitive decline prevention:** Maintaining a positive

mindset through affirmations can delay cognitive decline. *PLOS ONE* published a report that found having a positive outlook on aging lowers the risk of dementia.[5]

- **Heart health:** Positive affirmations cultivate a positive mindset, which is linked to better heart health. *JAMA Network Open* published a report noting that optimism is associated with a lower risk of heart disease.[6]

Three Simple Steps to Create Results-Oriented Affirmations

We are about to walk you through in-depth, step-by-step instructions on how to create your first set of Miracle Morning Results-Oriented Affirmations. It is important to draft your affirmations *in writing* so that you can continue to customize, edit, and add to them over time, and read them every day. While you can handwrite your affirmations in a journal or on paper, we recommend using a digital device, such as a word processing document on your computer, a notes app on your smartphone, or using the *Miracle Morning* app, which offers a built-in affirmations creator that follows the three steps you're about to learn. One of the benefits of using a digital device is that you're able to go back and easily update your affirmations as often as you'd like since, as you continue to learn, grow, and evolve, your affirmations should evolve as well.

Through this daily repetition, your mind inevitably acclimates to new, more effective ways of thinking and begins to accept the possibility of a new reality for you. The constant repetition of an affirmation spurs the thoughts, feelings, and actions necessary to make and sustain meaningful improvements in your life.

So, before moving on, we encourage you to either grab a pen and paper or open up a document on your computer or a note on your phone so that you can immediately begin drafting your written Miracle Morning Results-Oriented Affirmations.

Now, let's break down these steps so you can design your first draft of practical, actionable, customized affirmations that will actually produce results!

Step 1: Affirm What You're Committed To

What do you want to improve, create, achieve, or experience in your life? We all want things, but we rarely get what we want just because we want it. Instead, we usually get what we are willing to commit to. One could even argue that the most determining factor in whether we reach any goal or make any meaningful change is our ability to commit to something thoroughly and remain committed for as long as it takes. When we're committed, there is always a way.

Repeatedly affirming what you're committed to each day keeps your commitments at the top of your mind and increases your level of commitment over time. So, your affirmations should begin by clearly articulating an outcome (i.e., goal, result, improvement, etc.) or an activity (i.e., action, habit, ritual, etc.) that you are committed to. To help you consider the difference between an outcome and an activity, think of it this way: An outcome would be "losing 10 pounds," while an activity would be "exercising five days a week."

Here's what Step 1 looks like in the form of a simple, written affirmation:

I am committed to _____
no matter what—there is no other option!

The more consistently and confidently you affirm your commitments, the more committed you will become to following through and making them happen.

You may notice an exclamation point (!) after the example affirmation. That is intentional, reminding you to read and embody it with emotion and conviction. Real commitment isn't something you do haphazardly. The more you can incorporate your affirmations with emotion and conviction, the more effective they will be.

Now, it's your turn to apply Step 1. Choose one area of your life. It could be your health, finances, your mental well-being, an important relationship, or any area you want to improve. What do you want to accomplish or change in this area that you need to commit to? Do you have an important goal that you've been putting off? Is there an area of your life that is a source of pain and frustration? Is there a change you've attempted to make but haven't succeeded (yet)?

Start by writing down a specific, meaningful outcome or activity that would improve your life, and that you are ready to commit to—even if you're not exactly sure how you will do it or are afraid of falling short.

Once you've identified a meaningful outcome or activity, you must commit to making it a reality. Write or type your outcome using the following template to fill in the blank and make it your own. We encourage you to do this now by choosing one area—any area—of your life that you'd like to improve.

I am committed to _____
no matter what—there is no other option!

If you're unsure or hesitant about what you want to commit to, you may be censoring yourself because of a lack of clarity or confidence in your ability to follow through. That's normal. However, you don't have to have everything figured out to begin your affirmation. It is often after you commit to something that the "how" reveals itself. You figure it out along the way.

Writing down your affirmation can be the first step in establishing your commitment, and affirming your commitment each day keeps it at the top of your mind and increases your commitment level over time. Remember: There's always a way when you're committed.

Step 2: Affirm Why It's a Must for You

Next, it is time to support, enhance, and reinforce your commitment by including your why—the most meaningful, compelling reason(s) that will continually fuel you to remain committed and take the necessary actions until what you affirm becomes your reality. The clearer and more compelling your reasons are, the more likely you are to follow through.

Let's continue drafting your first Miracle Morning affirmation. Underneath your commitment (Step 1), begin listing why following through with this commitment is essential to you. Why is it meaningful to you? Why is it a must for you? In what ways will it enhance your life and the lives of those you care about? What are the most compelling reasons/benefits that inspire you to do whatever it takes?

This commitment is a must for me because:

- _____

[Insert meaningful reason/benefit]

- _____

[Insert meaningful reason/benefit]

- _____

[Insert meaningful reason/benefit]

Remember that these reasons are personal; you'll never have to share your affirmations with anyone unless you want to. Also, remember that this is your rough draft. You can always edit your affirmations, so don't worry about getting anything perfect. A poorly written affirmation is far more effective than a nonexistent one.

Step 3: Affirm Which Actions You'll Take and When

Writing an affirmation that follows the first two steps but leaves out this third step might make you feel better and somewhat motivated. Still, clarifying the necessary actions to produce the outcome is required. It can also be counterproductive, tricking your subconscious mind into thinking that the result will happen automatically, without any effort.

In this third and final step, you'll ask yourself what you need to do to progress toward your ideal outcome or your predetermined activity and when you will do it. This step may seem obvious and come to you quickly. We often already know what to do to improve; we just haven't committed to doing it. For example, "To ensure I follow through with my goal of improving my health and losing 10 pounds of unwanted body fat, I will go to the gym Monday through Friday, from 7 a.m. to 8 a.m., and exercise for 30 minutes."

However, it might sometimes be more complicated. Depending on your desired outcome, you may have yet to learn what to do to get started. In that case, the initial action you'll commit to will be scheduling time to figure out which other actions you need to take. For example, let's say you want to plan for retirement, improve your marriage, or live to be 100, but you're unsure where to start. In that case, your first action is scheduling time to determine the next steps. A simple Google search for "how to plan for retirement," "how to improve my marriage," or "how to live to be 100" can get you started.

Of course, an endless supply of resources (articles, YouTube videos, podcasts, etc.) is accessible on just about any topic. And if you want to go deeper, countless books are available from experts with experience with whatever you're trying to accomplish.

Here are a few examples of different outcomes you might have and specific actions you could take to ensure you make meaningful progress:

To ensure that I follow through with my goal to set myself up for a comfortable retirement, I will schedule time to:

- Read 10 pages per day from a book on retirement planning, such as *The Ultimate Retirement Guide for 50+* by Suze Orman, *The Retirement Miracle* by Patrick Kelly, or *The 5 Years Before You Retire* by Emily Guy Birken, so that I can learn practical strategies to model.
- Schedule adequate time each day to implement what I read.
- Ask my friends to recommend good retirement advisors and meet with a few to find the best one for me.

To ensure that I follow through with my goal to improve my marriage, I will schedule time to:

- Read books on marriage every morning before reading any other books to learn how to be the best spouse I can be.
- Every morning, I will identify at least one thing I can do that day to enhance my wife's life or make it easier.
- Bring romance and connection back into our relationship by scheduling a date night on Wednesday nights twice a month (to avoid the weekend rush).

To ensure that I follow through with my goal to improve my health and live to be 100, I will schedule time to:

- Read *The Blue Zones: 9 Lessons for Living Longer from the People Who've Lived the Longest* by Dan Buettner.
- Exercise for 10 minutes every morning during my S.A.V.E.R.S. When the weather is nice, I will also go for a 10-minute walk every day after dinner.
- Eat fresh organic fruits and vegetables with every meal.

As you implement this third and final step, clarify which actions you will take, and keep in mind that some actions may be repetitive and recurring (such as going for a walk every day or taking your spouse on a date night each week), while others may be sequential and follow steps (such as writing a book or retirement planning—step 1, step 2, step 3, etc.). The more specific your actions are, the better. Be sure to include frequency (how often) and precise time frames to clarify when you will begin and end your actions. If you're unsure which actions to take, simply affirm when you will schedule time to discover and determine what those actions will be. You don't need to have everything figured out to get started. That false belief often prevents us from ever taking our first step.

Keep this as simple as possible. Don't overwhelm yourself. Choose one area of your life and follow the three steps to create your affirmations for it. Once you've done it for one area (i.e., health), you can then repeat the process for another (i.e., money) and another (i.e., marriage), etc.

To ensure I follow through with my commitment, I will schedule time to take the following action(s):

- _____
- _____
- _____

The key to achieving any goal or improving any aspect of your life is harnessing your ability to commit and maintain your commitment for as long as it takes, even when you don't feel like it. Your Miracle Morning Results-Oriented Affirmations are designed to help you do exactly that by ensuring that you stay focused on what you're committed to, reinforce why your commitments are a must for you, and clarify which specific actions you'll take (and when) to ensure that you follow through. Remember: When you're committed, there is always a way.

Hal says . . .

In 2016, I was diagnosed with a rare, aggressive form of cancer (acute lymphoblastic leukemia) and given a 20 to 30 percent chance of surviving. Upon being admitted to the hospital, I was already on the verge of death. My heart, lungs, and kidneys were failing. Fearing for my life, I devoted all six of the S.A.V.E.R.S. to one objective: beating cancer. And I used *Affirmations* as the foundation of my healing journey, which I believe played a crucial role in saving my life. Following the three-step formula outlined above, here were my affirmations:

1. **My commitment:** I am committed to healing my body from cancer and living a long, happy, healthy life (to 100+ years old) alongside Ursula and the kids—no matter what. There is no other option!

2. **My whys:** I am committed to beating cancer . . .
   - For Ursula because I promised her forever and a day.
   - For Sophia and Halsten because they need their daddy's love and guidance.
   - For Mom and Dad because they've already lost one child and don't deserve to lose another.
   - For myself because I deserve to live a long, happy, healthy life.
   - For the millions of people who are themselves battling cancer or some other disease and may not have the knowledge, mindset, and resources that I've been blessed with, so it is my responsibility to do everything in my power to beat cancer so that I can help them on their healing journeys.

3. **My actions:** To ensure that I beat cancer, I will:
   - Take 100 percent responsibility for my healing and do everything in my power to heal my body.
   - Combine the best of allopathic (Western) medicine with the most effective holistic medicine protocols, which I will relentlessly research and implement.

- Devote my Miracle Mornings each day to healing my body—meditating, praying, affirming, visualizing, exercising, reading books and articles about people who have beat cancer and the methods they used, and following my scribing process.
- Maintain unwavering faith and put forth extraordinary effort to heal my body from cancer—no matter what, there is no other option!

I recited these affirmations every day, especially when I felt afraid, unmotivated, or like giving up. My experience has been that affirmations are the most effective form of personal development when approached following this three-step formula. That is because customizing your affirmations allows you total precision when focusing on what matters most to *you* and designing your present and future reality. And, you can continually edit, update, or add to them whenever you want. So, if you haven't already, simply choose one area of your life that you want to improve or your most important goal, and follow those three steps to write an affirmation that will keep you focused on what you deem to be most important. Then, once you've done this with one area of your life (such as health), duplicate the process with other areas.

Dwayne says . . .

I believe that, in many ways, the tongue is the most powerful muscle in the body. It has the power to create life (or death), so what we say matters. Affirmations play a crucial role in creating positive, even transformative, changes in our lives. So, when I first read *The Miracle Morning*, I knew that including affirmations as part of my Miracle Morning routine was a no-brainer. Hal's method for crafting personalized affirmations enhances their impact. I encourage you to write affirmations about other topics important to you as well, like your creativity, spirituality, will, persistence, and even things you like about yourself. By affirming yourself, you'll be healthier!

Also, be aware that the brain believes what you say. It's like a supercomputer, and it functions on the information it is fed. So if you say positive things about yourself—your life, your goals, your beliefs—it believes them and helps make those things come into being. Unfortunately, the opposite also holds true. If you are constantly saying negative things about yourself or your situation, nothing is likely to improve. So watch what you say; your brain is listening!

> The tongue is the most powerful muscle in the body. It has the power to create life (or death), so what we say matters.

If you're new to practicing affirmations, don't shy away from them. Initially, they may feel unfamiliar or uncomfortable, as is common with activities outside our comfort zones. However, with consistent practice, affirmations become more natural, and over time, both you and those around you will notice positive changes and personal growth.

Additional Ways to Approach Your Affirmations

There are countless additional ways to approach affirmations. Although there are certainly "wrong" (ineffective) ways to word an affirmation, there is really no one "right" way to phrase one.

Here is the key perspective to understand: An affirmation, at its most fundamental level, is simply a reminder of something you deem important and want to integrate into your life. That could be a thought, perspective, belief, or identity you want to embody. It could also be an action, habit, or behavior you want to implement. Written affirmations keep any important changes you want to make, internally or externally, top of mind by simply reading them every day.

For instance, if you're struggling with self-worth, self-doubt, or being happy, you could affirm, *I am just as worthy, deserving, and capable of being happy as any other person on earth* and remind yourself of this inherent truth. Repeating this every day will gradually reprogram your subconscious mind and replace your limiting beliefs with empowering ones, helping you create your new internal reality. If you're aiming to improve your health, you could affirm, *I am committed to nourishing my body with healthy foods and exercising for 20 minutes every day.* Reading either of these affirmations each morning will gradually reprogram your subconscious mind while helping to guide your conscious behavior to be consistent with what you're affirming.

Here are some affirmations for you to choose from or model, tailored toward common challenges of growing older. If you are heading into the next chapter of your life, or approaching a milestone birthday, you might face anxiety about aging. Affirmations like, *I embrace the wisdom and opportunities that come with age,* can help you adopt a positive mindset. To address health concerns, affirmations such as, *I am committed to making healthy choices that enhance my vitality and longevity,* can drive actions that support well-being.

Perhaps you are contemplating retirement or have just left the workforce. Though retirement is an occasion to celebrate, retirees often struggle with losing daily structure, and might feel a loss of identity. Affirmations can help them create a new routine and maintain a sense of purpose. For example, *I am excited to explore new hobbies and activities each day,* can motivate retirees to stay active and engaged. Affirmations like, *I bring valuable experience and wisdom to every situation,* can help them recognize their ongoing contributions and maintain their self-esteem.

You or someone in your life might also consider a move into an assisted living community (or may already live there). Seniors in assisted living might feel dependent on others, but also isolated. Affirmations such as, *I am capable of managing my daily tasks with grace and ease,* can empower them to take more control over their lives. Affirmations like, *I enjoy meaningful conversations and connections with others,* can encourage social engagement, improving emotional well-being.

Final Thoughts on Affirmations

How we talk to ourselves—our inner dialogue—influences how we feel about ourselves, others, and life. What we affirm repeatedly becomes our internal reality. By incorporating affirmations into your daily routine, you can experience profound transformations in your mental, emotional, and physical health, all of which contribute to a longer, healthier life.

Before you move on to the next section, if you haven't already done so, we highly encourage you to create your first Miracle Morning Results-Oriented Affirmation. Grab a journal, sheet of paper, or open up a blank document on your phone or computer, choose any area of your life that you want to improve—health, happiness, relationships, career, retirement, etc.—and follow the three-step formula detailed earlier. It's important you have at least a rough draft of your affirmations before moving on to Chapter 6 because you will use your affirmations as the content for what you visualize.

A Note from a Miracle Morning Community Member

"I am a real estate broker, and have always had a great career and income. I have always been a morning person, and my routine typically included exercise and reading. *The Miracle Morning* was recommended to me, and I thought it would just be another book I would add to my morning reading list. I read it within a couple days, and started my S.A.V.E.R.S. immediately.

"I never believed in affirmations, and when I started doing my S.A.V.E.R.S. consistently, and really manifesting my affirmations, my visualization became clearer, and I was able to take my business to the next level. Since then, I have been able to translate this to everything in my life: business, family, health, and spirituality! Even if I'm unable to do a full S.A.V.E.R.S. session, I still recite and scribe my affirmations without fail. A definite game changer!"

—Kelly Tingle
Age 50+

6

V IS FOR *VISUALIZATION*

Mentally Rehearse Showing Up at Your Best

*"Create the highest, grandest vision possible for your
life, because you become what you believe."*
—Oprah Winfrey, TV host, producer, actor, author, and media proprietor

O n May 6, 1954, Roger Bannister made history by becoming the first person to run a mile in under 4 minutes, clocking in at 3 minutes and 59.4 seconds. Before Bannister's achievement, many believed running a sub-4-minute mile was impossible. When asked about his success, Bannister credited his rigorous visualization techniques, which helped him create a profound sense of certainty within his mind and body, thus enabling him to achieve this historic feat.

Visualization, also known as mental rehearsal, a practice commonly used by elite athletes and performers, is not a skill reserved for Olympians and Broadway stars. It's a practice that anyone can adopt to mentally picture their desired outcome and rehearse the steps needed to attain it, while cultivating the most effective mental and emotional states to support taking action in real time. Visualization is a tool that can empower anyone to start taking the necessary actions to unlock their potential and transform their lives.

Take Helen, a 75-year-old resident of Aegis Living, the company Dwayne founded. When Helen arrived at the assisted living facility, she struggled with mobility issues and often felt disconnected from her previous active lifestyle. Then, a physical therapist introduced her to visualization techniques as part of her rehabilitation. Every morning, Helen would close her eyes and visualize herself walking confidently through the garden, feeling the sun on her face and the strength in her legs.

Over the weeks, this practice transformed Helen's mindset. She began to feel more positive and motivated. Her physical therapist noticed improvements in her gait and balance. Helen's renewed confidence and improved physical capabilities allowed her to participate in more activities at Aegis, enhancing her social life and overall well-being. Visualization became a cornerstone of her daily routine, significantly contributing to her extended healthspan and quality of life.

> Visualization is a powerful tool for anyone seeking to enhance overall well-being.

Visualization is a powerful tool for anyone seeking to enhance overall well-being—from athletes like Roger Bannister to people like Helen. By envisioning yourself in vibrant health, making positive choices, and mentally rehearsing those actions, you're primed to make those choices in real life.

Visualization Can Help Anyone Get Past Obstacles

Visualization can help us overcome the most significant obstacles between us and our goals: getting ourselves to do what we need to, even when we don't feel like it. Its versatility makes it a tool worth exploring for anyone seeking personal growth and development.

Whether it's due to a lack of inspiration, motivation, or physical energy, we often don't feel like doing what we need to do. We let our feelings determine our behavior, leading to procrastination. However, when you learn to generate the necessary clarity and motivation to take action, you'll find little to stop you from achieving your goals.

Hal says . . .

Allow me to share a personal story that illustrates precisely how you can use visualization to generate the clarity and motivation you need to do what you need to do when you need to, whether you feel like it or not.

As I shared in Chapter 2, for most of my life, I hated running. I realize that "hate" is a strong word, and I rarely use it, but I despised and avoided running for as long as I can remember. I vividly recall my aversion to the mandatory mile run in high school PE class. However, in early 2009, after roughly six months of doing my Miracle Mornings, I asked myself what a level-10 would be in the category of physical fitness. I had two friends who had both run ultramarathons (52 miles), and I considered the possibility that if they could do it, I could, too. Having never run more than a mile (which had been against my will back in high school), I figured that to run 52 consecutive miles, I would have to evolve far beyond who I had ever been, mentally and physically.

Although the prospect of becoming someone who could run an ultramarathon was somewhat exciting, it was primarily terrifying. A charity I sat on the board of, Front Row Foundation, was hosting its annual fundraising run at the Atlantic City Marathon that October. That gave me six months to train. So, I committed to the foundation and announced publicly that I would complete the ultramarathon to raise money for the Front Row Foundation. I immediately began using visualization to help me overcome my resistance to running.

Firstly, I dedicated roughly 1 to 2 minutes each day to envisioning my triumphant finish at the Atlantic City Marathon, immersing myself in the sensation of accomplishment. This practice clarified my goal and stoked my motivation to realize it.

Secondly (and this is key), I spent the next few minutes visualizing precisely what I needed to do that day to progress toward my ideal outcome. I did so while cultivating an optimal emotional state that would compel me to take action. I closed my eyes and vividly pictured my iPhone resting on our living room coffee table, displaying 7:00 a.m. and the alarm beeping to let me know it was time to go for my run. I saw myself reach down, turn off the alarm, stand up, walk into the bedroom, and head into my closet to get dressed. I pictured myself wearing my running clothes, then heading back to my living room and toward the front door. I saw myself opening the door, looking at the sidewalk, and smiling as I affirmed with conviction and enthusiasm, *I'm excited to go for a run today because it enables me to become the best version of myself!* As I visualized, I repeated these affirmations and created congruent physiology (the alignment between a person's physical body language and their emotional or mental state) by nodding my head and generating feelings of excitement to go for today's run.

I didn't *wish* or *want* or *hope* for the feelings that would compel me to go for a run; I *generated* those feelings. Within a few minutes, I mentally rehearsed myself, taking the necessary actions I knew I needed to reach my goal while putting myself in an optimal emotional state that would compel me to take those actions at the predetermined time.

The payoff for this visualization method was that when the alarm on my phone began beeping at 7:00 a.m., I didn't give in to the temptation to procrastinate and skip my run. That didn't happen because that's not what I rehearsed. Instead, when my alarm went off, I did exactly what I had visualized that morning, almost automatically and with virtually no resistance. I stood up, went into my closet, dressed, walked across my living room to the front door, opened the door, and as soon as I saw the sidewalk, I was flooded with the positive emotions I had generated that morning. Even the exact words of my affirmation ran through my head. And off I went, suddenly able and compelled to do what I had despised and avoided for my entire life. That's the power and primary benefit of visualization.

Visualization for Increasing Longevity and Healthspan

Various studies have explored how visualization can enhance mental well-being, physical health, and longevity, with exciting results.

- **Stress reduction and immune function:** Imagine sitting in a quiet room, closing your eyes, and visualizing yourself in utter relaxation. A study published in *Psychosomatic Medicine* revealed that daily visualization exercises can boost the immune system by reducing stress levels.[1] Lower stress means the body produces more natural killer cells, fighting viruses and cancer.
- **Chronic pain management:** Research in the *Journal of Behavioral Medicine* showed that visualization exercises significantly reduce chronic pain and improve quality of life.[2] By visualizing pain as manageable, patients reported a decrease in pain intensity.

- **Cancer treatment:** A study by the Cleveland Clinic Foundation found that cancer patients who practiced visualization alongside their medical treatment experienced more effective tumor reduction.[3] By visualizing their immune systems attacking cancer cells, patients saw a decrease in tumor size.
- **Recovery from surgery:** Visualization can also aid in recovery from surgery. For example, heart surgery patients who used guided imagery to envision a successful healing process experienced faster recovery rates, reduced pain, and a more positive outlook.[4]
- **Managing heart disease:** A case study showed that a patient with heart disease who visualized a healthy heart and clear arteries, alongside medical treatment, experienced significant improvements in cardiovascular health.[5]
- **Benefits for seniors:** Seniors who visualized themselves as healthy, active, and living their entire lives with joy saw improvements in mental health, physical strength, and attitudes toward aging. These factors are linked to increased longevity and a higher quality of life.

Three Simple Steps for Miracle Morning Visualization

The perfect time to visualize yourself aligning with your affirmations is right after you read them. Your affirmations articulate what you want and are committed to, why it's a must for you, and which actions you'll take to follow through. Visualization lets you imagine what it will feel like to achieve your goals and mentally rehearse yourself taking the necessary actions while putting yourself into a positive mental and emotional state that will compel you to follow through.

Your visualization can take just a few minutes, though many find it particularly enjoyable and do it for up to 15 to 20 minutes—it all depends on you and how long you decide to devote to each element of your S.A.V.E.R.S. Now, onto your specific visualization steps.

Step 1: Prepare Your Mindset

Our mindset going into any experience sets the tone for the experience itself. Remember, the primary objectives of visualization are to see and feel what it will be like to achieve what you've committed to in your affirmations, generating the clarity and motivation to fuel your drive to follow through; mentally rehearse taking the actions needed to achieve your ideal outcome; and get into a peak emotional state to feel more compelled to take the necessary actions. And remember that the science shows that visualization really works.

This famous quote from Marianne Williamson's book *A Return to Love* may resonate with anyone who feels mental or emotional obstacles when attempting to visualize:

> *Our deepest fear is not that we are inadequate. Our deepest fear is that we are powerful beyond measure. It is our light, not our darkness, that most frightens us. We ask ourselves, 'Who am I to be brilliant, gorgeous, talented, fabulous?' Actually, who are you not to be? You are a child of God. Your playing small does not serve the world. There is nothing enlightened about shrinking so that other people won't feel insecure around you. We are all meant to shine, as children do. We were born to make manifest the glory of God that is within us. It's not just in some of us; it's in everyone. And as we let our own light shine, we unconsciously give other people permission to do the same. As we are liberated from our own fear, our presence automatically liberates others.*

Consider that the greatest gift you can give to the people you love and those you lead may be simply to fulfill your potential so that you can lead by example and inspire them to achieve their own. What do you want your life to be like from now on? You are just as worthy, deserving, and capable of being happy as anyone else.

Now, let's visualize what that looks like for you. Sit comfortably, breathe deeply, close your eyes, and clear your mind. Get ready to visualize.

Step 2: Visualize Your Commitment (from Your Affirmations)

First, imagine what it will be like once you've made your commitment a reality. What area of your life would you like to improve? What goal would you like to achieve? Close your eyes and vividly imagine the positive feelings the experience will bring. For Hal, it was crossing the finish line of the Atlantic City Marathon. For you, it might be improving your health, growing your business, or connecting more deeply with someone you love.

As you visualize what you desire, make it as vivid as possible. You can even involve more than one of your senses to maximize the effectiveness of your visualization. See, feel, hear, touch, taste, and smell every detail of your vision. The point is to imagine yourself enjoying what you set out to accomplish and to experience how good it will feel to have followed through and made your vision a reality. The more vivid you make your vision, the more accurate it will feel and the more compelled you'll be to take the necessary actions to make it happen.

Dwayne says . . .

I have a cork board in my bathroom, which is my vision board. It is layered with affirmations that I review silently every morning, as well as notes of things that I want to accomplish. Also, as I mentioned earlier in Chapter 2, I use sticky notes to write motivational messages that keep me focused on how I want to feel for the day and what I'd like to achieve. Combining visuals that reflect my goals and dreams with my daily affirmations and visualizations make the results more tangible and help keep me focused and motivated.

Step 3: Visualize Taking Action (While in an Optimal Emotional State)

Next, determine which actions to take to achieve that outcome and mentally rehearse taking those actions. See yourself engaged in the activities you need to do today (exercising, working, researching, writing, making phone calls, engaging with other people positively, etc.), while enjoying the process and feeling positive emotions. See yourself smiling as you're running on that treadmill, filled with pride for your self-discipline in following through. Picture the look of determination on your face as you make those phone calls, work on that report or project you've been putting off, take that trip, start a new hobby, or pursue your second career. Generate feelings of love and playfulness as you rehearse greeting your family for the day. Visualize yourself in a peak mental and emotional state, doing whatever you need to do today to move toward your ideal outcomes.

Final Thoughts on Visualization

When you combine reading your affirmations every morning with daily visualization, you turbocharge the programming of your subconscious mind for success. Visualization aligns your thoughts, feelings, and behaviors with your vision, making maintaining the motivation and discipline needed to take the necessary actions easier.

Stay patient and consistent with your visualization practice. Like meditation, affirmations, exercise, or any other self-care practice, it takes consistency over an extended period of time to reap the full benefits. Whether you're seeking to generate feelings of motivation, confidence, stress relief, inner peace, or personal growth, visualization offers a powerful tool to help you achieve your goals and live a more fulfilling life.

A Note from a Miracle Morning Community Member

"I kept hearing about *The Miracle Morning* in a leadership group and decided to finally check out the book. Loved it and immediately started putting it into practice. Soon after starting the MM practice, friends and family noticed a difference in my energy level and also my calmness. I seemed to get more done, more easily. I share *The Miracle Morning* and have referred many to it.

"I was already a morning person, but with *The Miracle Morning*, I found myself getting up at 4:30–5:00 a.m. and starting my day off in a way that has truly changed my life. I've always liked the morning quiet time, and my favorite S.A.V.E.R.S. exercise is *Visualization*, followed by *Silence*. Why? It seems that prior to TMM, I would never slow down long enough to actually visualize and take care of myself. I was always running from place to place trying to get everything done instead of taking care of myself and finding balance. Now I'm able to do several things but in a much calmer, more peaceful and effective way. It's an amazing way to start my morning."

—Kelly Gerhardt
Age 62

7

E IS FOR *EXERCISE*

Enhance Your Physical, Mental, and Emotional Vitality

"Stay in shape. And remember, daily exercise is a must.
Plan for it, and do it. The rewards will be well worth it."
—Jack LaLanne, American fitness and nutrition guru, motivational speaker

Betty was an 82-year-old resident at Aegis Living. She struggled with mobility and feared falling, which made her reluctant to move much. One of the caregivers introduced her to chair exercises that she could do while sitting down. She also introduced her to gentle yoga tailored for seniors that would allow Betty to stretch her limbs more easily. At first, Betty was skeptical, but she decided to try it.

Over a few weeks, Betty noticed a significant improvement in her flexibility and strength. She felt more confident moving around and started participating in group activities again. Her energy levels improved, and she enjoyed her days much more. Incorporating regular, gentle exercise into her routine brought a sense of independence and vitality back into her life.

While you may be younger than Betty and can't conceive of ever being in her situation, it is important to remember that aging well into each decade means incorporating exercise into your daily routine. When it comes to fitness and ease of movement, the "use it or lose it" principle is all too true. As we age, our muscles tend to lose strength and mobility, our bones tend to weaken, and our metabolism tends to slow, unless we actively work to prevent these things from happening. Keeping your body moving—or getting it moving again if you've found yourself slowing down—is imperative to your physical vitality. Fortunately, there are things you can do to build strength and preserve or increase mobility regardless of your age or physical condition. And, since *Exercise* is built into S.A.V.E.R.S., you'll be starting your day with vital movement.

Dwayne says . . .

Don't wait for a wake-up call. When I was younger, I was passionate about the pursuit of health, but over time, I lost sight of that passion. I worked long hours, lived on a rich sugar/fat-food diet, partied late into the night, and slept very little. And exercise? Well, I fit it in when I "had the time." I had learned so much about caring for people well into their 100s, but ironically, I'd never consciously applied those lessons to myself. While I had been living and breathing questions about the health and longevity of my Aegis residents, I'd separated myself from what I'd learned.

Everything came to a head one Labor Day weekend with my wife when I began to experience the most acute abdominal pain of my life. It was so bad that I ended up in the hospital, where I was diagnosed with severe gastritis. Lying in that hospital bed, overnight, my commitment changed.

My rekindled obsession with health and longevity led me on a research journey to find every conceivable way to live a more vibrant, healthier, and fulfilled life. I became a "wellness warrior," traveling to over 80 countries to interview hundreds of people about what it means to age well into their 80s, 90s, and 100s. (My findings are part of the inspiration for my book *30 Summers More*.) As simple as it sounds, a big part of the longevity equation came down to movement. Again and again, centenarians told me that simply making movement a part of daily life was their longevity secret. It wasn't about having a heavy workout routine or becoming a gym rat. It was about taking the stairs over the elevator, taking short walks throughout the day, doing 5 minutes of yoga, parking the car a few more spots away from the store, and stretching as often as possible. Whatever it takes, just keep moving!

The Power of Morning Exercise

Exercise is an invaluable and flexible part of your Miracle Morning. It doesn't have to be a full-blown gym session right after waking up, especially if you are new or just returning to exercise. (We'll give you a few suggestions for getting started later in this chapter.) The goal here is to incorporate a few minutes of movement in the morning to experience the physical and cognitive benefits that will help keep you energized and focused all day long while improving your healthspan and longevity—especially after 50. Aging gracefully involves more than just a positive mindset and healthy habits; it's about maintaining functional strength, which is crucial for performing everyday tasks and preserving independence.

Functional strength supports the ability to perform daily activities independently, such as standing up from a chair, carrying groceries, and climbing stairs. It helps preserve our autonomy as we age. Difficulty getting out of a chair is a telltale sign of sarcopenia, the age-related loss of muscle mass and strength, which impacts mobility, balance, and overall physical function. It begins around age 50 and accelerates with time, increasing the risk of falls and fractures, which can drastically reduce quality of life.

Strength training improves glucose metabolism and reduces the risk of type 2 diabetes. The American Diabetes Association highlights that strength training enhances insulin sensitivity and glucose uptake in muscles, which is particularly beneficial for aging adults in managing their metabolic health.[1]

Higher levels of muscle strength are linked to increased longevity and lower mortality risk from all causes,[2] including cardiovascular disease, osteoporosis, and cancer. It significantly enhances energy levels in those over 50 by improving cardiovascular health, increasing muscle strength, and boosting overall stamina. Engaging in consistent physical activity strengthens the heart and enhances lung capacity, facilitating more efficient oxygen and nutrient delivery to muscles and tissues. This improved circulation supports sustained energy throughout the day.[3]

Exercise improves cognitive function, mental health, and memory.

In addition to all of these benefits to your body, exercise also benefits your brain. Exercise improves cognitive function, mental health, and memory; it can also prevent the development of certain neurological conditions, including dementia.[4] How? There are several interesting ways by which exercise might help protect your mind.[5] First, when we exercise, more oxygen reaches the brain, and blood vessels grow in areas of the brain associated with rational thinking and social, physical, and intellectual performance. Also, exercise upregulates proteins called neurotrophins that help protect our neurons and keep them functioning right.

Morning exercise, in particular, has also been shown to have a significant impact on energy levels throughout the day. When you work out, oxygen and nutrients are increased throughout your body, and particularly in your heart and lungs. This improves your cardiovascular system, endurance, and overall stamina. Exercise also stimulates the production of mitochondria—our cells' powerhouses responsible for energy generation. A higher mitochondrial count boosts the body's capacity to produce energy, leading to reduced fatigue.[6] By exercising early, you set yourself up to feel more energized throughout the day.

Last but not least, physical activity is a natural remedy for stress. During exercise, your brain produces more endorphins, the feel-good neurotransmitters behind a runner's high. (Neurotransmitters like serotonin and norepinephrine are also known to accelerate our brain's information processing.) Stimulating these neurotransmitters in the morning sets your emotional thermostat for the day.

When you exercise in the morning, not only are you helping to preserve your health and build up your energy, but you'll also feel a sense of accomplishment, which helps to foster an optimistic outlook for the day.

Choose the Right Exercise for You

After you hit 50, you'll want to focus on exercises that prioritize functional fitness and improve strength, flexibility, balance, and cardiovascular health, while being mindful of any existing health conditions or physical limitations. Here are some options that meet these criteria and can be done during your Miracle Morning:

- **Walking or hiking:** These are low-impact and can be easily adjusted to fit individual fitness levels. Consider walking outdoors for the benefits of light and fresh air or even just around the house to increase daily steps and maintain mobility. Hiking provides additional benefits of improved muscle strength and balance. Walking a minimum of 4,700 steps a day is very good for your health, and 7,000 to 8,000 steps is great. The more, the better!
- **Cycling:** Cycling is an exercise that places very little pressure on most joints. It's also an ideal exercise for improving balance

and strengthening muscles. Hal goes for a bike ride around his neighborhood three to four mornings a week, and he has an indoor exercise bike for when the weather isn't conducive to cycling outside.

- **Swimming:** Like cycling, swimming puts little to no pressure on your joints. It's a total-body workout that improves your flexibility, range of motion, and respiratory system, as well as strengthens your lungs and improves body balance.

- **Strength training:** Strengthen muscles to maintain mobility and prevent falls by using resistance bands or light weights to perform exercises that target major muscle groups. Resistance training helps maintain muscle mass and strength, crucial for functional movements.

- **Chair exercises:** These can be done while sitting or holding onto a chair for support. Examples include seated leg lifts, arm curls with light weights, seated marches, or rapid feet tapping to strengthen your lower body, elevate the heart rate, and improve cardiovascular health without stressing the joints.

- **Yoga:** Yoga can enhance flexibility, strength, and balance. If you're new to yoga and need some guidance at first, you can start with a YouTube video (just go to YouTube.com and search "yoga after 50, 60, 70, 80, etc.") or you can look for yoga classes designed specifically for your age group and fitness level, such as yoga for seniors or those with limited mobility. Many options are available online, so you can certainly do yoga at home as part of your S.A.V.E.R.S.

- **Tai Chi/Qigong:** These gentle martial arts practices involve slow, deliberate movements that improve balance, flexibility, and mental well-being. Many instructional videos are available for practicing these at home. A study in *Frontiers in Public Health* found that Tai Chi improves balance and reduces the risk of falls as we get older.[7]

- **Balance exercises:** Stand near a sturdy surface like a countertop or chair for support and practice exercises like heel-to-toe walking, single-leg stands, or standing on one leg with eyes closed to improve balance and stability.
- **Stair climbing:** Aging adults can use stairs for a low-impact cardiovascular workout if they are available. Start with a few steps and gradually increase the intensity as fitness improves.
- **Dancing:** Put on some music and dance around the living room! Dancing provides cardiovascular benefits and improves your balance, coordination, and mood.
- **Stretching:** Incorporate gentle stretching exercises for the major muscle groups to improve flexibility and range of motion. You can even start your day with gentle stretches while still in bed (see Chapter 2 for more on how to do this). Focus on holding each stretch for 15–30 seconds without bouncing. Stretching prepares your body for movement throughout the day.
- **Gardening:** Activities like gardening or light yard work can provide exercise while offering the benefits of being outdoors and connecting with nature.

During your S.A.V.E.R.S. practice, we recommend getting at least 10 minutes of movement. Whichever exercise(s) you choose, consult with your healthcare provider first, especially if you have any chronic health conditions or concerns. This will ensure that your exercise routine is safe and tailored to your needs, providing peace of mind as you work toward better health.

While movement is an obvious component of the *E* in your S.A.V.E.R.S. routine, you can also find ways to prioritize movement and functional strength during the other S.A.V.E.R.S. if you so choose. For instance, during *Silence*, you can incorporate mindfulness or meditation focused on body awareness and relaxation, which can help reduce stress and improve mental clarity. For *Affirmations*, use positive affirmations related to physical health and strength, such as *I am strong and capable,* or *I maintain my functional strength daily. Visualize* yourself performing daily activities with ease and confidence, reinforcing the importance of strength and mobility. *Read* materials that provide insights and tips on maintaining physical health and strength, such as books on fitness for people over 50 or articles on healthy aging. And finally, during *Scribing,* you can journal your progress in maintaining functional strength, set daily goals, and reflect on the benefits you experience from staying active.

Beyond the Morning: Developing Rituals of Daily Movement

With everything available at our fingertips, from grocery deliveries to banking, our daily routines have become increasingly sedentary. So, how do you break free from the sitting trap and get moving again? Here are a few tips to get you moving in the morning during S.A.V.E.R.S. and keep you moving throughout the day:

1. **Track your activity:** Start by tracking your steps from the moment you wake up. How many are you taking each day? Wearable trackers and smartphones can provide amazing insights here, but you can also do it the old-fashioned way with a pedometer! Aim to gradually increase your steps and decrease your sedentary time, starting with small increments and building up. Also, keep an eye on how much time you spend sitting or lounging and your screen time.

2. **Get those steps in:** If you find yourself sitting most of the day, you might only take around 2,000 steps daily. Try doubling that initially. While 10,000 steps a day

is the gold standard, if you've developed a sedentary lifestyle, hitting that number can feel like climbing Everest. Instead, aim for 5,000 to 7,500 steps, which can significantly improve your health compared to a sedentary lifestyle.

3. **Stand up regularly:** If you're desk-bound, make a habit of standing up or taking a short walk every 30 minutes. Set a recurring reminder on your phone, if you need a nudge.
4. **Incorporate movement:** Walk while talking on the phone, take the stairs instead of the elevator, or park farther away to add more steps.

Dwayne says . . .

You have to accommodate your lifestyle and health conditions and get creative with movement. Our exercise routines differ as we age and based on our career and family obligations, so it is important to be flexible with your exercise routine. For example, my wife and I travel with resistance bands so we don't miss a workout just because we're away from home. We do band workouts for stretching and improving muscle tone. They are great for mobility issues. We also travel with hand exercisers called eggs. They look like a rubber egg you hold in your hand and are great for strengthening your hands, fingers, and forearm muscles. They're also simple to use—while watching TV, reading, or walking. And, they fit in a purse or backpack so there's no excuse not to move your body in some way—no matter where you are. I have Aegis residents that are wheelchair bound who keep strong and mobile using resistance bands and eggs. They are great for all fitness levels.

Another tip: My physical therapist has me use various types of vibrating massage devices. Let's say I wake up and my knees or back are stiff. I grab one of these massagers, and the vibration gently loosens my muscles. I have one called the Peanut, and it is beneficial in keeping me motivated to move regardless of initial stiffness. (Actually, I have at least four. My wife has told me I have to stop buying them.) Some of these vibrating massage devices also have an infrared light attached to them. So not only do you have the healing from vibration, but you also have red light, which has its own therapeutic benefits around wound healing and reducing inflammation.

Bottom line: Don't let aches and pains stop you from keeping your body in a state of movement. That's the point.

Enhance Exercise with Cold Therapy

As you might guess from our earlier section on the Wim Hof Method (see Chapter 4), Dwayne is a big proponent of cold therapy. Studies have shown that cold exposure can increase the production of norepinephrine, a hormone that helps reduce inflammation and supports cellular health. This can be especially beneficial in warding off age-related ailments and promoting longevity.[8] Cold exposure can also boost your immune system and help eliminate senescent cells (zombie cells) that contribute to aging and inflammation.[9] Regular cold exposure also trains your body to handle stress better, both physically and mentally, enhancing your overall resilience.

Embrace the chill and enjoy the invigorating benefits it brings to your Miracle Morning! Here's how you can do it effectively and safely.

Begin with your usual exercise routine. This could be a brisk walk, yoga, strength training, or any physical activity that gets your blood flowing. Exercise warms up your body, making the transition to cold therapy more manageable. (Cold therapy also helps reduce muscle soreness and inflammation, promoting quicker recovery after exercise, so it's particularly effective after your chosen form of movement.)

Then, transition to cold therapy. If you have access to a cold plunge or ice bath, start by singing a song or doing some light stretching to mentally prepare yourself. (Seriously, Dwayne's favorite tip is to belt out your favorite tune for 30 seconds to a minute. Not only does it distract you, but it also helps regulate your breathing, which is crucial when you're about to take the plunge.) Enter the cold water and aim to stay submerged for 1 to 2 minutes initially. That's how long it takes for your body to start adjusting to the cold. Those initial moments are tough, but hang in there. As you get more accustomed, gradually increase the duration to 3 to 5 minutes. Focus on your breathing to help your body adjust. Take it from Dwayne—you'll feel like a superhero when you work your way up to those longer times.

If a cold plunge isn't available, a cold shower works just as well. Start with lukewarm water and gradually turn it colder. Begin with 30 seconds of cold water and work your way up to a full minute or more as your body adapts. (As always, consult with your healthcare provider before starting your cold therapy.)

Now, here's a critical part: When you get out, resist the urge to immediately warm up. Instead, give your body a few minutes to adjust. This helps prevent the shock of cold blood rushing to your heart. (If you have access to a hot tub or shower, wait a few minutes before jumping in to avoid shocking your system.)

So, give it a try. Sing your heart out, brave the cold, and know that every shiver is a step toward a healthier, more resilient you. And who knows, you might even start looking forward to that chilly embrace.

Final Thoughts on Exercise

While we all know how beneficial daily exercise is for optimizing our health, it can be far too easy to procrastinate and justify not exercising. Two of the most common excuses are, *I do not have time* and *I am too tired.*

Have either of those excuses ever stopped you from working out? That's what makes the *E* in your morning S.A.V.E.R.S. such a game changer: It ensures you get it done before you come up with excuses or deplete your energy throughout the day.

A Note from a Miracle Morning Community Member

"I have to thank my dad for helping me find the Miracle Morning. Although I cannot thank him in person (he passed away in February 2022), I do so often during my time of silence during my S.A.V.E.R.S. Even though he was 92, his health had deteriorated the last 10 years of his life and proved challenging, obviously for him but also for all our family. I never imagined the grief, sadness, and anger I would feel from his loss. I struggled and could not seem to find a way through!! Then I found a book given to me by my sister-in-law—*The Miracle Morning*. I picked it up and couldn't put it down. It totally resonated with me!! I'm now on my 294th consecutive day. The change in me has been recognized and voiced by my husband of 24 years and my 20-year-old twin girls. My life has improved so much through my positive mindset and much improved health both mentally and physically through *The Miracle Morning*. In fact, I am now reading a copious number of books, doing daily yoga exercises, and walking/running with our dog, Weston. 2022 was my worst year, but also my best year!!!"

—Jackie Davey
Age 50+

R IS FOR *READING*

Acquire the Knowledge to
Accelerate Your Transformation

"Reading is to the mind what exercise is to the body."
—Joseph Addison, English essayist, poet, playwright, and politician

It has been said that experience is our greatest teacher. Whoever said that may have failed to clarify if said experience must be our own or if we could take a shortcut and gain it from the experience had by others. If the latter is true, then that would help explain why the fifth practice in the S.A.V.E.R.S.—*Reading*—is one of the most efficient and effective methods for acquiring the knowledge, perspectives, and strategies you need to change, improve, or optimize any area of your life.

Want to be happier, healthier, and wealthier? Are you looking to start a business, improve your marriage, plan for retirement, or learn how to connect with your grandkids? There are countless books and articles written by those who have already done these things and will teach you how you can do the same, thereby shortening your learning curve and accelerating your success.

According to the National Institute on Aging, reading books and magazines can also help keep your mind engaged and sharp.[1] So, let's dive into how reading can help you live with vitality and joy well into your later years. (Ironically, this chapter on reading is one of the shortest in this book—but we think the evidence on reading speaks volumes!)

Science Says . . .

Studies have shown that reading can improve brain function, increase empathy, and reduce stress. Research published in *Neurology* indicates that engaging in mentally stimulating activities such as reading can delay the onset of cognitive decline.[2]

Furthermore, a Yale University School of Public Health study found that reading books contributed to a longer lifespan. Researchers examined data from 3,635 individuals over the age of 50 who participated in a nationwide health study. Based on their answers to the question, "How many hours did you spend last week reading books?" respondents were divided into three groups: those who read no books, those who read books for up to three-and-a-half hours a week, and those who read books for more than three-and-a-half hours a week. The results were heartening for book lovers. Over 12 years of follow-up, those who read for up to three-and-a-half hours a week enjoyed a 17 percent lower risk of dying compared to nonreaders, while those who read for more than three-and-a-half hours a week saw a remarkable 23 percent decrease in risk. On average, book readers lived 23 months longer than those who didn't read at all.[3]

Also, engaging with literature that promotes positive thinking and resilience can reduce the impact of negative thoughts and promote a more optimistic outlook. A study published in 2018 showed that reading self-help books can significantly reduce symptoms of depression and anxiety—which, as we know, become more prevalent as we age.[4]

How Much to Read

It's up to you how much of your Miracle Morning you want to devote to reading. (We'll get into various durations for each of your S.A.V.E.R.S. in Chapter 10.) Hal recommends reading for at least 10 minutes during your Miracle Morning. You can, of course, read for longer—and again later in the day!—if you'd like. Most of us can easily read 5 to 10 pages daily.

That may not seem like much, but let's do some math. Reading 10 pages daily multiplied by 365 days adds up to 3,650 pages per year, or approximately eighteen 200-page books. If you were to read 18 self-development books in the next 12 months (or even half that many at 5 pages per day), do you think you'll see improvements in your mindset and learn strategies that can significantly improve your life? Absolutely! Reading 5 to 10 pages daily won't break you, but it will make you. It's a journey of personal growth that can radically transform the quality of your life.

> Reading 5 to 10 pages daily won't break you, but it will make you. It's a journey of personal growth that can radically transform the quality of your life.

What to Read

To be clear, for your Miracle Morning, we are talking about reading non-fiction personal development and wellness content. We're not knocking fiction, but the goal here is to gain the knowledge and tools you need to live better. Look for content written by authors who have achieved results that are in alignment with those you aspire to, so you don't have to reinvent the wheel. You can achieve everything you want much faster by modeling someone who has already achieved it. With an almost infinite number of books available on nearly every topic, there are no limits to the knowledge you can gain through daily reading.

Hal says . . .

I can attribute some of the most life-changing and even life-saving advice I've ever received to the books I've read. When I lost over half of my income during the 2008 Great Recession, reading and applying the strategies in *Book Yourself Solid* by Michael Port enabled me to double my income in two months. When I wanted to run an ultramarathon and had no idea where to begin, *The Non-Runner's Marathon Trainer* was the book that showed me the way. When I was diagnosed with cancer and given a 30 percent chance of surviving, it was books like *Chris Beat Cancer* by Chris Wark and *Radical Remission* by Kelly A. Turner that provided me with much-needed inspiration and the specific instructions I needed to beat cancer and heal. Reading nonfiction books specific to areas of my life that I want to improve has been one of the most valuable aspects of my daily commitment to the S.A.V.E.R.S.

You're just a Google search away from an endless supply of free articles on how to overcome any challenge, improve any aspect of your life, develop any skill, or achieve any goal. In addition to articles, nonfiction books on virtually every topic enable you to delve deeper and learn more than you would in most articles. And if you want specific advice on a topic leveraging the somewhat controversial but extraordinary power of artificial intelligence (AI), tools like ChatGPT have emerged, which can give you instant, personalized information and assistance across a wide range of topics.

The advantages of reading a book (as opposed to an article or a response to a quick ChatGPT inquiry) is that you will likely go much deeper and spend significantly more time focused on that topic. And the more time you spend reading (and thinking) about a topic, the more knowledge, perspective, and insights you'll gain. Consider comparing the limited value of spending 5 minutes reading an article that may soon be forgotten with dedicating weeks or even months reading a book on the same topic. Not only will you learn more from the book's content, but you'll be thinking about how to apply it to your life, day after day, continuously gaining valuable insights and increased self-awareness.

Head to your library, local bookstore, or an online store, and you'll find more books than you can read in a lifetime to help you improve any area of your life. Whether you want to improve your mental or physical health, marriage, finances, relationship with your children, or learn any new hobby or thrive in retirement, you'd be unlikely to find a category that didn't have a wide variety of options to choose from. Because this book is specifically for readers over 50, here's a short list of top-rated books on longevity and the wisdom of aging to get you started:

- *30 Summers More: Adding Time Back to Your Aging Clock* by Dwayne J. Clark
- *Lifespan: Why We Age—and Why We Don't Have To* by David Sinclair
- *Outlive: The Science & Art of Longevity* by Dr. Peter Attia
- *Learning to Love Midlife: 12 Reasons Why Life Gets Better with Age* by Chip Conley
- *The Longevity Diet: Slow Aging, Fight Disease, Optimize Weight* by Valter Longo, PhD
- *Cheating Death: The New Science of Living Longer and Better* by Dr. Rand McClain
- *Consciousness Is All There Is: How Understanding and Experiencing Consciousness Will Transform Your Life* by Dr. Tony Nader

Dwayne says . . .

At Aegis Living, I had the pleasure of meeting a 75-year-old retiree named Jane. She moved into an Aegis Living community, not because she needed care, but because she wanted a simpler life than having to tend her home, garden, and daily needs after her husband passed away. She was a delightful lady who enjoyed group activities. One day, she mentioned to one of the resident managers that she often just felt bored, even with all the community activities. The manager asked her, "Read any great books lately?"

Jane responded, "I've never been a big reader." At the manager's suggestion, Jane started with just a few minutes a day, gradually increasing her reading time as she found books that truly resonated with her. She read about nutrition, exercise, and mindfulness, incorporating these practices into her daily routine. Jane even joined a local book club, making new friends and engaging in lively discussions. Her newfound love for reading not only kept her mind sharp but also enriched her social life and overall well-being. Jane is now an active, vibrant 85-year-old, living proof that it's never too late to start a new chapter in life.

Final Thoughts on Reading

Remember, it's not just about what you read or how often you read, but how you apply what you learn. Commit to reading each morning, and as you read, schedule time to take action on the insights you gain. You can also recall and incorporate useful content you read by writing it down in a separate note or adding it to your daily affirmations. That way you can reread it and integrate it into your life. By integrating this simple yet powerful habit into your daily Miracle Morning routine, you'll foster mental stimulation and continuously acquire knowledge to accelerate your transformations and enhance your quality of life.

A Note from a Miracle Morning Community Member

"I heard about *The Miracle Morning* about 12 years ago and was not a morning person at all. I didn't really implement anything until about 10 years ago when I was involved in a head-on motorcycle crash. Hal's story really resonated with me, given we had similar experiences. I started the Miracle Morning in the hospital and continued at home during recovery. Implementing the Miracle Morning was a game changer for me. It really helped me get my life back on track and I absolutely love waking up at 5 a.m. and having time for myself. I have consistently read a book a month and am on track to read over 20 books this year. I've also been able to take charge of my health and work out regularly. Hal has inspired me to create a podcast where I will be interviewing successful people on how they start their day."

—Albert Belo
Age: 50+

9

S IS FOR *SCRIBING*

Experience the Power of Solidifying Thoughts in Writing

"Journaling leads people to life changes, leaps of faith, new insights, and meaningful decisions."
—**Lynda Monk, author, coach, facilitator**

In 1789, Benjamin Franklin wrote a letter that famously stated, "In this world, nothing is certain except death and taxes." While Franklin was referring to the newly established Constitution, he may have left out at least one other certainty: *thoughts.*

There are few things that are more certain than the fact that our minds continuously generate countless thoughts each and every day. From our first moment of consciousness after waking until we close our eyes to sleep, we're generally thinking about *something.*

The problem is that many (or most) of our thoughts are unconscious and can be stressful, disempowering, unproductive, or counterproductive.

And since thoughts lead to feelings and emotions, which prompt us to take (or fail to take) certain actions that lead to outcomes, having tools to manage and direct your thoughts is essential to gaining more control of what you think and how you feel so that you can have more control over your life.

The need to be more intentional about our thoughts is one of the reasons affirmations are such an effective tool—because you get to carefully determine which thoughts best serve you, solidify them in writing, and affirm them every day. This intentionality puts you in the driver's seat of your life, enabling you to design affirmations that become the blueprint for creating the life you want.

Similarly, having a daily practice to manage the ongoing influx of thoughts is equally beneficial. That's where scribing becomes an invaluable aspect of your Miracle Morning.

Scribing may sound like a fancy word, but it's really just a more sophisticated term for journaling. Let's keep it real—Hal needed an *S* to fit into the S.A.V.E.R.S. acronym, because a *J* at the end would have been a bit awkward. Thanks, thesaurus! We owe you one.

Scribing allows you to observe your ongoing thoughts in real-time and discern which ones are worthy of writing down. This applies to both positive and negative thoughts. In terms of amplifying your positive thoughts, *Scribing* is where you capture your ideas, realizations, breakthroughs, and reflections, as well as record your successes, lessons learned, experiences, and aspects of your life that you're grateful for. In doing this, you'll gain new perspectives that lead to heightened clarity, self-awareness, and insights that might otherwise be missed. Leveraging these benefits sets you up to feel better and consistently make positive choices that will improve your life.

As a tool for managing and minimizing the potentially detrimental impact of your negative thoughts, *Scribing* enables you to express your fears, problems, or anything else causing you to feel stressed and overwhelmed. By transferring stressful thoughts out of your mind and capturing them in writing, you're able to relieve yourself of the burden that's caused by feeling you have to constantly remember (and worry about) every single thing. Similar to the benefits of keeping a to-do list, once something is in writing, you can release the need to constantly think (or worry) about it, and revisit it only as needed, when it best serves you.

Let's break these benefits down, one by one.

The Benefits of *Scribing*

When you commit to a regular journaling practice, you could get the following out of your morning *Scribing* time.

- **Gain clarity:** Writing helps you understand your past and present circumstances as well as your future aspirations. It's a tool for working through challenges, brainstorming ideas, prioritizing tasks, and creating exciting possibilities.
- **Capture ideas:** Jot down your ideas to keep track of them. This ensures you don't lose valuable insights and allows you to organize and expand on them.
- **Review lessons:** Your journal is a repository for recording and reviewing lessons learned. Celebrating wins and reflecting on mistakes help track your growth and development over time.
- **Acknowledge your progress:** Revisit past entries to see how far you've come. This can be incredibly rewarding and motivating, boosting your confidence and sense of accomplishment. Each entry is a testament to your growth and resilience, a tangible reminder of the progress you're making on your journey.
- **Improve your memory:** Here's a critical one for aging adults. Writing things down enhances memory retention. When you document your thoughts and experiences, you're more likely to

remember them, and you can always refer back to your journal for a quick refresh.

- **Let go of stress:** Whenever you feel stressed about something, grab your journal and write it down. Doing this immediately creates a feeling of relief and separation from your problems since they are now something that you can *observe* as opposed to having to keep them alive in your mind. In practical terms, think of something stressful that's been on your mind. Now, imagine writing it in a journal, closing the journal, and giving yourself permission to take a break from worrying about it, knowing that you can come back to it later. We all have difficulties in our lives, but we don't have to constantly worry about them. Life is meant to be lived and enjoyed, not a constant source of stress.

- **Improve emotional well-being:** Writing can improve emotional well-being, as noted in *JMIR Mental Health*.[1] Taking the time to write down and reflect on the aspects of your life that you're grateful for is an effective way to boost your emotional well-being. It's also completely free and available to us 24/7. We recommend going slowly, pausing, reflecting on each blessing and allowing yourself to feel deep, heartfelt gratitude for each aspect of this one life you've been given.

What's more, Rush University Medical Center found that engaging in mentally stimulating activities, including writing, can decrease cognitive decline by 32 percent.[2] This effect was evident even in individuals in their 80s. So, challenge yourself to maintain your scribing practice into your later years.

Getting Started with Scribing

First, choose a journal format—physical or digital. Decide whether you want to write by hand in a traditional physical journal or if you'd prefer to type in a digital journal on your computer, phone, or tablet. If you're not sure, experiment with both to see which feels best.

If you prefer writing by hand, consider investing in a quality journal that you'll want to keep and revisit. Make it your own, whether you choose lined paper for guided handwriting or a blank canvas for more creative expression. If you prefer to type and be able to easily edit your journal entries in the future, consider using a word processing program on your computer or a notes app in your smartphone.

Additionally, there are two journaling options specifically created for Miracle Morning practitioners. The first is *The Miracle Morning Journal* (available on Amazon.com), which is a lined physical journal that is formatted with a week at a glance, gives you room to write a short daily entry for all seven days of the week, has checkboxes to track your S.A.V.E.R.S., includes daily inspirational quotes, and more.

Another option is using the digital journal inside the *Miracle Morning* app. It includes daily prompts to help you reflect and get your thoughts flowing, along with space for anything else you want to write. It's a simple way to make journaling part of your morning routine.

Tips for Effective Journaling

Start by listing things you're grateful for, clarifying your top priorities for the day, or releasing any stressful thoughts. Write down whatever might optimize your mental and emotional state. There are infinite aspects of your life that you can scribe about and countless types of journals. Gratitude journals, dream journals, food journals, workout journals, and more. You can write about your goals, dreams, plans, family, commitments, lessons learned, and anything else that you feel you need to focus on in your life.

Here is a simple, three-step Miracle Morning *Scribing* practice:

Miracle Morning Daily Scribing Prompts

- Am I holding on to any stressful thoughts, fears, or painful emotions that aren't serving me and that I need to release or be at peace with? Note: It can be helpful to use Deep Breathing (Chapter 4) to aid in identifying and releasing any negative energies you're holding onto.

- What can I be grateful for today? Note: If you practiced Gratitude Meditation (Chapter 4) during your *Silence*, reflect on what you were grateful for and solidify your gratitudes in writing.

- What are my top one to three priorities for today that I will feel accomplished to complete or make progress on? Note: If you have a to-do list, identify the activities that will make the most positive impact in your life.

Write freely and don't worry about grammar, spelling, or punctuation—this is for your eyes only.

Dwayne says . . .

Scribing is a valuable part of the Miracle Morning for all the reasons we just discussed. It's writing about what we want for our lives, our dreams and desires. But there are other things I also write about. I have taken to scribing for my health. Every day, I track various health points in my health journal. I log entries about my weight, blood pressure, hours of sleep, any changes in medications, and exercise—35 push-ups and a 2-minute plank are my current threshold! If I don't journal this now, how will I know in a year, or five years, how I'm progressing?

Also, as I rounded 65, I decided to scribe about the lives of centenarians. My goal is to interview 100 amazing 100-year-olds and write about their stories and their wisdom. At the time of this publication, I've had the privilege of writing about over 30 of these insightful and entertaining people.

Final Thoughts on Scribing

We encourage you to revisit your journal entries periodically. Whether weekly, monthly, or annually, reviewing your journals can offer valuable insights and perspectives. For instance, looking back at a year's worth of entries can transform how you feel about your accomplishments. Writing down what you're grateful for enables you to be present to the blessings in your life, and reviewing those entries during tough times can shift your mindset.

Activities like scribing align with the understanding that mental stimulation is crucial for optimal aging. These practices are essential tools for maintaining cognitive health and overall quality of life as we age, helping us get better as we get older.

A Note from a Miracle Morning Community Member

"The Miracle Morning routine has been a huge blessing to me and my entire family. As a wife, mom, grandma, realtor, writer, and creek wader, I have many roles to fulfill. When my young nephew and then my daughter were both diagnosed with cancer, I had to find a way to improve myself in body, mind, and spirit so that I could lead by example. I have shared my success in these areas with my family, and several of them now implement Miracle Mornings, too. After my nephew passed away, I encouraged my sister to begin a new life with the help of the S.A.V.E.R.S. They have literally been life S.A.V.E.R.S. to our family. I am now writing a book as well, thanks to the *Scribing* routine."

—Angela Wilson
Age: 50+

10

CUSTOMIZE YOUR S.A.V.E.R.S. TO FIT YOUR LIFESTYLE AT EVERY AGE

"Anyone who stops learning is old, whether at 20 or 80. Anyone who keeps learning stays young."
—Henry Ford, American industrialist and business tycoon

Aging better is about focusing on optimizing cellular health and establishing habits that support mental, emotional, and physical well-being. These elements are paramount to living a longer, healthier, happier, and more fulfilling life. Think of it as upgrading your internal software and hardware simultaneously. On the cellular level, keeping those tiny building blocks of your body in top shape helps combat inflammation, fend off diseases, and keep your energy levels high. Meanwhile, nurturing your mental and emotional health ensures you stay sharp, positive, and resilient, able to enjoy every moment and ready to tackle whatever life throws at you.

Your Miracle Morning isn't just about starting your day on the right foot; it's about creating a foundation for becoming the best version of yourself. By integrating the S.A.V.E.R.S. into your daily routine, you give yourself a powerful one-two punch that enhances both your cellular health and your mindset. Of course, your Miracle Morning might not look the same for you at age 50 as it will at 80. As you age, it's essential to modify your routine to match your energy levels, physical capabilities, and schedule as well as adapt it to your shifting personal goals. But your S.A.V.E.R.S. routine can always remain your toolkit for optimal aging. Customizing your S.A.V.E.R.S. as you age means tailoring each component to meet your changing needs.

Customizing for Time

Remember that virtually every aspect of the Miracle Morning is customizable to fit your lifestyle. You can decide how much time to devote to each of the S.A.V.E.R.S. (as little as 60 seconds), which specific practice you do for each of your S.A.V.E.R.S. (i.e., meditation or breathwork for *Silence*, audiobooks for *Reading*, etc.), and in which order you do them (i.e., you could start with *Reading* to help activate your mind or *Exercise* to energize your body). For reference, roughly 72 percent of the global Miracle Morning Community devote an hour to their Miracle Morning routine. Investing the first 60 minutes of your day into your personal development allows you to relax, take it slow, and allocate an average of 10 minutes for each of the S.A.V.E.R.S. (although you'll see below that you don't have to allocate the same amount of time for each activity).

> Every aspect of the Miracle Morning is customizable to fit your lifestyle.

However, finding a full hour to devote to a new practice might seem daunting, especially in the beginning. If that's the case, we have good news: approximately 20 percent of Miracle Morning practitioners spend 30 minutes doing their S.A.V.E.R.S. We want you to just *start*, which will establish momentum and carry you forward. So, here are some customizable templates depending on how much time you have to invest in your Miracle Morning.

The 60-Minute Miracle Morning

Here is an example of how you might allocate time to each of the S.A.V.E.R.S. over the course of 60 minutes. Of course, you can adjust the time for each practice according to your preferences and priorities:

- **Silence:** 10 minutes (to pray, meditate, and/or experience breathwork)
- **Affirmations:** 5 minutes (to read and internalize your affirmations)
- **Visualization:** 5 minutes (to visualize the future and mentally rehearse today's activities)
- **Exercise:** 10 minutes (to stretch and move your body)
- **Reading:** 20 minutes (to read a book)
- **Scribing:** 10 minutes (to write in your journal)

If you have only 30 minutes, then simply allocate 5 minutes for each of the S.A.V.E.R.S.

The 6-Minute Miracle Morning

One of the most common concerns we hear from people new to the Miracle Morning is the idea of adding anything else to their already hectic life. Of course, adding the Miracle Morning makes life less hectic, as you become more at peace, focused, productive, and capable of handling anything life throws at you. Still, there will always be some mornings when you simply don't have a full 30 to 60 minutes to dedicate to your Miracle Morning.

Many of us tend to have an all-or-nothing mentality when it comes to how much time we believe we should allow to do something. Early on, Hal found himself doing exactly that with his Miracle Mornings. If he didn't have the full hour that he wanted, he just skipped it altogether. As this became a pattern early on, he realized this wasn't ideal. For one thing, doing anything related to personal development is almost always better than doing nothing. So, one morning, Hal had an early appointment, and after he got dressed, he only had 15 minutes until he needed to leave the house. He was about to skip his Miracle Morning when he thought, *What if I just did one minute for each of the S.A.V.E.R.S.?*

Hal sat down on his couch, set the timer on his phone, and began his first 6-minute Miracle Morning. Imagine if the first 6 minutes of your morning began like this:

- **One minute of *Silence*:** Imagine spending the first minute sitting quietly and enjoying a period of peaceful, purposeful silence. You sit, taking slow, deep breaths, with no one and nothing demanding your attention. Maybe you say a prayer of gratitude to appreciate the moment or pray for guidance on your journey. Maybe you enjoy a minute of meditation. As you sit in silence, you're totally present to this moment. You calm your mind, relax your body, and allow all your stress to melt away.

- **One minute of *Affirmations*:** As the first minute passes, you shift into your affirmations. With conviction, speak aloud the truths you want to embody today: *I am confident and capable. I embrace challenges as opportunities to grow. I am committed to becoming the best version of myself.* Each word resonates within you, reinforcing your belief in your limitless potential.

- **One minute of *Visualization*:** Closing your eyes, you move into visualization. You see yourself navigating the day with grace and purpose. You picture successful meetings, joyful interactions, and obstacles being effortlessly overcome. The vivid images play out in your mind like a movie, filling you with excitement and anticipation for what's to come.

- **One minute of *Exercise*:** Feeling inspired, you stand up for a quick burst of exercise. For 60 seconds, you engage in jumping jacks, feel your heart rate elevate, and blood flow invigorate your muscles. Energy surges through your body, shaking off any lingering drowsiness and awakening your physical self to match your mental state.

- **One minute of *Reading*:** Catching your breath, you reach for an inspiring book and spend the next minute reading. You absorb a powerful passage that offers wisdom or a new perspective. Even in this brief time, the words stimulate your mind and provide insights that you can carry with you throughout the day.

- **One minute of *Scribing*:** Finally, you pick up your journal and begin scribing. You jot down your intentions, things you're grateful for, or any thoughts that surfaced during your silence and visualization. The act of writing crystallizes your ideas and sets a clear roadmap for the day ahead.

See, it *can* be done! In just 6 intentional minutes, you've centered your mind, calmed your nervous system, energized your body, and ignited your spirit. You're now ready to step into the world with clarity, confidence, and purpose, fully equipped to make the most of the day that awaits you. So, please don't tell us you "don't have time." You *can* do this consistently, and consistency is key to building the habit of a daily practice.

Customizing Your S.A.V.E.R.S. Practice by Decade: 50s, 60s, 70s, 80s, and Beyond

As we age, our needs, energy levels, priorities, and life circumstances evolve. That's why the Miracle Morning isn't a one-size-fits-all routine—it's a customizable framework designed to meet you wherever you are in life. Below are some ways you can adapt each of the S.A.V.E.R.S. to align with the unique season of life you're in.

In Your 50s: *Reclaim, Reinvent, and Reignite*

Many people in their 50s are in a time of transition—careers may be shifting, kids might be growing up or moving out, and the question "What's next?" begins to stir.

- **Silence:** With your mind busier than ever, silence is your sanctuary. Try mindfulness meditation or prayer focused on clarity, reinvention, and letting go of past pressures or regrets. Also, consider using apps like *Headspace, Calm,* or the *Miracle Morning* app to experience guided meditations and breathwork tracks.

- **Affirmations:** Follow the Results-Oriented Affirmations formula taught in Chapter 5 to write specific affirmations that focus on your most important goals and commitments in areas such as your career, health, family, and personal development. Reinforce identity beyond titles (e.g., *I am not defined by my job; I'm defined by who I am and who I am becoming*). Reaffirm these commitments daily.

- **Visualization:** Close your eyes, and vividly picture successful outcomes in the areas of your life that you articulated in your affirmations. Envision your next chapter with boldness— whether it's starting a new business, writing a book, or traveling the world.

- **Exercise:** Focus on functional fitness and stress relief—yoga, brisk walking, cycling, or strength training to protect bone density. The Fred Hutchinson Cancer Center notes that moderate-intensity exercise improves health and reduces the risk of chronic disease.[1]
- **Reading:** Choose books on personal growth, leadership, or midlife renewal to fuel this powerful transition. Learn how to be healthier and happier; improve your marriage; be a better parent; earn more money; plan for retirement; or develop any mindset, skill, or ability.
- **Scribing:** Journal on purpose, passion, and priorities for your "second act." Reflect on what truly matters moving forward. Write down things you've accomplished to remind you of your capabilities and increase your confidence. Set goals for the next decade from a place of strength and optimism.

In Your 60s: *Freedom, Fulfillment, and Legacy*

The 60s often bring more freedom—retirement or semi-retirement, grandparenting, or more time for personal passions.

- **Silence:** Practice gratitude meditation or breathing exercises to deepen joy and presence in daily life.
- **Affirmations:** Focus on health, vitality, wisdom, and legacy (e.g., *I am a source of wisdom, energy, and love to those around me*). Use affirmations to reframe your relationship with aging: *I am older, wiser, and my best is yet to come.* Or, *I am committed to cultivating gratitude daily and choosing to be the happiest I've ever been.*
- **Visualization:** Create vivid mental images of yourself enjoying your retirement lifestyle, spending time with the people you love, while *doing* the things that you love. See yourself living each day with freedom and purpose—volunteering, mentoring, traveling, or pursuing long-held dreams.

- **Exercise:** Gentle but consistent movement—Tai Chi, swimming or water aerobics (if you have access to a pool), or Pilates to support mobility and longevity. Walking and cycling are also great joint-friendly activities.
- **Reading:** Dive into memoirs, spiritual books, or topics that challenge and inspire lifelong learning.
- **Scribing:** Write legacy letters, capture family stories, or reflect on lessons you want to pass on. Consider writing your memoir. Reflect on your life and share your wisdom with your family and future generations. Whether or not you publish it, writing your life story has immense value, especially at this stage of life.

In Your 70s: *Simplify, Savor, and Share*

In your 70s, simplicity and meaning often take center stage. There's wisdom in doing less, but doing it well.

- **Silence:** Use *Silence* for spiritual connection or simply to savor the moment with mindfulness and presence.
- **Affirmations:** Emphasize peace, purpose, and contribution (e.g., *I am at peace with who I am and the life I've lived*). Reinforce beliefs in maintaining physical health and healthy relationships. Affirm things like, *I am grateful for my health* or *I am grateful for the people in my life.*
- **Visualization:** Use *Visualization* as a joy generator. Picture family gatherings, laughter, meaningful travel, or writing that memoir. Imagine vibrant health, meaningful moments with loved ones, and simple pleasures fully enjoyed. The brain responds to imagined joy just like the real thing!
- **Exercise:** Prioritize joint-friendly movement like stretching, balance work, and short walks to maintain independence, preserve flexibility, and prevent falls. Daily stretching is key.

- **Reading:** Select uplifting content that nurtures the soul—scripture, poetry, or books on aging with grace.
- **Scribing:** Use journaling for reflection and celebration. Capture life's "greatest hits" or write letters to your future self and loved ones. Writing and reflecting on life experiences can improve cognitive health. Even a few lines a day creates a beautiful record of your life.

In Your 80s and Beyond: *Presence, Peace, and Purpose*

At this stage, your Miracle Morning can be gentler, more introspective, and deeply meaningful.

- **Silence:** Quiet prayer, contemplation, or simply sitting in peace can become the most sacred part of the day.
- **Affirmations:** Focus on inner peace, worthiness, and impact (e.g., *My presence is a blessing to others, just as I am*). Keep it simple and powerful: *Each day is a gift*. Encourage self-compassion and celebrate who you've become.
- **Visualization:** Visualize joy in everyday moments—a grandchild's laugh, the feel of sun on your skin, or sharing stories that matter. Boost your mood by remembering or envisioning happy moments.
- **Exercise:** Engage in low-impact activities like gentle stretching or chair yoga to keep energy flowing and the body engaged. Consistent, gentle activity is key.
- **Reading:** Enjoy short, heartwarming pieces or reread favorite books that bring comfort and connection. Keep the mind active and engaged with varied reading in diverse genres. Even audiobooks count, and bonus if you later discuss them with a friend.
- **Scribing:** Reflect on a lifetime of lessons. Write blessings, memories, or thoughts you want to leave behind as gifts for

the next generation. Write through a lens of gratitude for your experiences. Research shows it boosts immune function and lowers depression—plus, it just feels good.

Remember: The purpose of the Miracle Morning isn't perfection. It's about progress. No matter your age, the S.A.V.E.R.S. can be modified to honor your body, respect your time, and elevate your spirit. This is your time, your morning, your miracle.

Customizing Your S.A.V.E.R.S. *for Couples Over 50*

At this stage of life, your relationship likely has deep roots. And with more time and wisdom, it's the perfect season to grow even closer. Practicing the Miracle Morning together can help you stay connected, healthy, and purposeful as a team.

- **Silence:** Begin with quiet reflection, prayer, or gratitude together, establishing your day with peace and presence. Couples who meditate together experience increased relationship satisfaction, according to the Greater Good Science Center at the University of California, Berkeley.[2] Synchronize your breathing to deepen your connection.
- **Affirmations:** Create affirmations that honor your shared journey and your next chapter (e.g., *We are growing closer, stronger, and more joyful every day, I am grateful to be sharing my life with you,* or *I am committed to loving you the way you deserve to be loved*). Post your couples affirmations on the bathroom mirror or fridge to revisit throughout the day
- **Visualization:** Imagine the future you want to create— whether it's travel, legacy projects, grandparenting, or simply

enjoying life side-by-side. Imagine the sights, sounds, and feelings of achieving these goals together.

- **Exercise:** Do joint-friendly movement you both enjoy, like brisk walking, stretching, or gentle yoga, to stay active and support each other's health. Exercising with a partner improves adherence to exercise routines, as noted in the *Journal of Aging and Health*.[3]
- **Reading:** Choose uplifting or insightful books to read together or separately, and share your reflections over coffee or breakfast. It could be a book on marriage or any topic you're both interested in, such as health, finances, or a memoir or fiction book. Share one inspiring quote, passage, or insight with each other each morning. Shared reading can enhance mental stimulation and relationship satisfaction.[4]
- **Scribing:** Write down what you're grateful for in your relationship, or keep a shared journal capturing favorite memories, inside jokes, or dreams for the future. Writing and sharing gratitude notes can improve relationship satisfaction and emotional well-being, as found in *Psychological Science*.[5]

Customizing Your S.A.V.E.R.S. *for People with Limited Mobility*

Whether due to age, injury, illness, or disability, limited mobility doesn't have to limit your ability to transform your mornings—or your life. The Miracle Morning is flexible and can be fully adapted to meet you exactly where you are.

- **Silence:** Sit comfortably in a chair, or lie in bed. Practice deep breathing, guided meditation, or prayer to calm your mind and connect inward.

- **Affirmations:** Repeat affirmations to strengthen your mindset, resilience, and self-worth (e.g., *I am strong and capable*, or *I am grateful for my life, the people I share it with, and my ability to choose to be at peace and happy*).
- **Visualization:** Close your eyes and visualize joyful experiences or meaningful goals. No movement required, just imagination.
- **Exercise:** To the best of your abilities, move your body for a predetermined amount of time. Try chair yoga, stretching, arm raises, or any safe movement your body allows—even small actions count. Don't let what you can't do limit what you *can* do.
- **Reading:** Choose a book of daily inspirations or a collection of quotes. Select one passage or quote to read each morning. Books like *The Daily Stoic* by Ryan Holiday or *Meditations* by Marcus Aurelius are great options. After reading, take a moment to reflect on how the passage or quote applies to your life and how you can integrate its wisdom into your day. Audiobooks are great options, too.
- **Scribing:** Write one thing you're grateful for and really *feel* it. Keep it simple: "I'm grateful for my breath" or "for a phone call with a friend." Then set a small goal like "I'll finish my Miracle Morning" or "I'll spend time outside in nature." If writing is difficult, use voice dictation. Set a small, achievable goal for the day. Writing down your goal helps you stay focused and motivated throughout the day. It could be something like, *I will drink 8 glasses of water today*, or *I will spend 15 minutes reading*.

Final Thoughts on the S.A.V.E.R.S.

Everything is difficult before it's easy. Every new experience is uncomfortable before it's comfortable. The more we practice the S.A.V.E.R.S., the more natural and beneficial they will feel. Each S.A.V.E.R.S. practice should be manageable and beneficial, and align well with the needs and abilities of older adults.

The bottom line: Don't let your perceived limitations—whether it's your time or your age—stop you from making each morning a celebration of life.

A Note from a Miracle Morning Community Member

"One of the best things about the Miracle Morning is the community. I feel like I have found my tribe—people who love continuous learning and self-improvement. I am so grateful!"

—Katrina Kelly
Age: 50+

Join the Miracle Morning Community

By practicing the S.A.V.E.R.S., you're joining millions of people worldwide who are redefining what it means to age well. If you haven't already, we invite you to join The Miracle Morning Community at **MiracleMorningCommunity.com** to connect with like-minded Miracle Morning practitioners and get support as you're about to start the Miracle Morning 30-Day Life Transformation Journey in Chapter 11. You're not alone on this journey; you're part of a global community of aging adults committed to living their best lives and helping each other do the same. Let's get to living better and longer with more joy, vitality, and purpose—together!

11

THE MIRACLE MORNING 30-DAY LIFE TRANSFORMATION JOURNEY

"An extraordinary life is all about daily, continuous improvements in the areas that matter most."
—**Robin Sharma, author, speaker, leadership expert, humanitarian**

Welcome to the Miracle Morning 30-Day Life Transformation Journey, otherwise known as the I-can't-believe-I'm-waking-up-this-early challenge. In all seriousness, the next 30 days can become a significant opportunity to begin transforming any area of your life, one morning at a time. Transformation doesn't happen overnight, but it does begin the moment you decide to improve any aspect of your life and commit to taking consistent (daily) actions that will all but guarantee progress. Over the next 30 days, you'll harness the power of your Miracle Mornings and S.A.V.E.R.S. practice to create real, measurable progress in whatever area of your life matters most to you right now. Whether it's your health, relationships, finances, your overall sense of purpose, or a specific goal, the next meaningful step in your journey begins today.

For those who have read the original or updated and expanded edition of *The Miracle Morning* and have already completed one or more 30-Day Life Transformation Journeys, this is an opportunity to recommit to transforming one area of your life over the course of the next 30 days. In fact, Hal lives by a philosophy of living life in a rhythm of 30-day challenges/journeys, where every 30 days, you highlight one area of your life and set a goal to learn, grow, and improve in that area.

Human potential is limitless, and you always benefit when you commit to improving an area of your life. Research shows that having one or more meaningful goals to work toward can significantly enhance your motivation, sense of purpose, and results. Imagine how your life would be enhanced if, every 30 days, you chose one area of your life to improve and set a goal to improve it. Constant and never-ending improvement is the key to a perpetually fulfilling life.

One of the most effective ways to accelerate your transformation is to choose a single area of life to focus your Miracle Mornings on. While daily Miracle Mornings will inevitably enhance your overall mental, emotional, and physical well-being, remember that when Hal created the Miracle Morning back in 2008, he was in a financial freefall—deep in debt, losing his home, and struggling to stay afloat. So, he used each of the S.A.V.E.R.S. to turn his financial situation around and was able to do so in only two months. As mentioned earlier, he read *Book Yourself Solid* by Michael Port to learn how to book more clients. He prayed and meditated daily in a state of abundance, recited affirmations that reminded him what he was committed to and why it was a must, and which actions he needed to take and when. He then visualized himself taking the appropriate actions, exercised to boost his physical energy and mental clarity, and journaled each day to cultivate gratitude as well as prioritize his to-do list so that he could maximize his productivity. As a result, even though the economy was out of his control and continued to get worse, he focused on what he could control, using the S.A.V.E.R.S. to get better, and within two months, he had doubled his income.

Similarly, years later, when he was diagnosed with a rare, aggressive form of cancer and given just a 20 to 30 percent chance of surviving, he once again turned to the S.A.V.E.R.S. This time, he focused all of his energy on healing, using each practice to strengthen his mindset, his faith, and his body. Once again, Miracle Mornings helped him beat the odds. These timeless practices are more than just habits; they are proven tools that, when used intentionally, can help you overcome even the most difficult circumstances and achieve extraordinary results.

So, what about you? Which area of your life do you want to transform? Over the next 30 days, you can use your S.A.V.E.R.S. to make powerful, targeted progress toward improving that area. Or, if life already feels pretty good and you're not facing a pressing challenge and nothing specific comes to mind, this is your opportunity to elevate your self-care, strengthen your mindset, and take your personal development to the next level. Either way, you're about to create the momentum that leads to lasting transformation—starting with how you begin each day.

A Note from a Miracle Morning Community Member

"I am married, mother to a grown daughter, and a top Realtor in our valley. I have RA, so the Miracle Morning is just what I needed to change my focus.

"The biggest change for me is clarity that I have to come first. Checking the box for each of the S.A.V.E.R.S. is visual progress and has made me learn to focus on the process rather than the results. Results end. Processes continue for a lifetime. That's why I keep repeating the 30-Day Life Transformational Journey . . . the results can't help but come. It has me not wanting to leave a box unchecked (visual progress), and I have worked out daily for 63 days, which has led to being very conscientious about my choices of food, reading materials, podcasts, etc. I feel a sense of childlike wonder and newness that has lit a raging passion in me for life!! I feel blessed to have had the opportunity to read *The Miracle Morning* three times now, in addition to reading *The Miracle Morning for Real Estate Agents* and *The Miracle Morning for Entrepreneurs*. Miracle Morning has completely changed my joy. I am so grateful!!"

—Karen McLean-Wilson
Age: 59

From Unbearable to Unstoppable: The 3-Phase Strategy to Successfully Implement Any Habit in 30 Days

As you prepare to embark on a journey of transformation, it's normal to feel both excited and uncertain, with thoughts of self-doubt creeping in. We all have moments when our inner voice whispers things like, *Will I have the discipline to stick with this? What if I fail? I don't know if I'm ready for this.* That's fear trying to protect us from the discomfort of growth, and it's to be expected. But what if, instead of fearing the unknown, you embraced it? What if you acknowledged that on the other side of this 30-Day Life Transformation Journey is an even better, more capable version of yourself?

You don't have to be fearless, just brave enough to start. Thankfully, you're not alone. This path is one that has already been paved by millions of Miracle Morning practitioners. If you're willing to commit to this for 30 days, you'll discover that you're capable of far more than you've ever imagined. To help set you up for success, we're going to give you a 3-phase strategy to successfully implement any habit in 30 days.

There's much debate about how long it takes to implement a new habit. In his 1960 book, *Psycho-Cybernetics*, Dr. Maxwell Maltz observed that his patients typically took about 21 days to adjust to physical changes after plastic surgery, such as a nose job or leg amputation. This observation was then generalized to other areas of life, including habit formation, leading to the widespread belief that any new habit could be formed in 21 days.

However, modern research has shown that this may be a myth and that habit formation typically takes longer. A study from the *European Journal of Social Psychology* indicates that, on average, it took 66 days for a new behavior to reach a plateau of automaticity, meaning it became a habit.[1] Yet Hal's grandfather, known fondly as Papaw, maintained the habit of smoking cigarettes every day for 50 years, and he was able to permanently change that habit and quit smoking after a single hypnosis session.

The reality is that there is no fixed number of days required to change a habit. It ultimately comes down to whether or not we're committed to initiating and sustaining that change. You're about to learn a simple but powerful strategy that has proven successful for establishing the Miracle Morning as a lifelong habit in only 30 days. As you embark on your 30-Day Life Transformation Journey, the following 3-phase strategy will give you realistic expectations as well as the mindset and approach to stick with your new routine.

Days 1–10:
Unbearable → Days 11–20:
Uncomfortable → Days 21–30:
Unstoppable

Phase 1: Unbearable (Days 1–10)

Unbearable might be a strong word and risk turning you off, but sometimes the first few days of establishing or changing a habit can feel that way. If you've ever tried making any significant change to your behavior, you've likely experienced feelings of fear or resistance. This is completely normal and to be expected.

On the other hand, the first few days of implementing a new habit—and this is especially true for the Miracle Morning—can also be exciting and even easy because it's something new, and you are looking forward to the benefits. However, even with the Miracle Morning, as soon as the newness wears off and reality sets in, it's normal to resist and reject any type of change to our normal routine. We are tempted to go back to the way things were before.

Phase 1 is when any new activity requires the most conscious effort, and implementing the S.A.V.E.R.S. routine is no different. You're combatting existing habits that have been entrenched for years. The brain's prefrontal cortex, which handles decision-making and self-control, can tire quickly when adjusting to new routines. So, it's mind over matter and ultimately comes down to your level of commitment. When you're committed, there's always a way and you can do anything.

Thankfully, our resistance to change is only temporary, and we soon acclimate to our new habits, behaviors, and routines. In Phase 1, as you contend with existing patterns and limiting beliefs, you'll discover what you're made of and capable of. Sure, the first few mornings might look like you're auditioning for a zombie movie, but before you know it, you'll be bouncing out of bed like you've got springs for legs and a smile that says, *I've got this!* Keep pushing, stay committed to your vision, and hang in there. You can do this!

Phase 2: Uncomfortable (Days 11–20)

You might be thinking, *Wait a second . . . my reward for making it though the "unbearable" phase is that I get to be uncomfortable for the next 10 days? That doesn't sound very exciting.*

Well, when you put it that way . . . We're kidding, of course. Allow us to explain.

After you make it through the first 10 days—what was likely be the most exciting and simultaneously challenging 10 days—you begin Phase 2, which is considerably easier although it presents the risk of getting too confident too early before your new habits are cemented. You will be getting used to your new habit. You will also have developed some confidence and positive associations with the benefits of your Miracle Mornings. In Phase 2, your body and mind acclimate further to waking up earlier. You'll notice that getting up starts to get easier, but it's not yet cemented as a sustainable habit.

Experts, including Charles Duhigg, author of *The Power of Habit*, note that consistency is critical. The biggest temptation at this phase is to reward yourself by taking a break, especially on weekends. A common question in the Miracle Morning Community is, "How many days a week do you get up early for your Miracle Morning?" The answer from longtime practitioners is *every single day*. While we have been conditioned by society to think that the weekends are meant to be lazy, when you realize that every day is better when you begin it with your Miracle Morning routine, you find that weekends are no different. That doesn't mean you can't choose to sleep in on Saturdays or Sundays and start your Miracle Morning a bit later; it just means that you may soon find that doing your S.A.V.E.R.S. on the weekends is just as beneficial as they are during the week.

> When you realize that every day is better when you begin it with your Miracle Morning routine, you find that weekends are no different.

While days 11 through 20 are no longer unbearable,

they may still be uncomfortable and tempt you to take days off and thus will require discipline and dedication on your part. Stay committed. You've already gone from *unbearable* to *uncomfortable,* and you're about to find out what it feels like to elevate yourself to being *unstoppable.*

Phase 3: Unstoppable (Days 21–30)

Phase 3 is where the magic happens. You've proven to yourself that you're far more disciplined than you may have believed was possible just 20 days ago. You've transcended many of your fears and self-imposed limitations. The Miracle Morning routine has become part of your everyday life. You're feeling proficient with the S.A.V.E.R.S., and every morning presents you with a new opportunity to learn, grow, and become an even better version of yourself.

Days 21 through 30—the homestretch—are largely about cementing your new habit through positive reinforcement and enjoyment. A quick word of caution: Just as during Phase 2, it's normal to face the temptation to rest on our laurels. It feels good to pat ourselves on the back and think, *I've done it for 20 days so I'm just going to take a few days off.* It's not that you can't take a day off. Just be aware that those first 20 days—the unbearable and uncomfortable phases—are arguably the most challenging part of the process. Taking a few days off before you've invested the necessary time into positively reinforcing the habit can make it difficult to get back on track.

Others make a potentially detrimental mistake and adhere to the popular philosophy that it takes only 21 days to form a new habit. The experts who support this claim may be partly correct in that it does take 21 days—the first two phases—to *form* a new habit. But the third 10-day phase is crucial to *sustaining* your new habit in the long run, as it is where you positively reinforce and associate increasingly positive mindsets and emotions with your new habit. This is where you turn that mindset of resistance around and begin to fully acclimate to and enjoy your new routine.

It's days 21 through 30 where you start to experience exponential benefits, which is what supports you in making your Miracle Morning a lifelong habit. Instead of dreading your alarm clock in the morning, you are excited to wake up and start your S.A.V.E.R.S. because you've been experiencing the life-changing benefits in real-time for 20-plus consecutive days, and not just reading about them.

Phase 3 is also where the actual transformation occurs, as your new habit becomes part of your identity. It transcends the space between *something you're trying* and *who you're becoming.* You inevitably begin to see yourself as a morning person. You'll rightfully identify as a Miracle Morning practitioner.

This isn't just about trying some new fad; it's about adopting a life-long habit that continuously enables you to show up at your best every day while molding you into the person capable of realizing your deepest desires. You'll nurture your physical, intellectual, emotional, and spiritual well-being through the S.A.V.E.R.S. and tap into your limitless potential, experiencing results beyond what you previously imagined.

If you're still feeling that nervous energy, it's a sign that you're ready to commit and take charge of your mornings and, ultimately, your life. You've got this, and you're more than ready for this transformative journey.

Get Started in 4 Easy Steps

Here are the steps to help you get started on your 30-Day Life Transformational Journey.

Step 1: Schedule Your Miracle Morning for Tomorrow

If you keep a calendar, add your inaugural Miracle Morning S.A.V.E.R.S. session for tomorrow. If you use a digital calendar, set it as a recurring daily appointment. If you're like Hal and find that colorful emojis spark joy for you, consider adding a bright sun or happy face to your calendar appointment. Take a minute to do this now. (Seriously, putting it in your calendar is an easy but crucial first step to set yourself up for success. Do that now, and we promise, we'll be here when you come back.)

Next, decide where you're going to do your Miracle Morning. Pick a spot that resonates with you—your living room, a serene outdoor setting, or a cozy corner in your home. The key is choosing a place to immerse yourself fully without distractions. Remember, we recommend creating some distance between you and your bed so you're not tempted to crawl back under the covers and fall asleep.

Also keep in mind that this is about progress, not perfection! You don't even have to do all of the S.A.V.E.R.S. on day one. You can just stick with *Reading* as you continue on to Part 2 of this book, Not-So-Obvious Self-Care Strategies to Thrive After 50. You could also incorporate *Scribing* and begin filling out your Life Transformation Kit outlined in the next step. Or you can download the *Miracle Morning* app and utilize the guided S.A.V.E.R.S. experiences. What's most important is that you start your day with one or more of the S.A.V.E.R.S., for the next 30 days.

Step 2: Download The Miracle Morning After 50 Life Transformation Kit

Download your free Miracle Morning After 50 Life Transformation Kit at **TMMAfter50.com.** This comprehensive kit helps you gain clarity on what's most important in your life and provides you with goal-setting exercises, pre-written affirmations, as well as customizable templates, journaling prompts, daily checklists, tracking sheets, and more—all of which were designed specifically for readers of this book. You'll get everything else you need to support you in completing the 30-Day Life Transformation Journey as easily as possible. The purpose of this is to help you identify which goal(s) you want to achieve and/or area(s) of your life you want to improve, consider any obstacles you may need to overcome, clarify which actions you'll take, and then align your daily Miracle Morning and the S.A.V.E.R.S. to help you stay focused and follow through.

While completing the Life Transformation Kit is optional, we do recommend it. Like anything in life that's worthwhile, setting yourself up for a successful 30-Day Life Transformation Journey is best done by starting with a bit of preparation, so it's important that you do the initial exercises. Again, you can work on this during the allotted Scribing time during your Miracle Morning.

Step 3: Set Your Alarm and Move It Across the Room

Of course, this step will only apply if you use an alarm clock to wake up. If that's you, set your wake-up time for anywhere from 30 to 60 minutes earlier than normal to give yourself adequate time to complete your personal hygiene practices and start your Miracle Morning.

Next, if you tend to hit the snooze button and let the minutes slip away, consider moving your alarm clock across the room so that you start your day upright and in motion. You may remember from Chapter 2 that keeping your alarm clock across the room or in a nearby room (Hal keeps his on his bathroom counter) ensures that you get out of bed to turn it off, and being upright makes it much easier to stay awake than when you're able to reach over to your nightstand, hit the snooze button, and keep sleeping.

Step 4: Find an Accountability Partner

Consider teaming up with a friend, family member, or colleague for support and motivation. You can also find an accountability partner at **MiracleMorningCommunity.com**. Having someone to support, encourage, and hold you accountable can significantly increase your commitment to following through—and it's usually more fun to share new experiences with others! Reach out to someone in your circle or someone in the Miracle Morning Community, and invite them to join you.

You Deserve This

As you embark on your 30-Day Life Transformation Journey, you're not just committing to a daily personal development routine, you're also investing time and energy into improving your physical health and optimizing your mental and emotional well-being. You're also leveraging scientifically proven methods to increase your longevity and healthspan.

Imagine unlocking the full potential of the second half of your life, regardless of your age, health status, or past experiences. Consider what lies beyond your current level of personal growth and which areas of your life are waiting to be transformed. No matter what your age is, you have the power to decide that your best is yet to come! Over the next 30 days, you'll cultivate discipline, clarity, and continuous personal development, unlocking the keys to elevating yourself to the next levels of joy, vitality, and purpose. You'll feel the burdens of stress lift, replaced by a sense of control over who you're becoming each day. Energy, clarity, and motivation will become your companions, driving you toward your loftiest goals—goals you may have postponed for far too long.

Your First Reading Assignment

Now that you're ready to start your Miracle Morning 30-Day Life Transformation Journey, we'd like to make a recommendation for your first S.A.V.E.R.S. reading assignment, namely Part 2: Not-So-Obvious Self-Care Strategies to Thrive After 50. In the following chapters, you will discover powerful strategies to realize your purpose, optimize your energy, embrace self-care, and enhance your mental clarity and overall well-being as you age. This section is a blend of practical advice, scientific insights, and engaging tips to help you thrive!

Now, give yourself permission to let go of any self-imposed limitations you may be holding onto in exchange for the person you can choose to become—the best version of yourself—from this day forward. And give yourself the gift of making a commitment for just 30 days—a fraction of your lifetime—to initiate significant improvements, one day at a time. Seize this moment, embrace the challenge, and let the next 30 days be the catalyst for a lifetime of growth, resilience, and boundless potential. Embrace it with open arms, and watch as your life unfolds and transforms in ways you may not have even imagined were possible. Your journey starts now.

Part 2

NOT-SO-OBVIOUS SELF-CARE STRATEGIES TO THRIVE AFTER 50

12

SELF-CARE HOURS

Extend Restorative Rituals Beyond the Morning

*"You need to be proactive, carve out time in your schedule,
and take responsibility for being the healthiest person
you can be—no one else is going to do it for you."*
—Dr. Mehmet Oz, cardiothoracic surgeon and television personality

D o you ever feel like you're running on empty? So busy taking care of others that there's no time left to take care of yourself? Or perhaps you feel selfish or even guilty when you *do* carve out a moment to do something for yourself, so you avoid it altogether. Many adults over 50 have spent decades prioritizing the needs of others while quietly neglecting their own. If any of this resonates with you, you're certainly not alone. Been there. Done that. Worn out the T-shirt!

While often overlooked, the concept of self-care has emerged as a vital aspect of maintaining well-being as we navigate the inevitable changes that accompany aging. While our parents or grandparents may have spent their later years sitting on the couch and watching reruns on television (which we would argue is fine—in moderation), that's hardly the recipe for a fulfilling and purposeful life. In order to feel and be at our best, our bodies and minds require more attention and care than they did in our youth. Self-care is the secret sauce to unlocking youthful energy and vitality—nurturing your body, sharpening your mind, uplifting your spirit, and regulating your emotions—so you can show up as your absolute best self for the decades still to come.

> Self-care is the secret sauce to unlocking youthful energy and vitality.

To be clear, the S.A.V.E.R.S. are in and of themselves six of the most effective self-care practices, which are already embedded in your Miracle Morning routine. These morning habits lay the foundation for how you think, feel, and function throughout the day. And while the morning is your launchpad, they are not the be-all and end-all of personal well-being. You are about to discover that you get bonus points (and benefits) for weaving self-care into other parts of your day.

In this transformative chapter, we delve into the profound impact that maintaining self-care hours will have on every facet of your life. We'll address the impact self-care makes on your cellular health and introduce a wide variety of self-care activities to implement throughout your entire day, in addition to your Miracle Morning practices. It's time you take better care of the most important person in your life . . . you!

The Mindset of Self-Care

Fifty is the new 40 and *60 is the new 50* are widespread mindsets in the aging community. However, some argue that 50 should be embraced as the new 50, not the new 30 or 40, acknowledging the unique experiences, challenges, and benefits that come with aging. These include everything from physical

changes and challenges such as menopause (for women) and decreased testosterone (for men), to the need for more rest and the simultaneous opportunity to slow down and enjoy each moment of our lives.

To deny or resist the aging process is to deny or resist reality. The
good news is that your quality of life at any age is ultimately based on your
mindset and how well you take care of yourself more than on the amount
of years you've been alive. So, don't get caught up on, or feel limited by,
your biological age. Instead, embrace it and enjoy every moment.

At 67 years young, Hal's mom still exercises, gardens, prepares healthy
meals at home each day, and goes out dancing and singing karaoke with
her friends every week. These are her favorite self-care activities. She also
regularly volunteers in her community, sits with hospice patients in their
final days, and donates blood as often as possible. She does all of this
despite enduring a traumatic accident last year, when a ladder suddenly
collapsed beneath her, shattering both her left foot and wrist. Although
she now walks with a limp and has only partial use of her left hand, she
will tell you enthusiastically that neither age nor injury will stop her from
living her best life and helping others live theirs! She takes care of herself
so she can help take care of others. While most people would've been
sidelined and discouraged, her quality of life and the positive impact she
makes for other people are determined by her mindset more than anything else.

The truth is, the mindset of self-care isn't about resisting aging—
it's about redefining it. It's about choosing to see each new decade as
an opportunity to grow wiser, stronger, and more intentional about
how you live. When you believe that your best years can still be ahead
of you, you begin to treat
yourself like someone worth
caring for—because you are.
Self-care becomes less of a
chore and more of a privilege,
a daily act of self-respect that

> Self-care becomes less of a chore and more of a privilege, a daily act of self-respect that fuels everything else in your life.

fuels everything else in your life. It's a mindset that says, *I'm not done yet. In fact, my best is yet to come.*

Ultimately, adopting the mindset of self-care means refusing to let age define your limits. It means showing up for yourself each day with compassion, courage, and commitment. As you'll discover in the rest of this chapter, self-care isn't just about bubble baths or green smoothies (although those are certainly included). It's a science-backed strategy that strengthens you from the inside out. In addition to adopting this mindset, it's important to understand the physical component for leading a long, vibrant life: maintaining healthy cells.

Your cellular health and your mindset are always influencing your well-being, and they're either working for you or against you. Research indicates that cellular turnover (the process of producing new cells to replace existing cells) slows down as we age, leading to a decline in various bodily functions. This decline necessitates an offsetting increase in self-care activities to counteract the effects of aging. Without intentional support, this slower regeneration can contribute to fatigue, weakened immunity, slower healing, and even cognitive decline. However, by proactively engaging in self-care activities that support cellular repair (we'll give you 22 of them to choose from shortly), you can help your body function more effectively, even as the years advance.

Dwayne says . . .

As a husband, father, and grandfather to nine energetic grandkids, I know firsthand the demands life can throw at you. Add in the responsibility of thousands of employees and nearly 2,700 residents at Aegis Living, and you can see why staying at the top of my game is nonnegotiable. This is why I dedicate 18 to 20 hours a week (2 to 3 hours a day) to self-care. This includes the S.A.V.E.R.S., red light therapy, cold plunge, massage, physical therapy, swimming, sauna, doctor's appointments, and research on the latest and proven health and wellness protocols. It might sound like a lot, but it's the best investment of time, money, and energy that I've ever made.

Half of aging well is about our mindset. Having a forward-focused mindset can transform how you age. It's about staying positive, engaged, and ready to embrace what's next. Starting my day with the Miracle Morning routine helps set this tone. Meditation and mindfulness keep me mentally sharp and emotionally balanced. At the same time, fun activities, like singing in the shower or trying out cold plunge therapy, add a splash of joy to my routine.

The other half of aging well is about our cellular health. Cells are the building blocks of your body, and keeping them in top shape is crucial. Regular blood tests help me monitor my health markers and ensure I'm on the right track. Quality sleep? Essential—it's when your body repairs itself. And, of course, we have to keep those troublesome pesky zombie cells at bay. These senescent cells hang around past their prime and cause inflammation, accelerating aging. By tackling them as part of my S.A.V.E.R.S. and self-care hours (see below), I'm boosting my lifespan, healthspan, and overall longevity.

Something else that has been a game changer for my cellular health is cold plunge therapy. It reduces inflammation, boosts my immune system, and helps eliminate zombie cells. When I brave the cold water, I know I'm boosting my cells and setting myself up for a great day. Revisit Chapter 7 for more on cold therapy.

Investing in self-care is not selfish; it's essential. By dedicating these hours to myself, I can show up fully for my family, work, and community. You'll

> Did you know . . . There is no test in the world more effective at detecting changes in your body than a blood test? Your blood changes with conditions in and around you—the seasons, stress, underlying medical conditions. Ideally, have your blood checked every two to three months, always looking for warning signs of things that need to be addressed.

notice the benefits even if you start with just 30 minutes a day. Remember, keeping your cells healthy and having a positive mind-set are the keys to aging well. Trust me, your future self will thank you!

Self-Care Hours (SCH)

Now, you may feel that you don't have the time or ability to match Dwayne's level of commitment. That's fine. Self-care isn't an all or nothing pursuit. Similar to how your Miracle Morning S.A.V.E.R.S. routine can be done in as little as 6 minutes or as much as 60 minutes, you can incorporate self-care activities throughout the day and week in as little or as much time as you have. The key is to consciously commit to building self-care activities into your daily and weekly schedule, empowering you to take control of your health and well-being beyond just your mornings. This is what we refer to as self-care hours (SCH).

Think of self-care hours as dedicated blocks of time—roughly 60 minutes throughout the week—where you intentionally focus on your physical, mental, emotional, spiritual, or social well-being. It's like putting an appointment on your calendar, but instead of a meeting, it's time set aside just for you. Now, within that hour, you fill it with self-care activities—whether it's a workout, meditation, journaling, dancing, singing, hiking, boating, spending time in nature, getting a massage, or just sitting outside and breathing in fresh air. Your self-care hours are your structured time to recharge, while self-care activities are the things you do within that allotted time frame or throughout the day to make sure you're taking care of yourself—anytime, anywhere.

By incorporating SCH into your day, you can reduce stress, increase energy, and improve your mental and emotional well-being. Self-care for those over 50 can also reduce the risk of heart disease, stroke, and cancer. And from a spiritual standpoint, it can help you connect with a higher power, experience deeper feelings of gratitude, and help you to enjoy this one life you've been blessed to live. When you say yes to self-care hours, you're saying yes to a healthier, happier, more fulfilling life, now and into the future.

What Counts as Self-Care?

Self-care is personal and should reflect activities that make you feel whole and revitalized. As we clarified earlier in this chapter, your S.A.V.E.R.S. routine in itself is a form of self-care. As we discussed in Chapter 4, engaging in mindfulness exercises, such as meditation, helps increase self-awareness and allows you to observe your emotions without judgment, thereby reducing stress and promoting emotional stability. And as discussed in Chapters 4 and 9, regularly acknowledging and appreciating the positive aspects of your life can shift your focus from negative to positive experiences, enhancing overall happiness.

Choosing activities that resonate with you, excite you, and prioritize your well-being is critical to sticking with your commitment. So here are just a few—okay, 22—examples of self-care activities for your consideration, which you could start adding to your life as soon as today:

1. **Taking a bath:** Relax in a warm bath with soothing essential oils.
2. **Listening to music:** Create a playlist of your favorite songs and unwind.
3. **Spending time in nature:** Hike, visit a park, or simply sit outside.
4. **Art therapy:** Engage in drawing, painting, or other creative activities.
5. **Digital detoxing:** Unplug from screens and spend time offline.
6. **Cooking:** Experiment with new recipes and nourish your body with homemade meals.
7. **Socializing:** Connect with friends or loved ones in person or virtually.

8. **Laughter:** Watch a comedy show or funny videos to brighten your mood.

9. **Setting boundaries:** Say no to activities or commitments that cause you stress.

10. **Dancing:** Dance to your favorite music and let loose.

11. **Singing:** Sing along to your favorite songs, find a local karaoke spot, or join a choir.

12. **Volunteering:** Give back to your community and help others in need.

13. **Pet therapy:** Spend time with pets and enjoy their company.

14. **Massage therapy:** Treat yourself to a professional massage or even a self-massage.

15. **Attending therapy:** Seek professional support from a therapist or counselor.

16. **Listening to podcasts:** Tune in to podcasts on topics that inspire and educate you.

17. **Watching sunsets or sunrises:** Witness the beauty of nature's transitions.

18. **Stargazing:** Spend an evening observing the stars and contemplating the universe.

19. **Playing games:** Engage in board games, puzzles, or online games for leisure.

20. **Attending church:** Join a congregation or attend a service to experience spiritual renewal and community.

21. **Acupuncture:** Use this traditional Chinese healing practice to stimulate energy flow, restore balance, and promote physical and emotional well-being.

22. **DIY projects:** Get creative with DIY crafts, gardening, or home improvement projects.

Now, don't get overwhelmed. You clearly don't have to do all of these. Instead, think of this list of ideas as a buffet of options for you to choose from. Pick out your favorites and add them to your plate, one at a time. Do what works for your schedule and makes you feel excited! Your personal self-care evolution isn't a one-size-fits-all concept, and even something that was great for you in your younger years may no longer satisfy your needs as you enter each new decade; it evolves with you as you progress through the different stages of life.

The Connection Between Self-Care and Self-Talk

One of the most overlooked aspects of self-care isn't what you *do*—it's what you *say* to yourself. While self-care is often thought of as external actions like eating well, exercising, or meditating, it actually begins with the internal conversation you have every day. Your self-talk—the thoughts, beliefs, and stories you repeat to yourself—shapes your identity, influences your behaviors, and ultimately determines whether or not you believe you're worth the time and energy that self-care requires.

If your inner voice is critical, dismissive, or rooted in guilt (*I don't have time for myself, I'm too old for that,* or *I should be doing something more productive*), it becomes nearly impossible to practice consistent, meaningful self-care. On the other hand, when your self-talk is rooted in kindness, compassion, and encouragement, it becomes the internal permission slip you need to prioritize your well-being. The way you speak to yourself either reinforces your self-worth or erodes it—and self-care is simply the outward expression of that worth.

Research professor and author Brené Brown highlights the importance of self-compassion and setting boundaries as essential self-care practices. Her work on vulnerability and courage resonates with many seeking to improve their mental and emotional health. She insists, "Talk to yourself like you would to someone you love." This is critical for maintaining an optimal mental outlook and an optimistic mindset.

In many ways, self-care and self-talk work in a powerful feedback loop. When you treat yourself with care, you send the message to your subconscious mind that you matter. And when your internal dialogue is loving and supportive, you're far more likely to take actions that nurture your physical, mental, and emotional health. Over time, this creates a positive cycle: Healthy self-talk leads to more self-care, and self-care reinforces healthier self-talk.

If you're struggling to maintain consistent self-care habits or positive self-talk, it might be worth asking: *What am I saying to myself that's getting in the way?* Rewriting that script—one thought at a time—can be just as important as any morning routine or wellness strategy. Because ultimately, how you treat yourself on the outside begins with how you speak to yourself on the inside.

Of course, remember that's where affirmations—the "A" in S.A.V.E.R.S.—come in, as we detailed in Chapter 5. Affirmations are intentional statements that help you replace negative self-talk with empowering thoughts that help you cultivate positive mental and emotional states. By incorporating affirmations into your Miracle Morning that reinforce your commitment to self-care—such as, *I am worthy of time for myself,* or *Caring for my body and mind is a priority, not a luxury*—you begin to rewire your thinking and shift the way you see yourself. Over time, this practice trains your brain to default to supportive, compassionate self-talk, making it easier and more natural to follow through on the self-care habits that support your health, happiness, and longevity.

The Mind-Body Link: How Emotions Shape Your Well-Being

In the West, we often separate emotions from physical health, treating mental and physical wellness as two distinct categories. Traditional Chinese Medicine (TCM), which has been practiced for thousands of years, sees them as inseparably linked. According to TCM, every major organ in your body is directly affected by your emotional state—and vice versa. In fact, emotions are considered one of the primary internal causes of illness when they are excessive, suppressed, or left unresolved. TCM teaches that emotions can either support or disrupt the flow of qi (life energy) depending on how they're experienced.

Each organ is associated with both positive and negative emotional influences. For example, anger and resentment can cause stagnation in the liver, while kindness and patience help it function smoothly. Fear can deplete the kidneys, while courage and inner calm can strengthen them. Grief weakens the lungs, but acceptance and openness restore their balance.

Here's a quick snapshot of the emotion-organ connection:

- **Heart** – *Harmed by:* overexcitement, anxiety; *Healed by:* joy, love, compassion
- **Liver** – *Harmed by:* anger, frustration; *Healed by:* kindness, forgiveness, patience
- **Lungs** – *Harmed by:* grief, sadness; *Healed by:* acceptance, courage, openness
- **Spleen** – *Harmed by:* worry, overthinking; *Healed by:* trust, gratitude, groundedness
- **Kidneys** – *Harmed by:* fear, insecurity; *Healed by:* peace, willpower, wisdom

The key takeaway? Emotions are not just "in your head"—they are felt and processed throughout your entire body. Traditional wisdom reminds us that true healing is holistic. Your mind, body, and spirit are all connected, and when your emotions are flowing freely and positively, your organs—and your entire being—can function at their best. On the other hand, holding onto painful emotions for too long can lead to imbalances in your energy, blood flow, and overall health. If we do not take care of our emotions, we stand a greater chance of developing sicknesses or diseases. That is why cultivating positive emotional states is a form of deep self-care, one that strengthens your organs, balances your energy, and promotes longevity.

What should you do with this information? First, recognize just how important—and beneficial—it is to actively cultivate positive, healing emotional states. Second, feel assured that your commitment to your daily S.A.V.E.R.S. routine is already helping you move forward on the path to emotional well-being. Third, make it a priority to intentionally set aside and schedule time for self-care hours throughout your week.

By integrating additional self-care hours throughout your day, you're not just managing emotions—you're supporting your body on a cellular level and building the foundation for a state of sustained inner harmony—supporting both your mind and your body.

Dwayne says . . .

Inspired by my studies of Traditional Chinese Medicine, I have acupuncture done once a week, and I love it! Not only are my qi (energy flow) and mood better, but I know I'm taking care of my organs as acupuncture reduces inflammation (which is the source of so much disease). Also, as mentioned earlier, I practice Transcendental Meditation for 20 minutes twice a day. This also helps me manage any stress I might be feeling and brings a sense of emotional balance back to my day.

Easily Integrate Additional Self-Care Hours into Your Days

Here are several examples of how you can integrate additional self-care hours into your daily routine beyond your Miracle Morning:

- **Midday breaks:** Take short breaks throughout the day to recharge. Whether it's a brief walk outside, deep breathing exercises, or simply stepping away from your desk to rest your eyes, these moments of self-care can help alleviate stress and boost productivity.
- **Lunchtime wellness:** Use your lunch break as an opportunity to prioritize self-care. Prepare and enjoy a nutritious meal, practice mindfulness while eating, or do a quick workout or stretching session.
- **Afternoon pick-me-up:** Combat the afternoon slump with an energizing self-care activity. This could be anything from a walk outside to a short dance break or listening to uplifting music.
- **Evening wind-down:** Create a calming evening routine to signal your body that it's time to unwind. Incorporate activities, such as gentle yoga, reading, or a warm bath, to promote relaxation and prepare for restful sleep.
- **Digital detox:** Designate specific times during the day to disconnect from electronic devices and focus on self-care. Turn off notifications, set boundaries around screen time, and engage in offline activities that nourish your mind and body.
- **Mindful movement:** Integrate movement into your day in small increments. Whether taking the stairs instead of the elevator, stretching at your desk, or taking a short walk during breaks, find opportunities to move your body regularly.
- **Breathing exercises:** Incorporate brief breathing exercises into your daily routine to reduce stress and promote relaxation. Practice deep breathing techniques whenever you need a moment to reset.
- **Reflective pause:** At the end of each day, reflect on your experiences, accomplishments, and challenges. This can promote personal growth and self-awareness.

Social Connection = Self-Care

When we think of self-care, we often imagine solo activities like meditation, journaling, or a relaxing bath. But one of the most powerful and often overlooked forms of self-care is *connection with others*. As human beings, we are wired for social interaction. Meaningful relationships not only uplift our mood, but as studies have shown, they also play a crucial role in maintaining our physical health, emotional resilience, and even longevity.

The U.S. Centers for Disease Control and Prevention (CDC) highlights that high-quality relationships can help reduce the risk of chronic diseases such as heart disease, stroke, and dementia, as well as mental health conditions like depression and anxiety.[1] *Harvard Health Publishing* reports that strong social networks and active participation in social activities are associated with a reduced risk of cognitive impairment and dementia, suggesting that social engagement supports brain health as we age.[2]

Regular social interaction and consistent connection with friends and loved ones have been linked to a longer lifespan—on par with the benefits of exercise and a healthy diet. Laughing with a friend, sharing a heartfelt conversation, or simply feeling seen and heard can recharge your spirit in a way that no supplement or workout ever could.

> Regular social interaction and consistent connection with friends and loved ones have been linked to a longer lifespan—on par with the benefits of exercise and a healthy diet.

Especially as we get older and routines change, intentionally making time to socialize becomes even more important. Whether it's a weekly lunch date, joining a local club, calling a friend just to catch up, or saying yes to that karaoke night, these small acts of connection are not just good for the soul; they're essential for your self-care routine.

In the same way that movement nourishes your body and meditation calms your mind, connection fuels your heart. Surrounding yourself with people who uplift, inspire, and support you is one of the most life-affirming choices you can make. Because self-care isn't just about *how* you care for yourself, it's also about *who* you let into your life to care with you.

Dwayne says . . .

As we age, we need to have things to look forward to every day. It really is so important. This is why we see such success with our 80- and 90-year-olds at Aegis Living, with men and women living longer with more energy, spirit, and joy—because they have ample opportunity to be with other people. When you think about building your Miracle Morning routine, consider adding friends to do it with you.

Here's why: Have you heard the saying "Two heads are better than one"? Well, it turns out that it's true, especially regarding your brain health. Socializing with friends stimulates your brain, creating new connections between brain cells. And this boost in brainpower can help ward off conditions like Alzheimer's. Plus, it's a natural mood lifter, keeping those pesky feelings of depression at bay.

When you're socializing, you're also more likely to be active—whether it's strolling in the park, joining a yoga class, or just keeping up with your buddies. And all that movement is like a magic potion for your body, lowering blood pressure, reducing the risk of heart problems, and even potentially staving off conditions like osteoporosis. So, lace up those sneakers and hit the town with your crew!

Consider joining a social community to ramp up your social life further. These places aren't just for those needing care; they're hubs of activity and connection. From shopping outings and game nights to neighborhood hikes and movie marathons, these communities offer an array of social activities to keep you engaged and happy.

Hal says . . .

Great point, Dwayne. In the Miracle Morning Community, we have seen the power of socialization make a difference. Being able to share your goals and wins with like-minded people is magical!

Final Thoughts on Self-Care Hours

Incorporating self-care hours in your life is one of the most powerful commitments you can make to your long-term well-being. As you age, your body, mind, and energy levels naturally shift, making self-care not just helpful, but essential. These aren't indulgent luxuries or things to squeeze in when everything else is done. They are foundational habits that replenish your energy, elevate your mood, and help you thrive—not just survive—through every subsequent decade of life. Your daily Miracle Morning, and especially the S.A.V.E.R.S. practices, are the anchor, and your self-care hours throughout the day serve as reinforcements to help you stay centered, energized, and aligned.

Making self-care a priority sends a powerful message to yourself: *I matter.* Whether it's 15 minutes of quiet reflection, a morning walk, meaningful social time, or simply taking a break when your body asks for rest, these moments add up to a healthier, more vibrant you. The S.A.V.E.R.S. are designed to give you a head start on this each morning, but carrying that mindset into your self-care hours ensures you're recharging throughout the day. You've spent years caring for others, meeting responsibilities, and pushing through. Now is the time to create space to care deeply for yourself—because, when you're feeling rested, nourished, grateful, at peace, and re-energized, you can show up at your best for everyone and everything that matter most.

A Note from a Miracle Morning Community Member

"I am a homebirth midwife and a single parent. I put a lot of time and energy into my work and into parenting, but rarely feel like I am filling back up. Starting my day with *me*, by doing the S.A.V.E.R.S. every day, was what helped me figure out how to take care of myself."

—Ellen Levitt

Age 62

13

ENERGY OPTIMIZATION

Fuel Your Body and Mind to Thrive

*"I don't believe in age. I believe in energy. Don't let
age dictate what you can and cannot do."*

—Tao Porchon-Lynch, renowned yoga instructor who taught well into her 90s

As we age, one of the most common complaints isn't about wrinkles or gray hair. It's about *energy*. Or more accurately, the lack of it. Many people over 50 find themselves waking up tired, dragging through the day, and wondering where their vitality went. Consider that you can have a positive mindset, a plethora of knowledge, and a clearly defined action plan, but if you lack the energy to follow through, well, not much is likely to improve.

Growing older presents new energy challenges, such as decreased nutrient absorption and increased risks from chronic diseases, which can severely impact our energy levels. But here's the truth: Low energy isn't just a natural consequence of aging; it's often a result of how we're living.

No matter your age or circumstances, taking a holistic approach to optimize your energy levels is not just a possibility, but a necessity.

The good news? Your energy can be renewed, restored, and even elevated. This chapter will show you how to optimize your physical, mental, and emotional energy through intentional habits so you can wake up each day with the stamina and clarity to complete your Miracle Morning and create the miracle life you're here to live.

Factors That Influence Our Energy as We Age

Our energy levels naturally ebb and flow as we move through the years, shaped by a complex interplay of genetics and lifestyle habits. From hormonal changes in our 50s and 60s, affecting our vitality, to the physical declines and ailments of our 70s and 80s and beyond, there are certain variables that challenge our stamina and cognitive function, and each stage of life demands specific strategies to maintain energy.

Thankfully, as a species, human beings are biologically wired for resilience and renewal. Our bodies are designed to constantly repair, regenerate, adapt, and seek balance. Yet, how we live each day determines whether that innate potential is supported or suppressed. Here is a general overview of how our energy levels can fluctuate with each decade, starting at age 50.

Age 50–59

Energy levels can gradually decline. Hormonal changes, such as menopause in women and declining testosterone in men, can contribute to fluctuations in energy. Managing stress, maintaining a balanced diet, staying physically active, and getting quality sleep become increasingly important. Many people in their 50s may still feel energetic, especially if they have maintained a healthy lifestyle.

Age 60–69

Energy levels may decline slightly, mainly due to preexisting health conditions. Chronic health issues like arthritis, diabetes, or heart disease can impact energy levels. Muscle mass also tends to decrease, leading to reduced strength and endurance. The big danger here is that people aged 65 and older have an increased risk of breaking bones, including their femurs, after falling. This is why regular exercise, including strength training and aerobic activities, can help mitigate some effects of aging on energy levels as well as age-specific challenges like reduced balance.

Age 70–79

Energy levels may vary widely depending on health status and lifestyle choices. Chronic illnesses and age-related conditions may become more prevalent, affecting energy levels. Fatigue and decreased mobility can become more pronounced. Nutritional needs may change, requiring dietary adjustments to support energy levels.

Age 80–89

Energy levels can vary significantly depending on individual health, mobility, and cognitive function, and further energy and physical stamina can decline due to age-related changes. Chronic conditions and functional limitations may become more challenging. Maintaining social connections, engaging in stimulating activities, and receiving adequate support can help preserve energy and mental well-being.

Age 90–100 and Beyond

Increased frailty and dependence on others for daily tasks can contribute to fatigue. Cognitive decline, sensory impairments, and chronic health conditions can also play a role. Despite these challenges, maintaining a sense of purpose, staying socially connected, and receiving compassionate care can enhance overall well-being and quality of life.

Hidden Energy Zappers for People Over 50

Imagine your vitality is a treasure chest and hidden energy zappers are cheeky pirates trying to loot your reserves. You have to do what it takes to protect your treasure chest of vitality by identifying and addressing these hidden energy zappers. But first, you have to know what some of the more common ones are:

- **Dehydration**, which can result from age-related changes in thirst perception and reduced kidney function, is a stealthy thief of energy.
- **Nutritional deficiencies**, often due to poor dietary habits or digestive issues, can leave you feeling like a deflated balloon.
- **Undiagnosed health conditions,** such as thyroid disorders, anemia, sleep disorders, and depression, can make you feel perpetually exhausted, like you're dragging around a sack of rocks.
- **Medication side effects** can be a primary culprit, especially if juggling multiple prescriptions.
- **Chronic pain** from conditions like arthritis and back pain can rob you of restful sleep and make physical activity a daunting task.
- **Mental health issues**, including depression and anxiety, are like invisible weights, dragging down your energy, motivation, and cognitive function.
- **Sleep disturbances**, typical with age, can turn a once-peaceful night into a series of tosses and turns, leading to daytime fatigue.
- **Social isolation** can drain your spirit and zest for life, making your days feel longer and your energy levels lower.

Taking a holistic approach is crucial to fending off these sneaky energy zappers while considering your medical, nutritional, psychological, and social needs. By addressing these aspects, you can safeguard your energy treasure chest and enjoy a more vibrant, fulfilling life.

As we age, the foundations of lasting energy—movement, nourishment, and rest—become not just helpful, but absolutely vital. Regular exercise, which we explored in depth in Chapter 7, is only one piece of the

> As we age, the foundations of lasting energy—movement, nourishment, and rest—become not just helpful, but absolutely vital.

energy puzzle. Just as essential are the foods we fuel our bodies with and the sleep that allows our systems to repair, reset, and renew. Nutrition and sleep are no longer optional wellness strategies; they are the foundation of a life well-lived. In the pages ahead, we'll take a closer look at how these two pillars can either accelerate your aging or help you reverse it, depending on how you engage with them.

Eating for Energy

When optimizing our energy levels, what we put in our mouths plays a critical role. Most of us understand the importance of eating healthful foods, but we often overlook how the *quantity* and *quality* of what we eat directly impact our energy levels. Put simply, digesting food requires energy. If the food we eat provides less energy than is required to digest it, or if the amount of food we consume is more than our digestive system can comfortably handle, we will find ourselves in an energy deficit and feel sluggish. If, on the other hand, we are mindful about what we eat and consume reasonable portions of "living" foods (raw organic fruits and vegetables as well as sprouted nuts and seeds) that provide us with more energy than is required to digest them, then we will find ourselves in an energy surplus and experience greater mental clarity and physical vitality.

Of course, quantity also matters. The more we eat, the more we burden our bodies with digesting, which demands more energy and leaves us feeling drained. Think of how your energy level is affected after a large meal. Within an hour, your body is using all of its available energy to digest the food. The blood in your body has moved away from your brain and other organs and is in your stomach, and you feel tired and sluggish.

If you've ever taken part in the classic American Thanksgiving ritual, you know the drill. Everyone piles their plates sky-high with turkey, stuffing, mashed potatoes, cornbread, green bean casserole, mac and cheese, and enough pumpkin pie to make your ancestors proud. Then, they waddle to the nearest couch like it's a survival mission. Within minutes, belts are unbuckled, buttons are popping, and half the family is in a collective food coma, sprawled out like starfish across recliners, floors, or even a dog bed if it's available. It's less of a celebration and more of a culinary endurance event, followed by a three-hour nap you didn't plan but absolutely needed. Although this may seem comical, it's an extreme example of what many of us experience on a daily basis—eating a meal and then feeling tired in the hours that follow.

Before we talk about which foods will set you up for optimal energy, it's important to know what *not* to eat so you can avoid the foods that drain your energy. One of the biggest problems with the average American diet is that harmful, toxic, and even poisonous foods have been normalized through marketing and advertising—not for our health, but for profit. So, most people eat them as we have been conditioned to do. Every time you turn on your television—especially those during prime time, sporting events, or kids' programming—you see commercials that promote foods that fall into the least healthy categories. These ads are often designed to appeal to our cravings, emotions, and convenience-driven habits. We can't ever remember a time when we saw a commercial advocating for organic, healthy whole foods.

No matter what the advertisers tell you is "normal" and okay to consume, you must take responsibility for your own health. Here is a list of foods that disrupt your body's natural balance and are detrimental to your energy, health, and longevity:

- **Highly processed foods:** This includes packaged snacks, fast food, sugary cereals, soda, and any item with a long list of unrecognizable or artificial ingredients. These foods are typically high in empty calories, low in nutrients, and can lead to blood sugar spikes, energy crashes, and chronic inflammation.
- **Refined sugars:** Found in sweets, sodas, baked goods, and many processed foods, refined sugars provide a quick jolt of energy followed by a crash. Over time, they contribute to weight gain, insulin resistance, mood swings, and fatigue.
- **Artificial ingredients:** These include artificial colors, flavors, preservatives, and sweeteners. While they enhance shelf life and taste, they offer no nutritional value and may disrupt gut health and metabolic function.
- **Alcohol:** While moderate consumption may be fine for some, alcohol can dehydrate the body, disrupt sleep, impair liver function, and contribute to mental and physical fatigue— especially as we age.
- **Inflammatory seed oils:** Oils such as soybean, corn, vegetable, and canola are commonly used in processed foods and restaurant cooking. They are high in omega-6 fatty acids, which, when consumed in excess, can promote inflammation and oxidative stress in the body.
- **Low-quality animal products:** This refers to meat and dairy from animals raised with antibiotics, added hormones, and unnatural diets like grain-based feed. These products may introduce unwanted toxins and contribute to inflammation,

while lacking the nutrient density of grass-fed or pasture-raised options.

- **Refined grains:** White bread, white rice, and most pastries or baked goods made with white flour have been stripped of fiber and nutrients. These foods digest quickly, causing rapid spikes and crashes in blood sugar and leaving you feeling tired or hungry soon after eating.

In addition to spiking your blood sugar, these foods promote inflammation and burden your digestive and immune systems—leaving you feeling sluggish, foggy, or bloated. Over time, regularly consuming these foods also accelerates aging and increases the risk of chronic disease. If you regularly consume anything listed above, we implore you to start minimizing or eliminating these foods so that you can maintain optimal health, which will lead to noticeable improvements in how you feel, think, and move each day. If not now, when?

One of our collective problems as humans is that we tend to prioritize what we eat based more on flavor and pleasure than health and energy. Think about scanning the shelves of a grocery store or the menu at a restaurant and choosing which items will most satisfy us based on the taste and texture, regardless of the consequences to our health, energy levels, and longevity. Here's a big idea: *What if you started valuing the impact your food has on your health, energy, and longevity more than just how it tastes?* This is done by prioritizing eating for energy and longevity first, and then choosing the most delicious foods that will fuel your energy levels and enhance your health. Consider that taste provides a few minutes of pleasure, but the consequences of that choice impact the rest of your day—and, ultimately, your life.

So, how can you eat for the purpose of optimizing your energy level? Which foods should you consume each day to experience an ongoing supply of energy surpluses to fuel your mind and body throughout the day? Eating for energy and longevity means choosing nutrient-rich whole foods that are created by nature (not in a lab) and that stabilize your blood sugar, reduce inflammation, and support your body with vital high quality nutrients—fats, protein, carbohydrates, vitamins, and minerals—that you need to thrive. We recommend a diet rich in whole foods, such as organic fruits, vegetables, nuts, and seeds, as well as quality protein sources, including organic grass-fed, pasture-raised meats, wild-caught fish, and eggs, which will support your maintaining optimal energy levels.

Also, consider that raw (uncooked) organic fruits and vegetables, along with sprouted nuts and seeds, are some of the most energizing foods you can eat because they are alive with natural, bioavailable nutrients and enzymes. Whereas processed foods contain little to no living energy, so they require more energy from your body to digest than they contribute. So, rather than increasing your energy, processed foods tend to leave you in an energy deficit.

> We recommend a diet rich in whole foods, such as organic fruits, vegetables, nuts, and seeds, as well as quality protein sources, including organic grass-fed, pasture-raised meats, wild-caught fish, and eggs, which will support your maintaining optimal energy levels.

What follows are examples of energizing meals you can adopt, model, or modify.

Energizing Breakfast Ideas (to Fuel Your Morning and Nourish Your Cells)

- **Superfood smoothie** – organic berries, spinach, chia seeds, unsweetened plant milk, nut butter, and optional protein powder—packed with antioxidants, fiber, healthy fats, and plant-based protein to boost cellular repair, stabilize blood sugar, and kickstart your day with clean, sustained energy.
- **Oatmeal topped with banana, walnuts, and cinnamon** – a

warming, fiber-rich meal that supports heart health, promotes digestion, and offers sustained energy from slow-digesting carbs and healthy fats.

- **Avocado toast on sprouted grain bread with a soft-boiled egg and microgreens** – a nutrient-dense combo of healthy fats, protein, and fiber that fuels brain function, balances hormones, and keeps you full for hours.

- **Coconut milk chia pudding with mango, pumpkin seeds, and a dash of turmeric** – rich in omega-3s, anti-inflammatory compounds, and gut-friendly fiber to support brain health and immune function.

- **Grass-fed steak and pasture-raised eggs served with sautéed spinach or avocado slices** – a protein- and iron-rich breakfast that supports muscle maintenance, boosts metabolism, and delivers long-lasting energy.

Energizing Lunch Ideas (to Refuel Your Midday and Avoid Energy Crashes)

- **Big leafy green salad with mixed greens, sprouted seeds and nuts, avocado, bell peppers, and lemon-olive oil dressing** – a powerhouse meal full of antioxidants, plant-based protein, and healthy fats that fight inflammation, stabilize mood, and support digestion.

- **Grain bowl with quinoa or brown rice, roasted seasonal vegetables, and tahini drizzle** – provides complete plant protein, complex carbs, and minerals to keep blood sugar steady and energy flowing.

- **Vegetable soup with lentils or beans and a side of fermented sourdough** – a comforting, gut-friendly meal that supports gut health and mental clarity and is high in plant protein, fiber, and prebiotics.

- **Lettuce wraps filled with grilled chicken or tempeh, shredded carrots, and avocado** – low in carbs, high in protein, and rich in micronutrients to help you feel light, satisfied, and focused throughout the afternoon.

Energizing Dinner Ideas (to Support Recovery, Promote Sleep, and Restore Energy)

- **Grass-fed steak with roasted sweet potatoes and garlic green beans** – provides high-quality protein, B vitamins, and iron to support muscle repair, immune health, and deep sleep.
- **Pasture-raised chicken breast with steamed broccoli and wild rice** – a balanced plate offering lean protein, antioxidants, and complex carbs that replenish energy stores without spiking blood sugar.
- **Grilled salmon with quinoa, arugula salad, and lemon-olive oil dressing** – loaded with omega-3 fatty acids, anti-inflammatory compounds, and fiber to support heart, brain, and joint health.
- **Stir-fried veggies (bok choy, mushrooms, bell peppers, broccoli) with tofu or shrimp and coconut aminos** – a colorful, nutrient-dense meal that supports detoxification, hormone balance, and digestion.
- **Stuffed bell peppers with ground turkey, cauliflower rice, garlic, and herbs** – a low-carb, high-protein dinner rich in flavor, antioxidants, and essential nutrients to satisfy your body's repair processes overnight.

Eating whole, organic, made-in-nature (not in a lab), living foods typically gives you an abundance of energy—more energy than they require for digestion—thus empowering your body and mind with an energy surplus, which enables you to perform at your best. While quality meats will give you the protein you need, when you eat living, plant-based foods, you're not just consuming calories, you're taking in nature's life force, which translates directly into increased vitality, mental clarity, and sustained energy throughout your day.

Compounding Your Vitamins for Optimal Energy

As we age, we often need more than a healthy diet to keep our nutrient levels at their peak. Aging reduces nutrient absorption efficiency, so maintaining optimal vitamin and mineral levels becomes challenging. And even with a balanced diet, the body's ability to absorb nutrients diminishes due to reduced stomach acid, slower metabolism, and changes in gut microbiota.

Aging adults often experience deficiencies in essential vitamins and minerals, including vitamin D, B12, and calcium, despite adequate dietary intake. The digestive system's ability to assimilate nutrients declines with age, making supplementation vital to overall health.[1]

One empowering solution is compounding vitamins and minerals to your specific needs based on regular blood tests. Customized supplementation ensures you are not taking unnecessary vitamins or minerals, providing a sense of security. It also helps maintain optimal energy levels, improves immune function, and supports overall health by addressing specific deficiencies.

Here's a simple process to get started:

1. **Consult your healthcare provider.** Before starting any supplementation, consult a healthcare provider (frequently a nutritionist) who understands customized supplementation. This professional advice is essential to ensure your safety and well-being.

2. **Schedule regular blood tests.** Get a comprehensive blood test

to check your levels of essential vitamins and minerals. Work with your doctor or nutrition specialist to interpret your blood test results and identify nutrient deficiencies.

3. **Consult a compounding pharmacist.** A compounding pharmacist can use your blood test results to create personalized vitamin and mineral supplements tailored to your specific needs. Research and select a reliable compounding pharmacy in your area or online, and be sure it is accredited by the Pharmacy Compounding Accreditation Board because it will comply with all regulatory requirements.

4. **Monitor and adjust.** Regularly review your blood test results and adjust your supplements. This process allows you to take control of your health, providing reassurance as you monitor your health and nutrient levels with follow-up blood tests every two to three months, adjusting your supplements as necessary.

By taking these steps, you ensure that your body receives the proper nutrients tailored to your needs, helping you maintain peak health and energy as you age.

Dwayne says . . .

I know from experience that taking a bunch of supplements willy-nilly will not improve your health. It's all too easy to get seduced by magazine ads, store displays, and the latest thing your friend is trying. Most "experts" and websites are trying to sell you something, no matter how well-intentioned. Unlike medications, the FDA does not regulate supplements, and their quality varies; so, do your research and make sure the supplements you take are really what you need (ideally in consultation with a knowledgeable nutritionist).

I like compounded vitamins because they are built to supplement the deficiencies my blood tests reveal. My nutritionist helps me do this and it costs about $300 for a four-month supply, which is not much more than regular vitamins. My blood is tested every two to three months and the vitamins are reconfigured after each test to meet my body's changing needs. If you'd like to try this, work with a nutritionist who uses compounded vitamins to help his or her patients. When you take this approach, it will likely change your life, as it has mine.

Sleeping for Sustainable Energy

If you want sustainable energy, deep sleep isn't optional—it's essential. Sleep is when your body repairs itself, your brain clears out waste products including beta-amyloid and tau proteins—both linked to Alzheimer's and other neurodegenerative diseases—and your energy reserves are fully replenished. Yet as we age, quality sleep can become more elusive due to shifting hormones, stress, nighttime discomfort, or poor habits. The good news is, with a few intentional changes, sleep can become one of your most powerful aging allies. In this section, we'll explore how to create a sleep routine that supports your energy, sharpens your mind, and helps you wake up feeling refreshed and ready for your Miracle Morning.

> Sleep can become one of your most powerful aging allies.

If you don't sleep enough, you're gradually wearing yourself down and will lack the energy to do all that you want and need to do. But how much is enough? There is a big difference between the amount of sleep you can get by with and the amount you need to function optimally. In other words, just because you're able to function on five to six hours of sleep doesn't mean you wouldn't feel better and have more energy if you spent an extra hour or two in bed. It has been well-documented that enough sleep allows the body to function at higher levels of performance.[2] You'll not only work better and faster, but your attitude will improve, too.

The amount of nightly rest each individual needs differs, but research shows that the average adult needs approximately seven to eight hours of sleep to restore the energy it takes to handle all of the demands of living each day. However, sometimes we need less, and sometimes we need more. The best way to figure out if you're meeting your sleep needs is to evaluate how you feel as you go about your day. If you're sleeping enough, you'll feel energetic and alert all day from the moment you wake up until your regular bedtime. If you're not, you'll reach for caffeine or sugar mid-morning or mid-afternoon . . . or both. Ugh!

But here's a thought: What if you changed your beliefs about sleep? The mind-body connection is a powerful thing, and we must take responsibility for every aspect of our lives, including the power to wake up every day feeling energized, regardless of how many hours of sleep we get. In other words, our readiness to start our day upon waking up isn't based solely on how many hours of sleep we got but is significantly impacted the night before by how we told ourselves we would feel when we woke up.

Hal says . . .

Along with countless Miracle Morning practitioners, I have found that how we feel when we open our eyes in the morning is largely affected by our personal beliefs about how much sleep we need to feel rested. For example, if you have a belief that you *need* eight hours of sleep to feel rested, but you get into bed at midnight and have to wake up at 6:00 a.m., you're likely to tell yourself, *Geez, I'm only going to get six hours of sleep tonight. I'm going to feel exhausted in the morning.* Then, what happens as soon as your alarm clock goes off and it's time to wake up? What's your first thought? *Geez, I only got six hours of sleep. I feel exhausted.* It's a self-fulfilling, self-sabotaging prophecy. If you tell yourself you're going to feel tired in the morning, then you are going to feel tired. If you believe that you need eight hours to feel rested, then you won't feel rested on anything less. On the flipside, if you go to bed every night affirming that you're going to wake up feeling energized, excited, and ready to make tomorrow the best day of your life (!)—that becomes a self-fulfilling, self-empowering prophecy.

Also related to the mind-body connection, Dwayne likes to say—and believe—three positive things before going to bed. It helps him prepare his mindset for the night and new day ahead of him. Maybe it's saying something like, "I'm going to get a great night's sleep" or "I know tomorrow is going to be a great day filled with great accomplishments." Setting your mind on the positive, your brain (as mentioned earlier) will hear and believe what you say and prepare to accomplish it.

Ultimately, listen to your body to know if you're getting the restorative and energizing sleep you need while also believing that you will feel energized when you wake up in the morning! It's a one-two punch to having plentiful energy for your Miracle Morning and the whole day!

Tips for Getting Restful, Energizing Sleep

There are many things you can do—and not do—to ensure you get restful, energizing sleep. Here are a few things to do and avoid to awaken refreshed, with the energy to live your day well and to the fullest.

Limit caffeine: Did you know that the half-life of caffeine is 6 to 8 hours? Even more surprising is that the quarter-life of caffeine is 10 to 12 hours. That means one-quarter of the caffeine in your 4:00 p.m. coffee is still swirling around in your system at 2:00 a.m.! It might not *keep* you from falling asleep, but it might be detrimental to your *sleep quality*. Dr. Michael Breus, a clinical psychologist and sleep expert (aka, The Sleep Doctor), advises stopping caffeine consumption by 2:00 p.m. to prevent sleep disturbances.[3]

No strenuous exercise before bed: While regular exercise—such as what you do as part of your S.A.V.E.R.S.—is great for your sleep quality, exercising too close to bedtime can have the opposite effect. Physical activity raises your body's core temperature, and it typically takes about 90 minutes for it to return to baseline. A cooler body temperature is conducive to initiating sleep, so exercising too close to bedtime may delay this process.[4] Exercise also stimulates the release of adrenaline and elevates your heart rate, which can make it challenging to relax and fall asleep promptly.[5] Lastly, physical activity triggers the release of endorphins, which can create a feeling of euphoria and heightened alertness, potentially making it harder to wind down for sleep.[6] So, be sure to avoid exercise, especially cardio workouts, within 90 minutes of going to bed.

Adjust your thermostat: Did you realize that the temperature of your bedroom can make a significant difference to your sleep quality? We tend to sleep better in cooler temperatures due to the body's natural thermoregulation process, which is closely linked to our circadian rhythm. As bedtime approaches, the body initiates a drop in core temperature, signaling that it's time to sleep. A cooler sleep environment facilitates this temperature decline, making it easier to fall asleep and maintain restful sleep throughout the night.

Conversely, a warmer room can hinder the body's ability to cool down, leading to increased wakefulness and reduced sleep quality. According to SleepFoundation.org, the best room temperature for sleep is approximately 65 degrees Fahrenheit (18.3 degrees Celsius). This may vary by a few degrees from person to person, but most doctors recommend keeping the thermostat set between 65 to 68 degrees Fahrenheit (15.6 to 20 degrees Celsius) for the most comfortable sleep.[7]

Wake up at the same time every day: Maintaining a consistent wake-up time each day is crucial for regulating your circadian rhythm and various physiological processes. By rising at the same time daily, you reinforce this natural rhythm, leading to improved sleep quality and increased daytime energy. Consistency helps synchronize your body's functions, resulting in enhanced alertness, mood stability, and overall well-being.[8] Conversely, irregular wake-up times can disrupt this balance, leading to feelings of fatigue and decreased productivity. Dr. Breus advises that, even if you have a late night, it's beneficial to wake up at your usual time to preserve your circadian rhythm.[9]

Avoid fire brain: Many of us experience what Dwayne calls "fire brain" before bedtime, and it can be a significant issue in getting a restful night's sleep. Fire brain is best described as our thoughts being influenced by the activities of the few hours before going to bed. Whether watching a stimulating movie or a disturbing documentary, tackling work emails, reading something upsetting, or having a difficult or emotional conversation, engaging in any task that keeps our minds fixed on stressinducing thoughts negatively affects our ability to sleep. Even as we close our eyes, our minds continue to churn through these activities, profoundly impacting how well we fall asleep, remain asleep, and ultimately wake up. By reprogramming your nighttime routine to reduce fire brain, you will wake up easier and feel better all around.

Dwayne says . . .

My whole adult life, no matter how well I ate or how much I exercised, this is what it used to be like for me: Fire brain. At night.

During the day, I was full-on from morning to evening, though I was good about getting in a physical workout most days. After 45 minutes on the treadmill, I would be dog-tired and ready to collapse, except I had to get straight back to work. However, when bedtime came, I was so excited about all the things that I was doing that after 17.5 hours of go-go-go, I didn't know how to give my brain a break. I couldn't turn it off. My brain was so fired up that even when I slept, I didn't sleep deeply. My brain was taking all my body's energy, even during sleep.

On a typical night, I would lie down around 10:30, watch a violent, action-packed movie or a TV show like *Dateline* or *20/20* that was about a murder. With my iPad on my lap, I'd triple-task by answering e-mails and texting on my iPhone at the same time. Eventually,

I'd crash and my body would fall asleep from pure exhaustion, iPad on my lap, phone in my hand, TV blaring, lights blazing. I had many dreams that woke me up and disturbed my sleep. My body might have been asleep, but my brain was on fire.

I woke up tired, my weight was going up even as I tried to diet, and my blood pressure and fasting blood sugar levels were rising. Even my cortisol levels were getting higher. If I hoped to live a long and happy life, something—maybe everything—had to change.

So how did I overcome fire brain and give myself the best chance for a calm evening that would set me up for a restful night of sleep? I stopped engaging in the stimulating (and sometimes disturbing) activities that fired my brain up. I also did calming things, like taking hot showers or baths with Epsom salts, doing guided meditation, and listening to 528 Hz music (music composed at a frequency of 528 hertz, part of the ancient Solfeggio scale, and is believed to help prepare the body for sleep by promoting relaxation and reducing stress). That made all the difference.

Final Thoughts on Optimizing Your Energy

Energy is the foundation for living life to its fullest, especially during the second half of your life. By intentionally managing your physical, emotional, and mental energy, you can unlock the vitality needed to pursue your goals, maintain meaningful relationships, and enjoy life's simple pleasures. Regular exercise keeps your body strong and resilient, while a diet rich in nutrient-dense, living foods fuels your daily activities and long-term health. Quality sleep recharges your body and mind, setting the stage for focus and productivity.

As we age, it becomes even more important to be proactive about preserving and enhancing energy levels. By staying mindful of hidden energy zappers, maintaining healthy routines, and tailoring your nutrition and activities to your unique needs, you can sustain the stamina and clarity to embrace every chapter of life. Remember, energy is your most valuable resource; nurture it wisely, and it will serve you on your path to living with joy, vitality, and purpose.

A Note from a Miracle Morning Community Member

"My wife and I started Miracle Morning 13 months ago and are getting up at 5:30 a.m. to do our S.A.V.E.R.S. routine. We are blessed to be able to do this together and the results are miraculous. We get a lot more things done, are more energetic, and all our endeavors are picking up speed. Most importantly, we have more time together to either enjoy nature or discuss things during our morning walk."

—Andrea Vincenzo Braga
Age 50+

14

FIRST LIGHT AND EARTHING

Reconnect with Nature to Enhance Longevity

"When you arise in the morning, think of what a precious privilege it is to be alive—to breathe, think, enjoy, love."
—Marcus Aurelius, Roman emperor, Stoic philosopher

Imagine starting your day with a sense of connection to the natural world, setting the stage for a vibrant and healthy life. In this transformative chapter, you'll discover how to supercharge your Miracle Morning S.A.V.E.R.S. routine with two robust health and longevity tools: first light and earthing. These two simple, effective, natural, and affordable (FREE!) ways to improve your health and extend your lifespan have been around and practiced for millennia but have only recently been studied for their scientifically proven benefits. Both involve being outdoors (although earthing can be done indoors as well), can be done simultaneously, and have similar health benefits.

The Magic of First Light for Longevity

Our biological clock, an internal timekeeper, thrives on the rhythm set by the rising and setting sun. Morning sunlight does more than chase away the shadows; it kickstarts our body's sleep-wake cycle, keeping our circadian rhythms in harmony. This dance of light and dark isn't just poetic; it's crucial for our health.

Research underscores the profound impact morning sunlight has on us.[1] It's akin to nature's caffeine, invigorating us without a drop of coffee. Furthermore, this celestial light is our ally in vitamin D synthesis, a cornerstone for robust immunity and mental health, playing a vital role in diminishing stress levels. The morning light is not just a source of illumination but a powerful force that can rejuvenate and energize us for the day ahead, as well as improve our ability to fall asleep swiftly and rest well.

So why is morning light—first light—critical to our well-being? Isn't sunlight, well, sunlight? As it turns out, morning sunlight differs slightly from afternoon or evening sunlight.

> Morning light is akin to nature's caffeine, invigorating us without a drop of coffee.

Light comprises several wavelengths, from blue to red, and some invisible ones, such as infrared and ultraviolet (ultraviolet-A or UVA and ultraviolet-B or UVB). Morning sunlight is precious because it is saturated in infrared and blue lights. This is important because infrared light stimulates collagen, increases bone healing, and heals wounds. In addition, it is proven to have anti-aging properties, reducing wrinkles and scars.

Morning blue light wakes you up by increasing your cortisol levels, and it is activated when it hits your pituitary gland. It also sets your circadian rhythm for the day. Blue light is gone with the sunset and melatonin—the sleep hormone—comes out to play so you can fall asleep. Blue light is the switch that controls the ebb and flow between cortisol and melatonin.

You've probably heard that blue light is terrible. Perhaps you even wear blue-blocker glasses at night to protect your eyes from the evil blue light. (And good for you! You're a step ahead!) There is a tremendous difference between natural blue light from the sun and the artificial blue light emitted by your screens and light bulbs. Blue light in nature is always balanced by regenerative red light and other wavelengths, serving you well. So, get out and catch those infrared and blue rays in the morning's first light.

Health Benefits of First Light

Whether you're 22 or 82, exposure to morning sunlight is essential for a healthy lifestyle. After all, we are wired to wake with the sun. Sunlight significantly impacts our bodies, influencing everything from hormone production to sleep cycles. Let's look at a few of the most significant benefits of first light.

Circadian rhythm regulation and improved sleep quality: At night, when it's dark outside, your body starts releasing melatonin, which helps you sleep. Natural light in the morning signals your brain and body to enter its active phase by suppressing melatonin production. This helps synchronize the body's circadian rhythms, which, as just mentioned, are critical for regulating sleep patterns, metabolism, and hormone production. Morning sunlight helps set the stage for a restful night's sleep.

Proper circadian rhythm alignment reduces risks of chronic diseases such as obesity, diabetes, and heart disease. It also keeps the systems of the body working in perfect synchrony. Our circadian clock directs the suitable cells to correctly turn on the necessary genes, thus synchronizing the body's complex functions.

For example, the immune system relies on the circadian clock to accommodate the body's needs at different times of the day. During waking hours, you are more likely to encounter bacteria or viruses, so more immune cells will migrate through your tissues on the lookout for invaders. During mealtimes, some immune cells move to your gut, ready to fight any invading bacteria in your food. And it all starts with morning light.

Mood enhancement: Morning light is a powerful mood enhancer. Exposure to morning light increases serotonin production, a neurotransmitter associated with mood elevation. It also triggers the release of endorphins, which are natural mood lifters. These hormones can be particularly beneficial in reducing symptoms of depression and Seasonal Affective Disorder (SAD), contributing to overall mental health.

Vitamin D synthesis: Early morning sun exposure is a natural source of vitamin D, which is crucial for bone health, immune function, and reducing inflammation. The sun is the most important source of vitamin D, so getting it early in the morning ensures your body has what it needs throughout the day, especially as it partners with calcium to strengthen your bones. Vitamin D deficiency has been linked to various health issues, including osteoporosis and increased susceptibility to infections.

Eye health: Natural light exposure, particularly in the morning, is beneficial for eye health. As we just read, the sun helps the human body produce vitamin D, which also plays a vital role in slowing the aging process and improving your vision. Eyes that lack exposure to natural light tend to look dull and lifeless, not to mention are more inclined to develop photophobia, which is extreme sensitivity to sunshine. Natural light can facilitate normal eye development among children, not to mention maintain healthy biorhythms as we age.

Incorporating first light exposure into your daily routine can significantly benefit longevity and healthspan. By aligning our body's natural rhythms with the environment, improving sleep quality, enhancing mood, boosting vitamin D levels, and supporting eye health, we lay a foundation for a healthier, longer life.

Incorporating First Light into Your Miracle Morning

The key to harnessing the power of first light lies in its incorporation into our daily lives—a task easier said than done in our modern, often indoor-centric world. Here are some actionable tips to ensure you receive your daily dose of dawn, tailored for the seasoned life navigator but applicable to all.

- **Morning rituals with a view:** Begin your day by opening your curtains or taking your morning tea or coffee outside. This simple act invites the day's first light into your life, setting a natural rhythm for wakefulness and sleep.
- **A sunrise stroll:** A brief, leisurely walk in the early hours exposes you to beneficial sunlight, kickstarts your metabolism, and stimulates your senses, preparing you for the day ahead.
- **Greet the sun from your garden or balcony:** Gardening or enjoying breakfast outdoors can effectively absorb morning light, imbuing the start of your day with tranquility and a touch of vitamin D.
- **Adjust your environment:** For those days when stepping outside isn't feasible, eat breakfast or exercise near a window that welcomes the morning sun, ensuring you still benefit from its glow.
- **Adjust your schedule:** Try to align your morning routine with sunrise. Waking up with natural light can help set your internal clock more effectively. If this isn't possible during the week (due to having to wake up for work or other obligations before the sun rises), commit to trying it on the weekends.
- **Limit artificial light in the morning:** Reduce the use of bright artificial lights in the morning to allow your body to respond naturally to the gradual increase of natural light.
- **Make your bedroom sunlight friendly:** Ensuring your bedroom receives natural light in the morning can help regulate your body's internal clock and promote better sleep at night. Simple things like adjusting your blinds to point downward or leaving an opening in your curtains so sunlight can peek

through will make your bedroom environment more conducive to morning's first light.

- **For night owls:** For many people, especially those over 60, getting up in the middle of the night to use the bathroom is just a fact of life. So, if it's after 4 a.m. or 5 a.m., open your curtains if you're up anyway. The sunrise will pour natural light into your room.

Once you figure out what works, stick to a regular schedule. Waking up at the same time every day and getting morning sunlight is a good combination.

Dwayne says . . .

As we've already established, I'm not a big fan of traditional alarm clocks. Not because I don't like getting up in the morning but because I believe our biorhythms should be naturally set. Developing positive sleep habits will help with this. Thankfully, technology exists to wake us up more naturally.

Devices that simulate first light, often called dawn simulators or sunrise alarm clocks, gently wake you by gradually increasing light intensity, mimicking the natural sunrise. This approach aligns with our natural circadian rhythms, making it easier to wake up feeling refreshed. These devices are especially beneficial for individuals in the 50+ age group as they provide a natural wake-up method that doesn't rely on jarring alarm sounds.

When choosing a sunrise alarm clock, especially for someone over 50, consider factors like ease of use, brightness settings (to ensure they're not too harsh), sound options (for those who might also want an auditory cue), and overall simplicity of use. These devices can significantly improve the quality of waking up, making mornings more pleasant, and helping to maintain healthy sleep patterns.

Earthing for Longevity

When was the last time you walked barefoot in the grass, dug your toes into the soil, or sat directly on the sand at the beach? When was your body's last direct contact with the earth? Did you know that direct contact with the earth is good for you? It is, and here's how.

Beneath your feet is a truly amazing resource for health and longevity—planet Earth! It is a natural source of beneficial, negatively charged energy (i.e., electrons) that we can "plug" into to counter the positive charge our bodies build up from our 21st-century lifestyle, which bombards our body with excessive electromagnetic frequencies (EMFs) and often lacks regular contact with nature. We are essentially bioelectrical beings, and when we are "grounded" with the earth, our cells function better, stress decreases, and the parasympathetic system (the network of nerves that helps the body relax and perform life-sustaining functions when you feel safe and relaxed) is activated.

Earthing—also known as grounding—is the practice of physically connecting your body to the Earth's natural electric charge, typically by walking barefoot on grass, soil, or sand, swimming in a natural body of water, or by using grounding devices indoors. This simple act has been associated with a range of health benefits, particularly in reducing inflammation, improving sleep, and enhancing overall well-being.

> We are essentially bioelectrical beings, and when we are "grounded" with the earth, our cells function better, stress decreases, and the parasympathetic system that helps the body relax is activated.

While our current healthcare model doesn't provide us with extensive research on the importance of the bioelectrical component of our health, there is a growing body of evidence that supports the physiological effects and potential health benefits of earthing. Let's look at a few of the amazing benefits of earthing for better health, well-being, and longevity.

One of the primary benefits of earthing is its potential to reduce inflammation. As we've discussed, inflammation is a crucial contributor to many chronic diseases associated with aging, such as arthritis, heart disease, and Alzheimer's. Earthing is thought to help reduce inflammation by neutralizing free radicals. When electrons from the earth are absorbed, they have antioxidant effects, which can combat free radicals in the body that contribute to inflammation. A study published in the *Journal of Inflammation Research* found that grounding significantly reduced inflammation and improved immune response.[2] By allowing the body to absorb electrons from the Earth, grounding may neutralize free radicals, thereby mitigating chronic inflammation—a major contributor to aging and various diseases.

Improved circulation and sleep are two other notable benefits. Improved blood flow can aid in delivering oxygen and nutrients to the body's tissues, which is crucial for healing and overall health. Grounding has been shown to help regulate cortisol levels and align circadian rhythms, leading to deeper, more restorative sleep. In a study published in the *Journal of Alternative and Complementary Medicine*, participants who slept grounded reported better sleep quality and lower nighttime cortisol levels.[3]

Earthing also appears to have a calming effect on the nervous system, promoting a shift from the sympathetic (fight-or-flight) to the parasympathetic (rest-and-digest) state. This shift can lead to reduced stress and anxiety levels, contributing to improved mood and emotional well-being. A study in *Integrative Medicine: A Clinician's Journal* found that grounding improved heart rate variability, a key indicator of autonomic nervous system balance and cardiovascular health.[4]

In 2013, in the *Journal of Alternative and Complementary Medicine*, researchers also noted that grounding supports heart health by lowering blood viscosity and clumping, and stated, "Grounding appears to be one of the simplest yet most profound interventions for helping reduce cardiovascular risk and cardiovascular events."[5] Updated research from 2023 expands on the benefits of grounding for your heart, noting that, "Grounding outside on the earth can work synergistically to help naturally increase circulation and blood flow, decrease blood viscosity, increase heart rate variability, and reduce soreness after exercise. Not only will this benefit your entire cardiovascular system, but all of your bodily organs will benefit from the improved blood flow as well, in addition to your heart."[6]

While earthing has existed since ancient civilizations—until recently, physical contact with the ground was an ordinary way of life—today's earthing movement was popularized in the 1990s by Clint Ober, who began creating mats connected to the ground via conductive wire and a metal rod. When people sat and slept on these mats, they found that their energy increased, they slept more deeply, wounds healed faster, and even chronic pain improved, sometimes overnight.

How Does Earthing Work?

Does this all sound a bit out there? Skepticism about the earth's ability to connect with us and restore health and well-being is expected. So here are a few science-based points about earthing that will help make more sense.

Your body runs through a type of electrical current. As the *Journal of Environmental and Public Health* states: "It is an established (though not widely appreciated) fact that the Earth's surface possesses a limitless and continuously renewed supply of free or mobile electrons. The Earth's negative charges can create a stable internal bioelectrical environment for the normal functioning of all body systems, which may be important for setting the biological clock, regulating circadian rhythms, and balancing cortisol levels."[7]

Electrical first, chemical second. According to Clint Ober, "Everything in the body is electrical first, chemical second."[8] For example, the brain, heartbeat, and neurotransmitter activity rely on electrical signals, so other aspects of your health will also be off when your electricity is off.

Your skin acts as a "conductor," allowing your body to absorb electrical charges from the earth naturally. Your feet, and precisely specific points on the balls of your feet, are believed to be especially receptive to the earth's electricity. When you practice earthing, your body absorbs the earth's electrons like a sponge! Then, those electrons move throughout your body, providing beneficial impacts from your head to your toes.

The best part about earthing is that it's straightforward and completely free. It requires nothing but your bare body and a willingness to try something that might seem out of the ordinary.

Earthing Every Day

How can you most easily integrate earthing into your daily routine? Thankfully, earthing is one of the easiest, safest, and most natural things you can do to improve your health and increase longevity. Here are a few simple ways to start doing this.

- **Daily practice:** Incorporating 10 minutes of earthing into your daily routine can benefit individuals, particularly after 50. This can be as simple as walking barefoot on grass, soil, or sand.
- **Do it during existing activities:** Earthing can be conveniently combined with other daily activities. For example, practicing it during a morning walk, gardening, or simply sitting barefoot on the ground while reading or journaling can be effective.
- **Indoor options:** For those who find it challenging to spend time outdoors, grounding products like earthing mats, sheets, pillowcases, bands, and pads mimic the effects of direct earth contact and are available online.

Note that it's essential to practice earthing in a safe environment, avoiding areas with potential hazards, such as sharp objects or harmful substances. Individuals with neuropathy should consult with their healthcare provider before starting earthing practices.

A Compelling Case Study

By scientific standards, research into earthing is still in its early stages. But with the growing body of research currently being conducted, we are on the cusp of some significant discoveries that could be the missing puzzle piece in living healthier today and improving longevity.

The Earthing Institute reported a case study from Dr. Gregory Melvin, DC, of La Mesa, California.[9] On a routine basis, Dr. Melvin gets feedback from patients, telling them that grounding has accelerated healing on various issues, ranging from pain problems to poor digestion. Then he confirms their input through the use of thermal imaging. Dr. Melvin shares, "When I learned about [grounding], I wanted to see if and how it could affect vascular changes and the extremities. I gave some grounding pillowcases to patients and did pre- and post-grounding imaging. I wasn't treating them. I just asked them to be grounded for a few nights in bed. After seeing significant degrees of changes within three days, I went on to do about a dozen more patients. I saw similar significant improvements, and at that point, I knew I needed to include grounding in my treatment plans and imaging analysis.

"Since that time, grounding has become pivotal in my multifaceted approach to health. We are bioelectrical beings, and grounding rapidly loads up the body's electrical system. It's like charging a battery."[10]

Final Thoughts on First Light and Earthing

So, what's stopping you? It's like our grandparents used to say: "Get outside, let the sun see your face, and get some fresh air!" They were right. Regular contact with nature does improve our physical health and mental well-being. First light and earthing, as natural healing techniques, offer significant benefits relevant to aging populations. They're simple to do and can be incorporated to stack the healing benefits on top of each other.

As with any new health practice, especially for those with existing health conditions, consult with healthcare professionals before starting.

Incorporating first light and earthing into your S.A.V.E.R.S. routine can transform your morning and enhance physical energy, mental clarity, emotional well-being, and spiritual fulfillment. When the weather permits, begin with silence or meditation as you step outside to greet the morning sun, grounding yourself by standing barefoot on the earth. This practice helps regulate your circadian rhythm and infuses you with the earth's natural energy. Follow this with affirmations and visualization as you feel the warmth of the sunlight and the coolness of the ground, creating a powerful mind-body connection. Engage in exercise by taking a brisk walk or doing light stretches on the grass, allowing the first light and earthing to amplify the benefits of physical activity. You can also read and scribe outside to further your mind and spirit by blending these natural practices into your Miracle Mornings. You create a holistic morning ritual that supports longevity, independence, and a more vibrant life, catering to better health and well-being at any age.

As we navigate the chapters of our lives, let us turn the pages with the morning sun and Earth's energy, embracing their light and electrical charge as a source of strength, health, and rejuvenation.

A Note from a Miracle Morning Community Member

I am a Retired Night Nurse of 30+ years. I started Miracle Mornings five years ago and all areas of my life improved. My husband is an early riser, and I was dreading the day he would retire. Fortunately for me, TMM changed my routine before he did. I am eternally grateful for my Miracle Morning. The funniest thing that has happened since I started practicing is that I discovered the sunrise out of my bedroom window after nine years of living there! What a pleasant surprise!"

Tina Banton
Age 50+

15

LIVING ON PURPOSE WITH PURPOSE

Infuse Your Days with Meaning

"The two most important days in your life are the day you are born and the day you find out why."
—**Mark Twain, American author, humorist, and essayist**

There comes a time in life—often after 50—when you begin to reflect more deeply on the *why* behind everything you do. It's no longer enough to simply go through the motions or fill your days with busyness. You want meaning. Fulfillment. A reason to get out of bed in the morning that goes beyond obligation. *Living on purpose with purpose* means aligning your daily actions with your deepest values and living in a way that energizes you, contributes to others, and feels deeply true to who you are. This chapter is about rediscovering that purpose—or perhaps, uncovering it for the first time—and learning how to design a life that reflects it in every area.

For some, purpose means having a sense of direction and overarching goals, such as improving health or achieving financial freedom, or specific ones, like learning a new skill or taking time to enjoy your favorite hobby. For others, purpose represents an underlying way of being, such as spreading love and kindness to others, glorifying God, or a commitment to contributing, such as taking care of your family or volunteering to help those in need. Purpose can also be thought of as your reason for waking up in the morning because you're needed by an endeavor, spouse, family, or community.

Integrating a sense of purpose into your Miracle Morning practice can be a powerful motivator that drives you to set and achieve worthwhile goals. When you infuse your purpose into the S.A.V.E.R.S. each day, you create a holistic approach that supports and amplifies your ability to gain clarity and take consistent actions toward meaningful outcomes. For example, let's say your purpose is to create financial freedom for your family. In that case, you could start in silence by praying for guidance and spending time in meditation to gain clarity. Next, you can create and recite specific affirmations that articulate the goals you're committed to, why they're important to you, and which specific actions you need to take to achieve them. Use visualization to imagine your ideal future and mentally rehearse yourself taking the actions you affirmed and doing so in a peak state. Then, exercise to get the blood flowing, use your reading time to consume content (books, articles, etc.) to learn strategies for creating financial freedom, and, finally, utilize your scribing time to write down what you're grateful for and identify your top priorities for the day. Of course, you can do these in any order, and know that this synergy ensures the benefits of your S.A.V.E.R.S. are aligned with your purpose.

Here's a big idea: *Purpose is not something you find as much it's something you choose.* In other words, you get to decide what it is. Many people put unnecessary pressure on themselves to "figure out" their purpose, as if their life won't be complete until they discover what they were meant to do. Purpose doesn't work that way. You're the one who decides what gives you purpose. And it can change with each season of life you're in. Purpose isn't rigid; it's flexible, fluid, and can even be fun—a lifelong journey of ongoing exploration and fulfillment.

So do what you enjoy, what fulfills and is meaningful to you, and you will have discovered your purpose. No pressure!

Hal says . . .

I chose my first life purpose when I was in my mid-twenties. I was reading a book titled *Love Is the Killer App* by Tim Sanders, and he talked about how important it was to focus on adding value for other people, both in personal and professional settings. He emphasized that the more value we add for another person, group, or organization, the more valuable we become to them. Thus, our value and the strength of our relationships are increased. This really resonated with me and reminded me of Zig Ziglar's famous quote: "You can get everything you want in life if you help enough other people get what they want."

So, I chose my first purpose and put it in writing: *Selflessly add as much value as I can for as many people as possible.* I incorporated the word *selflessly* as a reminder that I was committed to adding value *for others* and not merely to serve my own selfish ambitions, though I was aware that this approach would inevitably benefit me as well. It was a win-win. I reviewed and affirmed my purpose each day during my Miracle Morning and began to live it. Professionally, I focused on going above and beyond to add value for my customers and colleagues, as well as the company I worked for. The results were hard to argue with, as I increased my sales by 102 percent over the previous year, doubling my income. I also built a reputation within the company as someone my colleagues and superiors could count on, which is still paying dividends more than 20 years later.

Having a clearly defined purpose organizes your time, focus, and even relationships. Purpose is about putting forth effort toward doing things that have meaning for you.

While research shows that finding purpose early in life is a prescription for health, finding a renewed sense of purpose enables people to thrive later in life.[1] If you are bored with gardening after many years, find a new way to garden or a new hobby or pursuit that excites you. If you live to 100 or beyond, you will have several lifetimes of purpose and passions to fulfill, each offering new opportunities for fulfillment.

Purpose is about setting goals and having a concrete reason to get up every morning. Purpose becomes critical as you sail into the second half of your time on this planet. Purposeful goals pull you into the future, so why not set meaningful goals and enjoy working toward them?

Purpose Is Powered by Resilience and Optimism

Resilience, the ability to adapt positively to adversity, has always seemed to be a hallmark of longevity. Recent longevity research suggests that adults with resilience age more slowly, live longer, and enjoy better health.[2] Cultivating resilience empowers us to tap into our inner strength and resourcefulness, enabling us to navigate life's inevitable challenges with vitality and grace.

Optimism also plays a crucial role in this process. It allows you to maintain the perspective that the best is yet to come, no matter how many years lie ahead. Optimism fuels your resilience by enabling you to maintain a hopeful and positive outlook, even in the midst of adversity. Optimistic individuals are more likely to believe they can find new purposes and meaning in life, making them more resilient. This positive cycle between optimism and resilience is essential for maintaining a sense of purpose as you age, and it offers a hopeful and optimistic view of the future. The good news is that cultivating optimism is a choice, and one that can be made each morning using your S.A.V.E.R.S. More on that in a minute.

Dwayne says . . .

Resilience is one of the qualities that led to my interest in aging when I started my career in my 20s. I remember I was a young boy and met a World War I veteran in my grandmother's nursing home. On one of our weekly visits, I wandered the hall and heard a man calling for help. I cautiously entered his room and retrieved his pillow, which had dropped to the floor, when I suddenly saw all his medals. We started talking, and I was spellbound by his war stories and the stories of his productive—and I now see, resilient—life. The next time I visited my grandmother, I went to look for him, eager to hear more of his stories, and found out he had died.

I always remembered him, and when I got my first job working with older people, the thing that made the work meaningful for me was spending time talking to the residents. My purpose is to continue to evolve how our aging population goes into each new year. I'm now working on a project I'm calling "100 X 100," where I will interview 100 centenarians. As of this writing, I've interviewed over 30 of these centenarians to hear their stories of tragedies, incredible persistence, resilience, and unbelievable optimism. So many of these amazing individuals, whom I refer to as my oracles, credit their long lives to these characteristics.

Optimism, the belief that good things will happen, is crucial in adapting to stressful situations and thus contributes to resilience. I've always felt that resilience and optimism work hand-in-hand. I've also observed that those who are more optimistic demonstrate more resilience. There seems to be a corresponding relationship between these two: Optimism leads to resilience, which brings about greater optimism.

These qualities become even more significant as we age, and yet they can be anything but straightforward for many people. Discovering or redefining your purpose later in life often involves navigating new challenges such as retirement, health issues, or changes in social roles; living alone, feeling lonely and isolated from friends and family; or retiring and missing the comradery that one might have experienced at work. Resilience allows you to adapt to these changes positively, seeing them as opportunities rather than setbacks. It helps you bounce back from difficulties and continue pursuing what matters most.

Discovering and choosing your purpose often involves trial and error. Without resilience, setbacks make it easy to become discouraged. However, resilience is the key to overcoming these setbacks. It helps you stay determined and persistent, even in the face of challenges. Optimism complements resilience by helping you stay motivated and open to new possibilities, increasing the likelihood of finding a fulfilling purpose. When you view challenges as opportunities for growth rather than obstacles, you are more likely to engage in activities that bring meaning to your life.

There's some good news if you struggle to be optimistic and focus on the positive. Nir Barzilai, MD, director of the Institute for Aging Research at the Albert Einstein College of Medicine, says there is evidence that people can change their attitudes and behavior, even at older ages. A study of 243 centenarians led Dr. Barzilai to discover that when it comes to personality, "We found qualities that reflect a positive attitude toward life. Most were outgoing, optimistic, and easygoing. They considered laughter an important part of life and had a large social network. They expressed emotions openly rather than bottling them up."[3]

Optimistic people are more likely to do things to care for themselves, including finding purpose in their later years. They believe they can make choices that will lead to better situations—and they don't have what psychologist Martin Seligman calls "learned helplessness," which is associated with pessimism. You may not know right away what you can do to change your situation or feelings for the better, but believing that opportunities will show up keeps you optimistic and resilient. That attitude causes a chain reaction of positive outcomes.

Purpose Improves Mental Health and Longevity

Evidence suggests that having a sense of purpose benefits mental and emotional well-being and has a tangible impact on physical health and longevity.

Having a strong sense of purpose does a great deal to lift one's mood and outlook on life no matter what a person's age, thus it's vital for improving mental health. It's been known for quite a while that people with severe mental illness, in general, have shorter lifespans. Still, researchers are starting to learn that milder conditions, such as depression and chronic anxiety, can also have significantly detrimental impacts on people's lives. Even low-level signs of depression and anxiety may be associated with a 20 percent increase in health risks. Chronic stress can lead to a string of problems, including increased cortisol and inflammation, a depressed immune system, metabolic changes, adverse changes in the gut microbiome, and brain disorders. To avoid this, especially as we age, we must keep our sense of purpose alive and well. Being stoic instead of flexible and resilient, living in the past, and living without purpose and a sense of happiness are not the prescriptions for good health and wellness.

A few studies on purpose and longevity are particularly interesting and encouraging. One of the most compelling case studies comes from Okinawa, Japan, known for its high number of centenarians. Researchers attributed the longevity of Okinawans not only to their diet and lifestyle but also to their strong sense of purpose or *ikigai*—a reason for being. Okinawans who maintained an active role in their community and clearly understood life purpose tended to live longer, healthier lives.[4]

Other research has focused on areas known as Blue Zones, where people live exceptionally long lives. And a common factor among residents of Blue Zones is having a strong sense of purpose. For example, in Sardinia, Italy, and Loma Linda, California, older people continue to be actively involved in their communities and pursue activities that give them a sense of purpose.[5] Another study, conducted as part of the Rush Memory and Aging Project, found that individuals with a high sense of purpose were 2.4 times more likely to remain free of Alzheimer's disease than those with a low sense of purpose.[6] A study in the *Journal of the American Medical Association (JAMA)* found that individuals with a strong sense of purpose had a lower risk of experiencing cardiovascular events like heart attacks and strokes.[7] The sense of purpose acted as a protective factor against cardiovascular diseases. Finally, research from the Boston University School of Public Health, that analyzed data from over 13,000 individuals, showed that people with a greater sense of purpose had a 15 percent lower risk of death, regardless of their age.[8]

Purpose is the elixir of longevity. Those with a clear sense of mission tend to wake up each day with more energy and vitality and weather life's storms with greater resilience, emerging unscathed and invigorated. In an age of stress and uncertainty, cultivating a sense of purpose becomes increasingly vital. Whether serving others or pursuing personal endeavors, embracing a higher calling can imbue life with meaning and vitality.

Purpose is the elixir of longevity.

Redefining Your Purpose After 50

There are numerous successful people who have found their purpose and lived/are living their best lives after they turned 50. Here are just a few.

Arianna Huffington: When Arianna Huffington was 55, she launched The Huffington Post (now HuffPost). After a decade as editor-in-chief, she left to start Thrive Global, a wellness and productivity company. Huffington's transition to a wellness advocate demonstrated her ability to adapt and pursue new passions, proving that success is not limited by age. She recently posted on X, "What I've learned as I've gotten older is how much we can gather steam as we gather years. So let's take away from ourselves the pressure of believing we must achieve it all at 30 or 40 or any age, for that matter, or all at once."[9]

Harland Sanders: Better known as Colonel Sanders and the founder of Kentucky Fried Chicken, Harland Sanders was a remarkable entrepreneur who didn't achieve his greatest success until he was in his 60s. Starting as a gas station owner, he began selling his secret-recipe fried chicken to truck drivers. At the age of 62, he decided to franchise his business, and it quickly became a global sensation. Sanders's perseverance and dedication to his unique recipe, combined with his late start, made him a culinary icon. He wrote in his autobiography, "I've only had two rules: Do all you can and do it the best you can. It's the only way you ever get that feeling of accomplishing something."[10]

Julia Child: At the age of 49, Julia Child released her influential cookbook, *Mastering the Art of French Cooking*. When she was 51, she created *The French Chef*, a successful television cooking show, which made her a household name in America. Her passion for cooking and teaching others how to enjoy food led her to a successful career in television and writing. Child's enthusiasm and dedication to her craft are evident in her quote, "Find something you're passionate about and keep tremendously interested in it." Her journey shows that pursuing your passion can lead to remarkable success, regardless of age.

Bernie Marcus: Bernie Marcus co-founded Home Depot at the age of 50, after being fired from his job at another hardware store at the age of 49. Leveraging his extensive experience and knowledge, he and his business partner, Arthur Blank, created a revolutionary retail concept that focused on providing customers with a wide selection of home improvement products and tools. Home Depot's success can be attributed to Marcus's vision, leadership, and ability to identify a gap in the market.

His late-career entrepreneurial venture proved that age is no obstacle to achieving significant success.

Laura Ingalls Wilder: Laura Ingalls Wilder published *Little House in the Big Woods*, the first book in her beloved Little House series, at age 65. Her stories, which are based on her childhood experiences, have captivated readers for generations. Wilder's success came later in life, proving that it's possible to start a new chapter and leave a lasting legacy at any age. She once said, "It is the sweet, simple things of life which are the real ones after all," highlighting the value of finding joy and purpose in everyday experiences.

These remarkable over-50 trailblazers illustrate that age is not a barrier to success. Whether you're starting a new business, pursuing a creative passion, or finding new ways to contribute to your community, defining your purpose in your later years can lead to profound fulfillment and achievement. Embracing resilience, maintaining an optimistic outlook, and staying committed to your goals are crucial components in this journey. By looking to the examples set by these amazing people, you can find inspiration and motivation to redefine your purpose and continue striving for your dreams.

Infusing Purpose into Your S.A.V.E.R.S.

Your S.A.V.E.R.S. aren't just morning habits—they're your daily opportunity to reconnect with who you are and why you're here. When each practice is intentionally infused with a sense of purpose, your Miracle Morning becomes more than a routine; it becomes a mission. Here's how to elevate each element of your S.A.V.E.R.S. by aligning it with what matters most to you.

Silence is your sacred space to listen to your inner wisdom, your intuition, and the quiet whispers of your purpose. When you sit in silence with intention, you're not just relaxing your mind; you're creating room for clarity to emerge. Use this time to reflect deeper questions: *How can I live in alignment with my values today? How can I show up at my best, for myself and others?* Ask God for guidance. Create space to tap into your intuition. The answers may not always come right away, but the space you create allows them to surface.

Affirmations become far more impactful when they're intentionally aligned with your deeper sense of purpose. Rather than generic feel-good phrases, they become personal declarations that anchor you to who you are and what you're here to do. For example, if your purpose is to inspire others, your affirmations might focus on your commitment to lead by example, uplift those around you, and take specific, meaningful actions that reflect that mission. When repeated daily, these purpose-driven affirmations don't just boost confidence—they reshape your identity, fuel your motivation, and keep your goals rooted in something far greater than yourself.

Visualization becomes a tool to mentally rehearse living your purpose. Instead of just picturing success or reaching your goals, visualize yourself embodying your purpose—how you show up in your relationships, how you make a difference, how you feel when you're aligned. See yourself navigating challenges with grace because you're grounded in something meaningful. The clearer your vision, the more powerfully your purpose can pull you forward.

Exercise is a way to energize your body *for* your purpose. Moving your body with intention reminds you that your health is not just about longevity; it's about being physically capable of living out your mission. Whether you're walking, stretching, lifting, or dancing, let your movement be an act of gratitude for the body that carries your purpose through the world.

Reading becomes a form of purposeful learning. Choose books, articles, or passages that challenge your thinking, deepen your self-awareness, or teach you something new that aligns with your values or passions. Read not just to accumulate knowledge, but to grow into the person you're meant to become—the one your purpose is calling you to be.

Scribing is where your purpose takes shape in words. Use this time to reflect on how you're living in alignment, where you may have drifted, and what's calling you forward. Write about your goals through the lens of your purpose. Capture your insights, intentions, and the lessons life is teaching you along the way. When you write regularly with purpose in mind, your journal becomes a personal roadmap to meaning.

Scribing a Purposeful Letter

There's something powerful—almost sacred—about putting pen to paper to capture the lessons life has taught you. Whether you're writing to your younger self, your children, a friend, or simply for your own reflection, the process of distilling decades of experience into meaningful words can be both healing and transformative. In the heartfelt letter from Dwayne below, we see a beautiful example of this form of expression: part wisdom, part humor, part soul-stirring wake-up call. It's raw, unfiltered, and beautifully human. Letters like this serve as a mirror, a compass, and a legacy. They remind us of who we are, what matters, and what we still have the power to do.

In the pages ahead, you'll be invited to write your own version—a letter filled with truths you've earned, dreams you still carry, and encouragement you'd offer to someone you love (especially if that someone is you). Because sometimes, the most life-changing words are the ones we write ourselves.

Dwayne says . . .

On my 60th birthday, I began to reflect on how old I was, not just biologically but where it matters—in my head and heart. Was I living in my purpose? One of the thoughts that stuck with me was to live out my purpose; I let go of any thoughts that kept me hesitant and prevented me from continuing to explore, learn, and try new things.

My mindset could not allow for notions that didn't move me forward. Moving forward is crucial to being able to live out your purpose fully. This led to writing the following letter to myself and sharing it as a gift with my guests at my 60th birthday party.

Over the last 60 years, I've gained a lot of wisdom. Most of the lessons come from the over 60,000 people whose care I've been responsible for, from the scientists on the Manhattan Project, the woman who invented Cheerios, to the actress who played Jane in the Tarzan movies. I call them my oracles. My elderly residents have made my career, molded my life's beliefs, and passed on their wisdom. One day, I politely asked Sam how old he was. A 93-year-old resident and an ex-boxer, he answered, "Old enough to kick your ass." Now, it didn't matter if he could. The fact that he believed it was tonic enough to grant him extended longevity.

So, Dwayne, stop wearing chinos and boat shoes. You have no contractual obligation to become your father! You don't have to have your hair cut the same way you've had it cut for the last 15 years. Go Big! Reverse the part. Don't fall prey to what you think aging is supposed to be. Hold on to your youth. Don't forfeit it too quickly. Hold on to it like you would a newborn baby dangling over the rail ten stories up. Letting go of it results in a terrible outcome. Einstein, Martin Luther King, Gandhi. They were never worried about fitting in.

Dance the Gator at your daughter's wedding. Better yet, at your granddaughter's wedding, and then beg for forgiveness. Sing in the shower and in the car loud and proud. Don't give away you. Don't conform. Don't rob the world of your uniqueness. You are old enough not to care what people think of you. Start being yourself. Otherwise, you'll be a prisoner in someone else's jail.

Do the unexpected. Take that fantasy trip now. Don't keep putting off your dreams, kicking the can down the road. Climb a mountain, enter a car race, become a speed walker. Hell, write a play! Stop waiting to spend your money or worrying about saving it for your kids. Spend it now. Don't cheat them of the lessons of figuring it out for themselves. Realize that today is the day you've been planning for. Tomorrow? Well, tomorrow, unfortunately, is not promised.

Stubbornness is the greatest enemy of learning and advancement. Try something new. Anything! Salsa dancing, rock climbing, hell, produce your Claymation video. Go to Ibiza. Dance like crazy with people 40 years younger until 5 a.m. Then, wink at the cutest girl in the room as though she has no chance. Don't forget to kiss your wife passionately. And don't give up on that sexual fantasy. Just make sure you involve your partner in these dreams.

Do an inventory of who your friends are every ten years and make them deliberate. Friends should not be friends alone because of history. Choose your friends. Don't let your friends choose you. Don't keep friends who don't challenge you, accept you, or love you. Your life's happiness will benefit from it. You never know when the last "I love you" will be the last "I love you." If you are in a miserable relationship, get out and get on with it. Love hard. Make it a habit to tell those you love that you love them daily.

You don't have to drive a Tesla just to show you're socially responsible. Fight for the underrepresented, not because you're socially responsible, but because it's how your parents raised you. Live with purpose. Volunteer. Mentor, give your time, and give your essence. Do more than write a check! It's so much more meaningful and precious.

Write this down. Life sometimes makes it too busy to listen, even to our pain. Stop that macho bullshit and cry! Cry when you're happy; cry when you're sad. If you don't let these emotions out, they'll live inside you and eventually kill you. Give your body an attentive audience. Sit and let it tell you what hurts. This is the only body you're getting this time around. Use your legs. Walk as much as feasibly possible. Run once a week, even for 30 seconds, just to ensure you still can. Don't decide you can't do it anymore. The big guy upstairs will determine that for you, and you won't even know it.

Live with gratitude. Optimism adds an average of seven years to your lifespan over pessimism. Write down your words of wisdom and what you've learned during your lifespan. Your words are of great significance to those who come after you. You have incredible wisdom. There are few moments to ponder, "Am I on the right road?" This is one of those moments. In this moment, I remind you, as my hero, the late Robin Williams, once said, "Make your life spectacular. I know I did." Make your life spectacular!

Now it's your turn. We invite you to carve out some quiet time, open your journal or laptop, and write a letter from your heart—to yourself, to your children, grandchildren, or even to a younger version of you. Don't overthink it or worry about getting it perfect. Just let your wisdom flow. Reflect on what life has taught you—about love, failure, health, aging, purpose, and joy. What would you want someone you care about to know before it's too late? What do you wish someone had told you sooner? Speak with honesty. Infuse it with humor, if that's your style. Be bold. Be real. This isn't about sounding wise—it's about being authentic. Your words have the power to inspire, heal, and live on.

Because here's the truth: Your life has meaning. Your story matters. And your voice—your raw, beautiful, imperfect voice—might be exactly what someone else needs to hear. Whether you ever share your letter or keep it tucked away, the act of writing it will reconnect you to what's most important. So write it for them. Write it for you. But most of all, write it as a declaration that you are still here, still learning, and still choosing to live on purpose with purpose.

> Your life has meaning. Your story matters. And your voice—your raw, beautiful, imperfect voice—might be exactly what someone else needs to hear.

Final Thoughts on Purpose

Living *on* purpose and *with* purpose isn't about having all the answers or following some perfectly laid-out plan. It's about waking up each day with intention—knowing that your time, your energy, and your presence matter. Purpose gives your life direction, but it also gives it depth. It turns ordinary actions into meaningful ones. It reminds you that even the smallest act of kindness, the quietest moment of reflection, or the boldest leap of faith can be part of something bigger.

You don't have to change the world to live a purposeful life. You just have to live *your* truth—consistently, authentically, and unapologetically. Whether your purpose is to create, serve, lead, love, or grow, what matters most is that you honor it. And the beauty is, it's never too late to start. As long as you're alive, you still have time to align with your purpose and make every day count. So ask yourself often: *What am I here to do? Who am I here to become?* Then live into the answer—one intentional step at a time.

A Note from a Miracle Morning Community Member

"I have been retired for three years. I first started doing the Miracle Morning almost a year ago. I feel so much more focused and finally feel I have a purpose for my life. It has become a habit that I really miss if I don't do it every day!"

Mary Unger
Age 50+

CONCLUSION

This Is Your Time

*"Know that you are the perfect age. Each year
is special and precious, for you shall only live it
once. Be comfortable with growing older."*
—Louise Hay, American author, speaker, publisher

You've made it to the final pages of this book, but in many ways, you're just getting started. *The Miracle Morning After 50* has been your invitation to wake up—not just in the morning, but to your full potential, your deepest purpose, and the extraordinary possibilities still waiting to unfold in your life.

In Part 1: Waking Up to Your Full Potential After 50, you learned how to reclaim your mornings with the power of the Miracle Morning and the life-enhancing S.A.V.E.R.S. practices—*Silence, Affirmations, Visualization, Exercise, Reading,* and *Scribing.* These six daily rituals give you the clarity, confidence, and momentum to live intentionally, no matter your age. They're more than a morning routine; they're a blueprint for becoming the best version of yourself—in body, mind, and spirit.

If you embraced the Miracle Morning 30-Day Life Transformation

Journey at the end of Part 1, then you've already felt the shift—the inner strength and confidence that comes from starting your day with intention, and the deep knowing that it's never too late to transform your life.

If you haven't yet downloaded The Miracle Morning After 50 Fast-Start Kit yet, which gives you goal-setting exercises, pre-written affirmations as well as customizable templates, journaling prompts, daily checklists, tracking sheets, and more—all that were designed specifically for readers of this book—you can do so now at **TMMAfter50.com.**

In Part 2: Not-So-Obvious Self-Care Strategies to Thrive After 50, you discovered how to sustain that growth and joy throughout the rest of your day. From scheduling dedicated self-care hours to energy optimization through nourishing food, quality sleep, and mindful movement, you've learned to treat your well-being as a sacred responsibility. You explored how waking with first light reconnects you to nature's rhythm, how earthing grounds your nervous system and restores your vitality, and how living on purpose with purpose gives every day new meaning. Each of these strategies isn't just about adding years to your life—it's about adding *life* to your years.

Here's the truth: In the second half of life, you're not winding down; you're waking up. This season of your life can be your most fulfilling, vibrant, and meaningful yet. You have the tools. You have the wisdom. You have the time. All that's left is the choice—to rise each morning with intention, to care for yourself without apology, and to live each day with clarity, courage, and purpose.

Because your life after 50 isn't the end of the story. It's the beginning of the miracle life you were always meant to live.

Help Others on This Journey

If this book has added value to your life, if you feel like you're better off after reading it, and you see that *The Miracle Morning After 50* can be a new beginning for you to take any—or every—area of your life to the next level, we're hoping you'll do something for someone you care about: Give this book to them. Let them borrow your copy or get them their own. It could be for no special occasion other than to say, "Hey, I love and appreciate you, and I want to help you live your best life. Read this."

If you believe, as we do, that being a great friend or family member is about helping your loved ones become the best versions of themselves, we encourage you to share this book with them. Together, we are truly elevating humanity's consciousness, one morning at a time.

GLOSSARY

A

Affirmation – In the context of S.A.V.E.R.S.®, *Affirmations* are consciously chosen, positive statements that reinforce desired beliefs, mindsets, behaviors, or outcomes to help optimize your thoughts, emotions, and actions.

Automatic negative thoughts (ANTs) – Involuntary, negative thoughts that can occur reflexively in response to certain situations or triggers; they are often irrational and can contribute to anxiety, depression, and a host of other mental health issues.

B

Bed stretching – Typically a 5-minute routine performed while still in bed to "wake up" key areas of your body; helps increase blood flow to muscles and joints; improves muscle flexibility and joint range of motion, reducing the risk of injuries caused by sudden movements or falls.

Blue light – A type of visible light with short wavelengths and high energy, emitted by the sun (natural) and digital devices like smartphones and computers (artificial); plays a crucial role in regulating our circadian rhythm.

Breathwork – Term that encompasses a variety of structured breathing techniques or exercises, often used for more specific purposes like emotional release, healing, or heightened states of awareness; practices may involve different rhythms, holds, and patterns of breathing, and they are commonly found in practices like yoga, meditation, and holistic therapies.

C

Circadian rhythm – The physical, mental, and behavioral changes an organism experiences over a 24-hour cycle; the 24-hour internal clock in our brain that regulates cycles of alertness and sleepiness by responding to light changes in our environment.

Compounded vitamins – The customized preparation of vitamin formulations by licensed pharmacists or physicians to meet the specific needs of individual patients; based on bloodwork ideally taken every two to three months; allows for tailored dosages, combinations, and forms of vitamins that are not commercially available, ensuring optimal patient care.

Cortisol – A steroid hormone produced by the adrenal glands; often called the stress hormone because it's released into the bloodstream when a person is stressed; helps the body respond to stress or danger by increasing blood sugar levels, improving the brain's use of glucose, and making substances available to repair tissues.

D

Deep breathing – A relaxation technique in which a person focuses on taking slow, deep breaths.

Diaphragmatic breathing – A relaxation technique in which a person focuses on taking slow, deep breaths; breathing in slowly through the nose and then out through the mouth using the diaphragm (the thin muscle that separates the chest from the abdomen) and abdominal muscles.

E

Earthing – A therapeutic technique that realigns your electrical energy by reconnecting to the earth.

Emotional optimization meditation – A type of meditation designed to help you identify, regulate, and elevate your emotional state by aligning your thoughts, breath, and focus with intentional, empowering feelings.

Epigenetics – The study of how cells control gene activity without changing the DNA.

Exercise – In the context of S.A.V.E.R.S.®, *Exercise* is the practice of engaging in physical activity within the first hour of the day in order to sustain or improve health and fitness, as well as increase the flow of blood and oxygen to the brain for the benefit of enhanced cognitive function.

F

Fire brain – Thoughts that are influenced by the activities of the few hours before going to bed that keep your mind fixed on stress-inducing thoughts; negatively affects your ability to and the quality of sleep.

First light – Morning light, including time before official sunrise; contains beneficial ultrared and blue lights and does not contain ultraviolet lights.

G

Grounding – see *Earthing*.

Guided meditation – A practice where an individual is led through the meditation process under the direction of a trained practitioner or teacher, either in person, via audio or video, or an app.

H

Healthspan – Living longer in optimal good health, free from chronic diseases and debilitating conditions; enjoying a life where you can remain active and fully functional.

I

Inflammaging – Low-grade chronic inflammation, associated with various age-related diseases.

Inflammation – A complex biological response to protect the body from harmful stimuli, such as pathogens, injuries, or toxins. While acute inflammation is crucial to the body's defense mechanism, chronic inflammation can harm health and longevity.

Infrared light – A type of electromagnetic radiation that is not visible to the human eye but can be felt as heat, typically from the sun or a fire; can penetrate deep into the body, reaching muscles, bones, and organs; increases bone healing, heals wounds, stimulates collagen; has anti-aging properties.

J

Journaling – see *Scribing*.

L

Life expectancy – Assesses how long someone is expected to live based on birth year and demographics.

Lifespan – Refers to our lifetime (how long we live).

Living food – Natural foods that are as close to their original form as possible, retaining their nutrients and active ingredients; consumed fresh, raw, and in a condition as close as possible to their original, vibrant, living state.

Longevity – Refers to living a long duration of life (especially beyond the average age).

Lymphatic system – A network of vessels, nodes, and organs that helps maintain fluid balance, absorb dietary fats, and support immune function by transporting lymph—a clear fluid containing white blood cells—throughout the body.

M

Meditation – The practice of calming your mind, cultivating inner peace, and developing present-moment awareness to reduce stress, enhance clarity, and improve emotional well-being.

Micro-habit – A small, everyday action that can lead to big changes over time.

Mindfulness meditation – A type of meditation in which you focus on being intensely aware of what you're sensing and feeling in the moment, without interpretation or judgment.

Miracle Morning® – A structured personal development routine created by Hal Elrod, consisting of six core practices—*Silence, Affirmations, Visualization, Exercise, Reading,* and *Scribing* (collectively known as the S.A.V.E.R.S.®)—intended to be practiced daily in the morning to enhance physical, mental, emotional, and spiritual well-being, and to support individuals in reaching their full potential at any stage of life.

Mitochondria – Membrane-bound cell organelles (mitochondrion, singular) that generate most of the chemical energy needed to power the cell's biochemical reactions; also known as your cells' powerhouses.

Morning Motivation Level (MML) – A way to gauge your eagerness to get out of bed and get moving; a scale from 1 to 10, with 10 indicating you're fully prepared to start the day and 1 meaning you're desperately longing to stay in bed.

N

Neuroplasticity – The brain's ability to change and adapt in response to new experiences, stimuli, or injuries.

Neurotransmitters – Any of a group of chemical agents released by neurons (nerve cells) to stimulate neighboring neurons or muscle or gland cells, thus allowing impulses to be passed from one cell to the next throughout the nervous system.

O

Oxidative stress – An imbalance between free radicals—unstable molecules that can damage cells—and antioxidants, which neutralize them; can lead to cellular damage and is associated with various health conditions, including aging, cardiovascular diseases, and neurodegenerative disorders.

P

Parasympathetic nervous system – A network of nerves that helps the body relax and perform life-sustaining functions when you feel safe and relaxed; part of the autonomic nervous system; is responsible for the body's "rest and digest" response.

Proprioceptive sensors – Sensory receptors that provide feedback about body and limb position.

Purpose – 1: Having a sense of direction and overarching or specific goals; underlying way of being; the reason to wake up in the morning because you're needed. 2: An abiding intention to achieve a long-term goal that's both personally meaningful and makes a positive mark on the world.

R

Reading – In the context of S.A.V.E.R.S.®, *Reading* is the practice of intentionally absorbing knowledge, wisdom, and inspiration from books or other resources to support your personal growth and help you become the person you need to be to create the life you want.

S

S.A.V.E.R.S.® – An acronym representing six of the most timeless, effective, and scientifically proven personal development practices—*Silence, Affirmations, Visualizations, Exercise, Reading,* and *Scribing*—designed to elevate your mindset, well-being, and productivity every day, enabling you to become the best version of yourself.

Scribing – In the context of S.A.V.E.R.S.®, *Scribing* is the act of keeping a record of your personal thoughts, feelings, insights to gain clarity, track progress, and consciously create the life you want.

Self-care – The World Health Organization defines self-care as, "the ability of individuals, families, and communities to promote health, prevent disease, maintain health, and cope with illness and disability with or without the support of a health worker."

Senescent cells – Cells that release inflammatory and tissue-degrading molecules, negatively impacting health.

Silence – In the context of S.A.V.E.R.S.®, *Silence* is the intentional practice of quieting your mind—through meditation, prayer, reflection, or deep breathing—to cultivate inner peace, clarity, and a sense of centeredness before beginning your day.

T

Telomere – The end of a chromosome; made of repetitive sequences of non-coding DNA that protect the chromosome from damage. Telomeres become shorter each time the cell divides.

Transcendental Meditation (TM) – A type of silent meditation that involves repeating a mantra in your head while trying to achieve a state of relaxed awareness; practiced for 15 to 20 minutes, twice per day.

U

Ultraviolet light – An invisible form of light beyond the violet end of the visible spectrum, known for its role in causing sunburns and its use in sterilization processes; stimulates the production of vitamin D in the skin, which is essential for bone health, immune function, and overall well-being.

V

Visualization – In the context of S.A.V.E.R.S.®, *Visualization* is a practice to mentally rehearse a desired outcome and the steps needed to attain it, while cultivating the most effective mental and emotional states to support taking action in real time.

W

Wim Hof Method – A technique that combines deep breathing exercises, cold therapy, and mental focus to improve health and well-being.

Z

Zombie cells – see *Senescent cells.*

NOTES

Chapter 1

1   "Life Expectancy at Birth, Age 65, and Age 75, By Sex, Race, and Hispanic Origin: United States, Selected Years 1900–2019," U.S. Centers for Disease Control and Prevention 2020–2021, last reviewed October 30, 2024, https://www.cdc.gov/nchs/data/hus/2020-2021/LExpMort.pdf.

2   Kenneth D. Kochanek et al., "Mortality in the United States, 2022," Centers for Disease Control and Prevention, *NCHS Data Brief* no. 492 (2024): 1, https://www.cdc.gov/nchs/products/databriefs/db492.htm.

3   "Sleep and Older Adults," National Institute on Aging, last reviewed February 6, 2025, https://www.nia.nih.gov/health/sleep/good-nights-sleep.

4   Thelma J. Mielenz et al., "Patterns of Self-Care Behaviors and Their Influence on Maintaining Independence: The National Health and Aging Trends Study," *Frontiers in Aging* 2 (2021): 770476, https://doi.org/10.3389/fragi.2021.770476.

5   "Older Adults with Regular Activity Routines Are Happier and Do Better on Cognitive Tests, Study Finds," University of Pittsburgh Medical Center, September 13, 2022, https://www.upmc.com/media/news/091322-cognitivetests.

6   Estela González-González and Carmen Requena, "Practices of Self-Care in Healthy Old Age: A Field Study," *Geriatrics* 8, no.3 (2023): 54, https://doi.org/10.3390/geriatrics8030054.

7   Christoph Randler, "Proactive People Are Morning People," *Journal of Applied Social Psychology* 39, no. 12 (2009): 2787–97, https://doi.org/10.1111/j.1559-1816.2009.00549.x.

Chapter 2

1   "Web-Based Injury Statistics Query and Reporting System (WISQARS)," Centers

for Disease Control and Prevention, accessed May 12, 2025, https://www.cdc.gov
/injury/wisqars/index.html.

2   Ramakrishna S. Kakara et al., "Cause-Specific Mortality Among Adults Aged ≥65
Years in the United States, 1999 Through 2020," *Public Health Reports* 139, no. 1
(2023): 54–8, https://pubmed.ncbi.nlm.nih.gov/36905313/.

3   Lisa Stathokostas et al., "Flexibility Training and Functional Ability in Older
Adults: A Systematic Review," *Journal of Aging Research* 2012, no. 1 (2012):
306818, https://doi.org/10.1155/2012/306818.

4   In-Hee Lee and Sang-young Park, "Balance Improvement by Strength Training
for the Elderly," *Journal of Physical Therapy Science* 25, no. 12 (2013): 1591–93,
https://doi.org/10.1589/jpts.25.1591.

5   Mayo Clinic Staff, "Health and Zombie Cells in Aging," *Mayo Clinic News Network*,
December 1, 2023. https://newsnetwork.mayoclinic.org/discussion/health-and
-zombie-cells-in-aging/.

6   Jennifer L. St. Sauver et al., "Biomarkers of Cellular Senescence and Risk of Death
in Humans," *Aging Cell* 22, no. 12 (2023): e14006, https://doi.org/10.1111/acel
.14006.

7   Stella Victorelli et al., "Apoptotic Stress Causes mtDNA Release During Senescence
and Drives the SASP," *Nature* 622, no. 7983, (2023): 627–36, https://doi.org/10
.1038/s41586-023-06621-4.

8   Barry M. Popkin et al., "Water, Hydration and Health," *Nutrition Reviews* 68, no. 8
(2010): 439, https://doi.org/10.1111/j.1753-4887.2010.00304.x.

9   Michael Boschmann et al., "Water-Induced Thermogenesis," *The Journal of Clinical
Endocrinology & Metabolism* 88, no. 12 (2003): 6015–19, https://doi.org/10.1210
/jc.2003-030780.

10 Abby Moore, "This Is the One Time a Sleep Expert Says It's OK to Sleep in," *MBG
Health*, February 14, 2022, https://www.mindbodygreen.com/articles
/minimum-amount-of-sleep-you-should-get-each-night.

11 Adriane M. Soehner et al., "Circadian Preference and Sleep-Wake Regularity:
Associations With Self-Report Sleep Parameters in Daytime-Working Adults,"
Chronobiology International 28, no. 9 (2011): 802, https://doi.org/10.3109
/07420528.2011.613137.

12 Jim Kwik, host, Kwik Brain, "How to Sleep Better During a Pandemic with Dr.
Michael Breus," ART19, October 5, 2020, 15 min., 35 sec., https://www.jimkwik.
com/podcasts/kwik-brain-194-how-to-sleep-better-during-a-pandemic-with-dr
-michael-breus/.

13 Sanjana Gupta, "What Is a Circadian Rhythm Sleep Disorder?," *Verywell Mind*,
February 11, 2023, https://www.verywellmind.com/circadian-rhythm-sleep
-disorders-types-causes-and-coping-7108090.

Chapter 3

1   Anne Craig, "Discovery of 'Thought Worms' Opens Window to the Mind," *Queen's Gazette*, July 13, 2020, https://www.queensu.ca/gazette/stories/discovery-thought -worms-opens-window-mind.

2   Michael Vallejo, "Automatic Negative Thoughts (ANTs): How to Identify and Fix Them," *Mental Health Center Kids*, October 26, 2022, https:// mentalhealthcenterkids.com/blogs/articles/automatic-negative-thoughts.

3   Neşe Mercan et al., "Investigation of the Relatedness of Cognitive Distortions with Emotional Expression, Anxiety, and Depression," *Current Psychology* 42, no. 10 (2021): 1007/s12144-021-02251-z, https://www.researchgate.net/publication /354298569_Investigation_of_the_relatedness_of_cognitive_distortions_with _emotional_expression_anxiety_and_depression.

4   Natalie L. Marchant et al., "Repetitive Negative Thinking Is Associated With Amyloid, Tau, and Cognitive Decline," *Alzheimer's Dementia* 16, no. 7 (2020): 1054–64, https://doi.org/10.1002/alz.12116.

5   Louis Frank and Saleh Mohamed, "Crisis Intervention and Emergency Preparedness in Care Facilities: Addressing Acute Psychosocial Challenges during the Pandemic," *Easy Chair*, no. 13253 (2024), https://easychair.org/publications /preprint/l56Qc/open.

6   Madhav Goyal et al., "Meditation Programs for Psychological Stress and Well-Being: A Systematic Review and Meta-analysis," *JAMA Internal Medicine* 174, no. 3 (2014): 357–68, https://jamanetwork.com/journals/jamainternalmedicine /fullarticle/1809754.

7   Alexander T. Latinjak et al., "Self-Talk: An Interdisciplinary Review and Transdisciplinary Model," *Review of General Psychology* 27, no. 4 (2023), https:// doi.org/10.1177/10892680231170263.

8   Simon E. Blackwell, "Mental Imagery: From Basic Research to Clinical Practice," *Journal of Psychotherapy Integration* 29, no. 3 (2019): 235–47, https://doi.org/10 .1037/int0000108.

9   Andrea N. Niles et al., "Randomized Controlled Trial of Expressive Writing for Psychological and Physical Health: The Moderating Role of Emotional Expressivity," *Anxiety, Stress, and Coping* 27, no. 1 (2013): 1–17, https://doi.org /10.1080/10615806.2013.802308.

Chapter 4

1   Madhav Goyal et al., "Meditation Programs for Psychological Stress and Well-Being: A Systematic Review and Meta-analysis," *JAMA Internal Medicine* 174, no. 3 (2014): 357–68, https://doi:10.1001/jamainternmed.2013.13018.

2   Dr. Elizabeth Blackburn and Dr. Elissa Epel, *The Telomere Effect: A Revolutionary Approach to Living Younger, Healthier, Longer* (Grand Central Publishing, 2017).

3   Thomas J. Dunn and Mirena Dimolareva, "The Effect of Mindfulness-Based Interventions on Immunity-Related Biomarkers: A Comprehensive Meta-Analysis of Randomised Controlled Trials," *Clinical Psychology Review* 92 (2022): 102124, https://doi.org/10.1016/j.cpr.2022.102124.

4   Supaya Wenuganen et al., "Transcriptomics of Long-Term Meditation Practice: Evidence for Prevention or Reversal of Stress Effects Harmful to Health," *Medicina* 57, no. 3 (2021): 218, https://doi.org/10.3390/medicina57030218.

5   Thomas Larrieu et al., "Nutritional Omega-3 Modulates Neuronal Morphology in the Prefrontal Cortex Along With Depression-Related Behaviour Through Corticosterone Secretion," *Translational Psychiatry* 4 (2014): e437, https://doi.org/10.1038/tp.2014.77.

6   Sarah McEwen, "Meditation & Mindfulness for Stress Reduction," *Pacific Neuroscience Institute*, March 11, 2020, https://www.pacificneuroscienceinstitute.org/blog/brain-health/meditation-mindfulness-for-stress-reduction/.

7   Manoj K. Bhasin et al., "Relaxation Response Induces Temporal Transcriptome Changes in Energy Metabolism, Insulin Secretion and Inflammatory Pathways," *PLOS ONE* 8, no. 5 (2013): e62817, https://doi.org/10.1371/journal.pone.0062817.

8   Su Qin et al., "Structural Basis for Histone Mimicry and Hijacking of Host Proteins by Influenza Virus Protein NS1," *Nature Communications* 5, no. 1 (2014): 1–11, https://doi.org/10.1038/ncomms4952.

9   "Mindfulness for Your Health: The Benefits of Living Moment by Moment," *NIH News in Health*, June 2021, https://newsinhealth.nih.gov/2021/06/mindfulness-your-health.

10   "In the Journals: Mindfulness Meditation Practice Changes the Brain," *Harvard Health Publishing*, April 1, 2011, https://www.health.harvard.edu/mind-and-mood/mindfulness-meditation-practice-changes-the-brain.

11   "Benefits of Mindfulness," *HelpGuide.org in Collaboration with Harvard Health*, October 4, 2024, https://www.helpguide.org/mental-health/stress/benefits-of-mindfulness.

12   Florian Kurth et al., "Promising Links between Meditation and Reduced (Brain) Aging: An Attempt to Bridge Some Gaps between the Alleged Fountain of Youth and the Youth of the Field," *Frontiers in Psychology* 8 (2017): 236970, https://doi.org/10.3389/fpsyg.2017.00860.

13   Amy Novotney, "Feeling Nostalgic This Holiday Season? It Might Help Boost Your Mental Health," *American Psychological Association*, December 18, 2023, https://www.apa.org/topics/mental-health/nostalgia-boosts-well-being.

14 Lúzie Fofonka Cunha et al., "Positive Psychology and Gratitude Interventions: A Randomized Clinical Trial," *Frontiers in Psychology* 10 (2019): 430258, https://doi .org/10.3389/fpsyg.2019.00584.

15 Jeffrey Klibert et al., "The Impact of an Integrated Gratitude Intervention on Positive Affect and Coping Resources," *International Journal of Applied Positive Psychology* 3 (2019): 23–41, https://doi.org/10.1007/s41042-019-00015-6.

16 Sunghyon Kyeong et al., "Effects of Gratitude Meditation on Neural Network Functional Connectivity and Brain-Heart Coupling," *Scientific Reports* 7, no. 1 (2017): 5058, https://doi.org/10.1038/s41598-017-05520-9.

17 Amy Morin, "7 Scientifically Proven Benefits of Gratitude," *Psychology Today*, April 3, 2015, https://www.psychologytoday.com/intl/blog/what-mentally-strong -people-dont-do/201504/7-scientifically-proven-benefits-of-gratitude.

18 Summer Allen, "Is Gratitude Good for Your Health?," *Greater Good Magazine*, March 5, 2018, https://greatergood.berkeley.edu/article/item/is_gratitude_good _for_your_health.

19 Morin, "7 Scientifically Proven Benefits of Gratitude."

20 "The Benefits of Deep Breathing and Why It Works," *Psychology Today*, September 25, 2024, https://www.psychologytoday.com/us/blog/evidence-based-living /202409/the-benefits-of-deep-breathing-and-why-it-works.

21 "Yogic Breathing Helps Fight Major Depression, Penn Study Shows," *Penn Medicine News*, November 22, 2016, https://www.pennmedicine.org/news/news-releases /2016/november/yogic-breathing-helps-fight-ma.

22 Joni Sweet, "The Science Behind Breathwork + 5 Benefits Of The Practice," *Mindbodygreen*, February 14, 2020, https://www.mindbodygreen.com/articles /the-benefits-of-breathwork.

23 Dallin Tavoian and Daniel H. Craighead, "Deep Breathing Exercise at Work: Potential Applications and Impact," *Frontiers in Physiology* 14 (2023): 1040091, https://doi.org/10.3389/fphys.2023.1040091.

24 Grzegorz Bilo et al., "Effects of Slow Deep Breathing at High Altitude on Oxygen Saturation, Pulmonary and Systemic Hemodynamics," *PLOS ONE* 7, no. 11 (2012): e49074, https://doi.org/10.1371/journal.pone.0049074.

25 Yu Liu et al. "The Effectiveness of Diaphragmatic Breathing Relaxation Training for Improving Sleep Quality Among Nursing Staff During the COVID-19 Outbreak: A Before and After Study," *Sleep Medicine* 78 (2021): 8–14, https://doi.org/10.1016 /j.sleep.2020.12.003.

Chapter 5

1 J. David Creswell et al., "Affirmation of Personal Values Buffers Neuroendocrine

and Psychological Stress Responses," *Psychological Science* 16, no. 11 (2005): 846–51, https://doi.org/10.1111/j.1467-9280.2005.01624.x.

2   J. David Creswell et al., "Self-Affirmation Improves Problem-Solving under Stress," *PLOS ONE* 8, no. 5 (2013): e62593, https://doi.org/10.1371/journal.pone .0062593.

3   Richard Cooke et al., "Self-Affirmation Promotes Physical Activity," *Journal of Sport & Exercise Psychology* 36, no. 2 (2014): 217–23, https://doi.org/10.1123/jsep .2013-0041.

4   Christopher N. Cascio et al., "Self-Affirmation Activates Brain Systems Associated With Self-Related Processing and Reward and Is Reinforced by Future Orientation," *Social Cognitive and Affective Neuroscience* 11, no. 4 (2016): 621–29, https://doi.org/10.1093/scan/nsv136.

5   B. R. Levy, et al., "Positive Age Beliefs Protect Against Dementia Even Among Elders With High-Risk Gene," *PLOS ONE* 13(2) (2018): e0191004. https://doi .org/10.1371/journal.pone.0191004.

6   Alan Rozanski et al., "Association of Optimism With Cardiovascular Events and All-Cause Mortality: A Systematic Review and Meta-Analysis," *JAMA Network Open* 2, no. 9 (2019): e1912200, https://jamanetwork.com/journals/jamanetwork open/fullarticle/2752100.

Chapter 6

1   Janice Kiecolt-Glaser et al., "Psychosocial Enhancement of Immunocompetence in a Geriatric Population," *Psychosomatic Medicine* 57, no. 1 (1995): 17–25.

2   E. A. Fors and H. Sexton, "Cognitive Control and Chronic Pain: A Follow-Up Study," *Journal of Behavioral Medicine* 25, no. 2 (2002): 181–93.

3   Liz Roffe et al., "A Systematic Review of Guided Imagery as an Adjuvant Cancer Therapy," *Psycho-Oncology* 14, no. 8 (2005): 607–17, https://doi.org/10.1002 /pon.889.

4   Diane Tusek et al., "Guided Imagery as a Coping Strategy for Perioperative Patients," *AORN Journal* 66, no. 4 (1997): 644–9, https://doi.org/10.1016/S0001 -2092(06)62917-7.

5   Karina W. Davidson et al., "Controlled Trial of Positive Affect Intervention to Reduce Depression, Anxiety, and Enhance Recovery from Heart Disease," *Archives of Internal Medicine* 170, no. 18 (2010): 1501–9.

Chapter 7

1   Sheri R. Colberg et al., "Physical Activity/Exercise and Diabetes: A Position Statement of the American Diabetes Association," *Diabetes Care* 39, no. 11 (2016): 2065–79, https://doi.org/10.2337/dc16-1728.

2   Darren Warburton and Shannon Bredin, "Health Benefits of Physical Activity: The
     Evidence," *American Journal of Epidemiology* 174, no. 10 (2006): 1231–43, https://
     www.researchgate.net/publication/25347587_Health_benefits_of_physical
     _activity.
3   Toni Golen and Hope Ricciotti, "Does Exercise Really Boost Energy Levels?,"
     Harvard Health Publishing, July 1, 2021, https://www.health.harvard.edu/exercise
     -and-fitness/does-exercise-really-boost-energy-levels.
4   Yves Rolland et al., "Physical Activity and Alzheimer's disease: From Prevention to
     Therapeutic Perspectives," *Journal of the American Medical Directors Association* 9,
     no. 6 (2008): 390–405, https://doi.org/10.1016/j.jamda.2008.02.007.
5   Michelle Plowman, "Exercise Is Brain Food: The Effects of Physical Activity on
     Cognitive Function," *Developmental Neurorehabilitation* 11, no. 3 (2008): 236–40,
     https://doi.org/10.1080/17518420801997007.
6   Golen and Ricciotti, "Does Exercise Really Boost Energy Levels?"
7   Weidong Chen et al., "Tai Chi for Fall Prevention and Balance Improvement in
     Older Adults: A Systematic Review and Meta-Analysis of Randomized Controlled
     Trials," *Frontiers in Public Health* 11 (2023): 1236050, https://doi.org/10.3389
     /fpubh.2023.1236050.
8   Jonathan Peake et al., "The Effects of Cold Water Immersion and Active Recovery
     on Inflammation and Cell Stress Responses in Human Skeletal Muscle After
     Resistance Exercise," *The Journal of Physiology* 595, no. 3 (2017): 695–711, https://
     doi.org/10.1113/JP272881.
9   Selim Chaib et al., "Cellular Senescence and Senolytics: The Path to the Clinic,"
     Nature Medicine 28 (2022): 1556–68, https://doi.org/10.1038/s41591-022
     -01923-y.

Chapter 8

1   "Cognitive Health and Older Adults," National Institute on Aging, last reviewed
     June 11, 2024, https://www.nia.nih.gov/health/brain-health/cognitive-health
     -and-older-adults.
2   Robert A. Gross, "Life-Span Cognitive Activity, Neuropathologic Burden, and
     Cognitive Aging," Neurology 81, no. 4 (2013): 307, https://www.neurology.org
     /doi/10.1212/WNL.0b013e31829ef315.
3   Avni Bavishi et al., "A Chapter a Day: Association of Book Reading With
     Longevity," *Social Science & Medicine* 164 (2016): 44–8, https://doi.org/10.1016
     /j.socscimed.2016.07.014.
4   Shuai Yuan et al., "Comparative Efficacy and Acceptability of Bibliotherapy for
     Depression and Anxiety Disorders in Children and Adolescents: A Meta-Analysis

of Randomized Clinical Trials," *Neuropsychiatric Disease and Treatment* 14 (2018): 353–65, https://doi.org/10.2147/NDT.S152747.

Chapter 9

1   Joshua M. Smyth et al., "Online Positive Affect Journaling in the Improvement of Mental Distress and Well-Being in General Medical Patients With Elevated Anxiety Symptoms: A Preliminary Randomized Controlled Trial," *JMIR Mental Health* 5, no. 4 (2018): e11290, https://doi.org/10.2196/11290.
2   American Academy of Neurology (AAN), "Does Being a Bookworm Boost Your Brainpower in Old Age?," *ScienceDaily*, July 4, 2013, https://www.sciencedaily.com/releases/2013/07/130704094454.htm.

Chapter 10

1   Kristen Woodward, "Exercise Reduces Chronic Disease Risks," *Fred Hutchinson Cancer Center*, July 1, 2007, https://www.fredhutch.org/en/news/center-news/2007/07/exercises-reduces-chronic-disease.html.
2   Jill Suttie, "Can Meditating Together Improve Your Relationships?," *Greater Good Magazine*, February 6, 2017, https://greatergood.berkeley.edu/article/item/can_meditating_together_improve_your_relationships.
3   Genevieve S. E. Smith et al., "Frequency of Physical Activity Done with a Companion: Changes Over Seven Years in Adults Aged 60+ Living in an Australian Capital City," *Journal of Aging and Health* 35, no. 9 (2023): 736–48, https://doi.org/10.1177/08982643231158424.
4   Meryl Roberts, "Why Reading Together Can Make or Break a Relationship: A Couple's Guide," *Morrigan Post*, July 10, 2023, https://morriganpost.com/couples-reading-together/.
5   Nathaniel M. Lambert et al., "Benefits of Expressing Gratitude: Expressing Gratitude to a Partner Changes One's View of the Relationship," *Psychological Science* 21, no. 4 (2010): 574–80, https://doi.org/10.1177/0956797610364003.

Chapter 11

1   Phillippa Lally et al., "How Are Habits Formed: Modelling Habit Formation in the Real World," *European Journal Social Psychology* 40 (2010): 998–1009, https://doi.org/10.1002/ejsp.674.

Chapter 12

1   "Improving Social Connectedness," Centers for Disease Control and Prevention, May 15, 2024, https://www.cdc.gov/social-connectedness/improving/.
2   Heidi Godman, "Get Back Your Social Life to Boost Thinking, Memory, and

Health," *Harvard Health Publishing*, October 22, 2023, https://www.health.harvard.edu/mind-and-mood/get-back-your-social-life-to-boost-thinking-memory-and-health.

Chapter 13

1   Institute of Medicine, *Providing Healthy and Safe Foods As We Age: Workshop Summary* (The National Academies Press, 2010) chap. 5, https://www.ncbi.nlm.nih.gov/books/NBK51837/.

2   "The Benefits of Slumber: Why You Need a Good Night's Sleep," *NIH News in Health*, April 2013, https://newsinhealth.nih.gov/2013/04/benefits-slumber.

3   Melissa Urban and Michael Breus, "Dear Melissa & Friends: Unpacking Diet and Sleep with Dr. Michael Breus," *Whole 30*, May 23, 2023, https://whole30.com/article/dear-melissa-diet-and-sleep-connections/.

4   Danielle Pacheco and Anis Rehman, "What's the Best Time of Day to Exercise for Sleep?," *Sleep Foundation*, October 11, 2023, https://www.sleepfoundation.org/physical-activity/best-time-of-day-to-exercise-for-sleep.

5   "Exercising for Better Sleep," Johns Hopkins Medicine, accessed May 12, 2025, https://www.hopkinsmedicine.org/health/wellness-and-prevention/exercising-for-better-sleep.

6   Johns Hopkins Medicine, "Exercising for Better Sleep."

7   Danielle Pacheco and David Rosen, "Best Temperature for Sleep," *Sleep Foundation*, March 7, 2024, https://www.sleepfoundation.org/bedroom-environment/best-temperature-for-sleep.

8   Jason Ong, "Consistent Wake-Up Time: Sleep's Surprising MVP," *Headspace*, October 17, 2023, https://www.headspace.com/articles/sleep-health-2-consistent-wake-up-time-sleeps-surprising-mvp.

9   Kwik, "How to Sleep Better."

Chapter 14

1   "Effects of Light on Circadian Rhythms," Centers for Disease Control and Prevention, archived April 13, 2023, https://archive.cdc.gov/#/details?url=https://www.cdc.gov/niosh/emres/longhourstraining/light.html.

2   James Oschman et al., "The Effects of Grounding (Earthing) on Inflammation, the Immune Response, Wound Healing, and Prevention and Treatment of Chronic Inflammatory and Autoimmune Diseases," *Journal of Inflammation Research* 8 (2015): 83–96, https://doi.org/10.2147/JIR.S69656.

3   Maurice Ghaly, and Dale Teplitz, "The Biologic Effects of Grounding the Human Body During Sleep as Measured by Cortisol Levels and Subjective Reporting of

Sleep, Pain, and Stress," *Journal of Alternative and Complementary Medicine* 10, no. 5 (2004): 767–76, https://www.liebertpub.com/doi/10.1089/acm.2004.10.767.

4   Gaétan Chevalier and Stephen T. Sinatra, "Emotional Stress, Heart Rate Variability, Grounding, and Improved Autonomic Tone: Clinical Applications," *Integrative Medicine: A Clinician's Journal* 10, no. 3 (2011): 16–24, https://www.terrapia.pl /files/imcj10-3-p16-24chevalier.pdf.

5   Gaétan Chevalier et al., "Earthing (Grounding) the Human Body Reduces Blood Viscosity—A Major Factor in Cardiovascular Disease," *Journal of Alternative and Complementary Medicine* 19, no. 2 (2013): 102–10, https://doi.org/10.1089/acm .2011.0820.

6   Laura Koniver, "Practical Applications of Grounding to Support Health," *Biomedical Journal* 46, no. 1 (2023): 41–7, https://www.ncbi.nlm.nih.gov/pmc/articles /PMC10105020/.

7   Gaétan Chevalier et al., "Earthing: Health Implications of Reconnecting the Human Body to the Earth's Surface Electrons," *Journal of Environmental and Public Health* 2012, no. 1 (2012): 291541, https://doi.org/10.1155/2012/291541.

8   Clint Ober, "The Benefits of Grounding: An Interview with Clint Ober," interview by Heather Sandison, *The Science of Grounding: How Earthing Improves Sleep and Reduces Inflammation,* Quaila, September 24, 2020, transcript, https://neurohacker .com/the-benefits-of-grounding-an-interview-with-clint-ober.

9   "From Pain Relief to Food Digestion: Grounding Benefits Confirmed Through Thermal Imaging," The Earthing Institute, May 2, 2017, https://earthinginstitute .net/from-pain-relief-to-unclogged-digestion-grounding-benefits-seen-through -thermal-imaging/.

10   The Earthing Institute, "From Pain Relief to Food Digestion."

Chapter 15

1   Association for Psychological Science, "Having a Sense of Purpose May Add Years to Your Life," *ScienceDaily,* May 12, 2014, www.sciencedaily.com/releases/2014/05 /140512124308.htm.

2   Chloe Many and Sheryl Leventhal, "Resilience and Longevity: Focus on Building Resilience Over Managing Stress," *Hudson Valley Longevity Medicine,* June 20, 2023, https://www.hvlongevity.com/2023/06/20/resilience-and-longevity-focus-on -building-resilience-over-managing-stress/.

3   Albert Einstein College of Medicine, "'Personality Genes' May Help Account for Longevity," *EurekAlert!,* May 24, 2012, https://www.eurekalert.org/news-releases /859879.

4   "Okinawa Centenarian Study," Wikipedia, accessed April 11, 2024, https://en .wikipedia.org/wiki/Okinawa_Centenarian_Study.

5   "Blue Zone," Wikipedia, accessed July 17, 2024, https://en.wikipedia.org/wiki
      /Blue_zone.

6   Patricia A. Boyle et al., "Effect of a Purpose in Life on Risk of Incident Alzheimer
      Disease and Mild Cognitive Impairment in Community-Dwelling Older Persons,"
      Archives of General Psychiatry 67, no. 3 (2010): 304, https://doi.org/10.1001
      /archgenpsychiatry.2009.208.

7   Aliya Alimujiang et al., "Association Between Life Purpose and Mortality Among
      US Adults Older Than 50 Years," *JAMA Network Open* 2, no. 5 (2019): e194270,
      https://jamanetwork.com/journals/jamanetworkopen/fullarticle/2734064.

8   Boston University School of Public Health, "Higher Sense of Purpose in Life May
      Be Linked to Lower Mortality Risk, Study Finds." *ScienceDaily*. November 15, 2022.
      Available online at: www.sciencedaily.com/releases/2022/11/221115184500.htm.

9   Arianna Huffington, "As I celebrate my birthday today, I'm reflecting on how much
      it's built into our youth-worshiping culture that we have to do everything by the
      time we're 30," Twitter (now X), July 15, 2023, https://x.com/ariannahuff/status
      /1680203064400134146.

10   Colonel Harland Sanders, *Col. Harland Sanders: The Autobiography of the Original
      Celebrity Chef* (KFC Corporation 2012), 14.

ABOUT THE AUTHORS

Hal Elrod is the bestselling author of 12 books, including *The Miracle Morning*, the revolutionary book that has transformed the mornings—and lives—of millions of people worldwide. He also recently wrote and published *The Miracle Morning Updated and Expanded Edition* to add over a decade of additional wisdom and experience to the original book. Now, with *The Miracle Morning After 50*, Hal brings his groundbreaking morning ritual and personal growth framework to those embracing life's second act, empowering readers to live with a proven path to joy, vitality, and purpose.

Hal has lived a life that would break most people, and yet he's managed to turn his adversities into perspectives and practices that have empowered millions. From witnessing the heartbreaking death of his baby sister at only 8 years old, to surviving a near-fatal car accident at age 20, and battling a rare, aggressive form of cancer in his late thirties—Hal is living proof that we can overcome any challenge we face. In the midst of his adversity, Hal discovered a powerful method for fulfilling the limitless potential that is within each of us, regardless of age or circumstance. His proven S.A.V.E.R.S. method (*Silence, Affirmations, Visualization, Exercise, Reading,* and *Scribing*) continues to inspire millions to unlock their fullest potential each day.

Hal is an internationally renowned keynote speaker, helping organizations and teams fulfill their collective potential. He is also the host of the acclaimed *Achieve Your Goals with Hal Elrod* podcast, which is in the top 0.1 percent of all podcasts in the world. When he's not writing or speaking, Hal's most important roles are as a faithful husband to his wife, Ursula, and a dedicated father to their two children, at their home near Austin, Texas.

To connect with Hal or to book him for media appearances or to speak at your event and deliver his inspiring Miracle Morning keynote message, visit **HalElrod.com**.

To watch *The Miracle Morning* movie, download the *Miracle Morning* app, and join the global Miracle Morning Community, visit **MiracleMorning.com**.

Dwayne J. Clark is the chairman, CEO, and founder of Aegis Living. With nearly 40 years of senior living experience, Dwayne is nationally known for redefining the industry—from innovative care models and building design to novel approaches to employee engagement and creating an employee-centric culture. When Dwayne founded Aegis Living in 1997, he recognized an industry that had great potential and intentions but was ultimately failing older adults. He coupled his personal experience with best practices from world-class companies such as Costco, Nordstrom, and Starbucks to create a new model for senior assisted living centered on helping residents live life to the fullest. He grew Aegis Living from a concept to a company that now has 39 communities along the West Coast, currently serving 80,000 residents and employing over 2,800 staff, with several additional properties currently in development.

Aegis Living has been widely recognized with industry accolades, including *U.S. News & World Report* Best Senior Living, *Fortune* Best Workplaces in Aging Services™, Best Assisted Living by *Seattle Business Magazine*, Top Corporate Philanthropist by *Puget Sound Business Journal*, Top 50 Best Places to Work by Glassdoor, among others. Under Dwayne's leadership, Aegis Living set new standards for senior living during the COVID-19 pandemic and continues trailblazing new territory today, including sustainable senior living.

Prior to forming Aegis Living, Dwayne worked in several major senior living companies. He has developed more than 250 senior living properties and continues to serve on several industry boards. He was named in the "Power 100" people in the Puget Sound region and Entrepreneur of the Year by Ernst & Young. He also received King County's highest honor as Man of the Year and the Mission Award from Bastyr University, among others.

Dwayne, with his wife Terese, has traveled to over 84 countries exploring different healing modalities—from working with doctors and alternative health specialists to engaging in mind, body, and spirit practices. These discoveries inspired his book and Amazon bestseller *30 Summers More*, which provides longevity and health tips.

An experienced author, Dwayne has also written two books that chronicle his mother and her journey with Alzheimer's, *My Mother, My Son* (currently being considered as a major feature film) and *Saturdays with GG* as well as *A Big Life,* a combination book/game to inspire families to connect and reflect on the powerful wisdom of older generations. He is the founder of True Productions and produced multiple documentaries, including one about NBA legend Spencer Haywood, *Full Court: The Spencer Haywood Story.* His first play, *Seven Ways to Get There,* premiered at Seattle's ACT Theatre. Since 2015, True Productions has been involved in the making of 13 documentary films.

Dwayne comes from humble beginnings and has remained dedicated to helping others throughout his life. He supports more than 70 local and global charities and has founded 5 of his own, including The Potato Soup Foundation, the Clark Family Foundation, March for Civility, D-ONE Foundation, and Queen Bee. Queen Bee Café, a coffee shop with multiple locations in the Puget Sound, was created as a tribute to his mother, and all the proceeds go to charity. Clark is chairman of the D-ONE Foundation, a mentorship program for Division I athletes. Clark also mentors several NFL players. He led the March for Civility in Washington, DC, where he had the honor of speaking on the steps of the Lincoln Memorial. He is also involved in the late Pope Francis's private foundation, the Galileo Foundation, aiming to end child slavery. In October 2022, he spoke at the Vatican Faith and Philanthropy Summit alongside other renowned business and world leaders. He has two children, Adam and Ashley, who both work for Aegis Living, and nine grandchildren. More information about Dwayne and interview opportunities can be found at **DwayneJClark.com.**